GW00808404

FIFTH-CENTURY ATHENS

DEMOCRACY & CITY STATE

ARTS: A SECOND LEVEL COURSE

The Open University

THE OFFPRINTS

THE OPEN UNIVERSITY

The Open University
Walton Hall, Milton Keynes
MK7 6AA

First published 1997

Edited, designed and typeset by The Open University.

Printed in The United Kingdom by Page Bros, Norwich.

ISBN 0 7492 1184 9

CONTENTS

GUIDE TO READING THE OFFPRINTS

Prepared for the course team by Paula James

Make sure you have worked through the first three sub-sections below, including 'How to approach the articles', before you read the individual articles and associated discussion. In the blocks themselves you will be told the point at which to study each article in detail.

The value of modern scholarship

The articles in The Offprints have been selected to enrich your understanding of the fifth century BCE: they all demonstrate how a range of primary sources can be critically evaluated. This guide will not cover all the articles in detail, but will introduce you to some tools of analysis so that you should feel more confident in your approach to the scholarship on the period.

The authors of the articles have been studying the period of classical Athens in depth over a number of years. I hope that our selections from a large body of secondary literature of this type will start you thinking about how scholars steeped in the period have developed and refined the sort of methodology you yourself are applying to the primary sources as you work through A209. You are by now used to working with the ancient sources; the articles demonstrate how this activity constantly opens up new areas of interpretation and debate about the ancient world.

The authors all make important contributions to central debates on Athenian life and culture, and in varying degrees they also advance our methods of approach to ancient societies. We have provided brief biographies of the authors for each article, focusing on the significance of their contributions. Some of the authors take a traditional approach to the material, but do so rigorously and comprehensively; others have responded imaginatively and creatively to the ancient evidence, advancing new methods of interpretation which now occupy an important place in that particular area of scholarship. You may also notice that some of the language seems a little old-fashioned: for example, reference is made to 'men' and 'he' where, today, we might prefer to say 'people' or 'he or she'. Such choices of words serve as a reminder of the extent to which scholars are influenced by the wider social context in which they write. At the same time, they illustrate the fact that – until relatively recently – classical research has largely been a male-dominated field. You might usefully consider whether such language merely reflects the academic conventions of the time at which the article was written, or whether it actually shapes the questions that are being asked of the evidence (and therefore the direction of the discussion).

Do keep in mind that these articles are not the last word on the subject: the ideas they contain are constantly being re-evaluated and extended. You should find them plausible and stimulating (they are interesting and powerful pieces), but you will soon feel confident about questioning and challenging their use of the evidence and the direction of any particular argument.

In conclusion, a close and critical reading of the articles in The Offprints will not only acquaint you with a number of important debates about the period you are studying; it will also encourage and help you to come to your own judgements about key issues in the cultural history of fifth-century Athens.

An introduction to the articles

The first two articles – by Momigliano and Dodds – are referred to in Blocks 1 and 2. The blocks indicate at what point you should be reading them. Similarly, the approaches and main propositions of the articles associated with Block 5 are discussed by Chris Emlyn-Jones within the block itself.

Before you start your programme of study, it is a useful exercise to take a critical look at your set text on the period, *World of Athens*. This is a piece of modern scholarship of a different kind from the articles in The Offprints and one which you are using as a factual database for significant events and structures in Athenian society. However, it also requires a critical methodology, once you are familiar with its contents and structure.

Lorna Hardwick suggests in Block 1, p.18, that you should 'dig beneath the smooth narrative of *WA*' and start to distinguish between established historical facts and interpretations of motives and causes – however attractively and seamlessly the authors combine the two. In other words, we need to keep in mind that the authors of *WA* are presenting us with their own readings of different types of source. Although they may not appear to be doing any more than stating the facts – the textbook format reinforces its role as guide and authority – they are actually making judgements about the significance of certain events and about who were the important figures of the time.

The authors of the Offprints articles have a more sophisticated agenda, one that requires them to argue a position and to justify their conclusions. They frequently engage in academic polemics at some stage in their investigations, and this invariably enlivens the narrative – but involves you in a process of judgement and interpretation too. The audio-cassette on handling the ancient sources will always repay a second – even a third – listening, as it will remind you of some of the basic methods all scholars have to apply to primary evidence, whatever level of sophistication their studies have reached.

Modern scholars, whether they are writing textbooks or controversial critiques, tend to draw heavily on the work of ancient historians for their reconstruction of events and attitudes in fifth-century Athens. However, they do not and indeed dare not use historians such as Herodotus and Thucydides uncritically. De Ste Croix's article, which you will be reading in association with Block 3, addresses the danger of responding to Thucydides simplistically. Several of the articles you will be reading in conjunction with Block 4 also challenge popular assumptions which the authors believe have been developed from unsound interpretations of the ancient evidence.

It has been observed that the works of ancient historians have a literary texture which cannot be removed like a superficial packaging from around the historical facts contained in their writing. In their own day the historians were expected to reproduce what really happened in the period under study, but it was also assumed that their histories would function as works of literature – we might say, as well crafted pieces to last for ever.

There is also a tendency in both Herodotus and Thucydides to 'expound moral truths', to bring out the broader patterns of causation behind complicated sequences of events, to lend structure and coherence to human history – which is why the course team suggests that you use the ancient historical writers with caution.

All the articles should widen your perspective on significant aspects of fifth-century Athens. Lissarrague, for instance, in the fourth article of The Offprints, gives a sophisticated analysis of vase scenes, highlighting their significance for the study of Athenian social life. This article complements the brief but pointed survey of the production and function of pottery in Section 3.2 of Block 4.

The work of Walcot, Gould, Hardwick and Finley is closely connected to the discussion you will find in Part 2 of Block 4 (in the section, 'The Athenian ethos'). The issue of Athenian democracy in practice (Finley) cannot be divorced from the part played by women in the society, so these articles enrich our perceptions of the way in which that society was organized. All the authors contextualize their specific themes and topics within the framework of Athenian attitudes and socio-political organization.

How to approach the articles

The articles in The Offprints will give you further practice in understanding historical methodologies and the particular challenges that ancient society presents to classical scholars. It is important, therefore, for you to feel confident that you are following the lines of the arguments in these articles and are identifying the main conclusions. When you make notes upon the content, you should at the same time be asking yourself whether you have grasped the central propositions of the authors.

It is useful to produce your own checklist of the different kinds of evidence they use to support their conclusions. When they quote from ancient literary sources, make sure you can distinguish between genres: for example, historical writing, legal digests, the written records of highly rhetorical speeches for the prosecution and defence, drama (tragedy and comedy), and philosophical dialogues.

- On a first reading you could make notes on the main points and stages of the argument.

- On a second reading, identify the direction of the argument, what evidence has been selected to support it, and whether you feel the author has produced more questions than answers concerning key issues.

- You may wish to summarize recurring areas of controversy *across the board*. Are there common problems in the evidence and in the interpretation of the evidence? And what strategies have the authors used to overcome them?

- Have the articles provided you with useful insights that have expanded your response in assignments?

A practice run

Please turn to The Offprints and read the opening few paragraphs of the articles by Walcot, Hardwick and Gould. Do the authors identify the same problems faced by scholars of the Ancient World?

Discussion _____

Any aspect of Athenian society presents challenges to the historian, not the least of which is the problem of modern perceptions applied to ancient societies. (You may recall the discussion in Block 1, Sections 1.1 and 1.2.)

The articles in The Offprints have been written by scholars with considerable and comparable skills in handling a variety of ancient source material. They map out their subject-areas coherently, and indicate at an early stage where their sympathies lie in the ongoing debates about life in fifth-century Athens. When you make notes on each of these articles, therefore, it is very useful to start by identifying the theme, the context, the problems and the author's declaration of intent.

Once you have these aspects clear in your mind, they are an important reference point when you move on to summarize, analyse and evaluate the author's arguments. Each author is asking for a reassessment of established and traditional views about the Athenian experience. You will certainly need to bear in mind, as you did with your primary historical sources, whether the author has a particular axe to grind. Even clear theoretical models may exclude some approaches to Athenian society and firmly espouse others: for instance, Gould quickly establishes his qualms about an uncritical use of the literary evidence about the position of women in Athens. As you work through the authors, you will find that they share certain concerns about how ancient evidence is used. ♦

The general reading strategies suggested in this introduction can be applied to all the articles and extracts you will find in this book. A number of the authors and the significance of their conclusions are alluded to in the block discussion. However, certain authors raise some fairly complex issues in an incisive but not so readily accessible way. Where this is the case, I have provided you below with a series of exercises to enable you to work through their pieces with a firm focus on the structure and argumentation.

The articles have been set out in sequence, in the order in which you will be reading them. Below are short biographies of each author so that you gain a wider picture of these authors' interests, specialisms, theoretical approaches and contributions to classical scholarship. It will be indicated in the blocks when you should refer to each article, and at that point you should also return to the relevant information given below.

Reading associated with Block 1, Part 2, Section 8

Arnaldo Dante Momigliano (1908–87) came from a Jewish Italian family. He was professor in Greek at Rome by 1932, and held the chair of Roman history in Turin until 1938 when he was dismissed under Mussolini's race laws. He continued to publish prodigiously on the history of Greece, Rome and Judaism. His later academic life was centred in England; he was professor of Ancient History at University College, London and it was in these years (1951–75) that he developed his very distinctive approaches to history, historiography and biography as interrelated disciplines. His *Studies in Historiography* (rev. 1969, Weidenfeld and Nicolson) and *Essays in Ancient and Modern Historiography* (Blackwells, 1977) illustrate this approach.

His book of 1975, *Alien Wisdom: the limits of Hellenization* (Cambridge University Press), suggested a wider cultural context for the study of Ancient History. His attention to the role of the intellectual, the influence of ideas and the responsibility of historians for their interpretations of the data single him out as a key figure in the development of the practice of cultural history. Note that the extract from Momigliano is also highly relevant to your study of Thucydides in Block 3.

Reading associated with Block 2, Sub-section 5.5

Eric Robertson Dodds (1893–1979), of Irish extraction, was professor of Greek at Birmingham and subsequently Regius Professor of Greek at Oxford.

His research concentrated on the areas of Greek and Roman religion and Greek literature, especially tragedy. These two interests came together in a series of definitive and pioneering studies of the role of the 'irrational' in Greek culture: *The Greeks and the Irrational* (University of California Press, 1951) and an edition of Euripides' *Bacchae* (Cambridge University Press, 1960) are two of his most influential works.

He also published a series of short analyses of particular tragedies, of which this article is one. Written for a non-specialist audience, it nevertheless raises in succinct form a number of key issues related to the Sophocles play, which are searchingly discussed.

Reading associated with Block 3, Section 9

Geoffrey Earnest Maurice de Ste Croix was a solicitor in his early career. He did war-service in the RAF and became a mature student at University College London in 1946. He was fellow and tutor of Ancient History at New College,

Oxford from 1953 to 1977. Key publications that brought him scholarly fame are *The Origins of the Peloponnesian Wars* (Duckworth, 1972) and *Class Struggle in the Ancient World from the Archaic Age to the Arab Conquests* (Duckworth, 1981); the latter won the Isaac Deutsch Memorial Prize. He has given numerous lectures around the world and contributed widely to journals and studies in the economy and culture of the ancient world.

His application of Marxist theoretical models to Greek and Roman society has set the agenda for many learned discussions in and out of print on the hierarchy and class structure of the pre-industrialized epoch. In the late 1970s, the classical periodical *Arethusa* devoted a whole issue to Marxism and the ancient world, and de Ste Croix's historical methodology was a constant reference point for the articles.

In your extract from de Ste Croix's substantial article on 'The Character of the Athenian Empire', a clear critical perspective on Thucydides emerges. We could say that de Ste Croix reads between the lines of Thucydides' history, but does so in an informed – not an instinctive – way. He demonstrates that even, in fact especially, when Thucydides is giving a highly partisan account of events and motivations, he can be a very valuable source for the tensions and transformations within Athenian society and within its relations with its subordinate allies.

Please read the fourteen pages you have of de Ste Croix's article and ask yourself what assumptions he is challenging and how he supports his own central ideas and interpretations.

Discussion

De Ste Croix challenges assumptions about Athenian despotism, a traditional picture which is based, he suggests, on an uncritical reading of the main primary sources. His aim is to demonstrate that Athenian hegemony over the Greek world was in large measure 'rule by consent'. 'Rule by consent', whatever historical period or society it is applied to, does not preclude the existence of political oppression and economic exploitation at home and abroad. De Ste Croix suggests, however, that even these features of modern imperialism within the Athenian Empire do not prove that the empire was detested by its allies.

Chief witness for the prosecution of Athens is an exiled citizen, Thucydides. Given Thucydides' jaundiced perspective on the democracy that banished him, you would expect de Ste Croix to discredit his evidence above all. However, he uses Thucydides first and foremost in Athens' defence. I would focus on paragraph two of pp.32-3 as crucial in de Ste Croix's method. There he distinguishes between the 'editor' Thucydides who interprets and comments on situations, and Thucydides the 'objective reporter' whose specific, narrative accounts apparently contradict his overall conclusions. You might feel that another dimension of the *logos/ergon* dialectic is emerging at this point. (See the summarizing discussion in Block 3, Section 4.)

During the course of the detailed instances that follow, de Ste Croix does refer to other ancient writers (for example, Diodorus, p.37). You will have noticed, too, the use made of inscriptions to support the line of argument. De Ste Croix compares and contrasts Thucydides' conclusions with other kinds of documentation. In regard to a general theoretical framework, he is especially concerned with the re-examination of terms such as *eleutheria* and *douleia* (usually rendered into English as 'freedom' and 'slavery') and with the tendency to impose twentieth-century preconceptions on Athenian and Greek attitudes and values, in regard to the conduct of the war.

Elsewhere in the article, de Ste Croix discusses the ranges of meaning implied by the terms 'democracy' and 'oligarchy' and their cognates. Marxists invariably question the blanket use of such terms and resist the tendency to see them as universal and unchanging concepts. The discussion is important so I have summarized it briefly as follows.

De Ste Croix draws upon Aristotle's fourth-century definition of *demotikos* as 'the poor'. 'Democracy' can be translated as rule by the *demos*, but the *demos* itself is a fluid term used to refer to the whole citizen body on some occasions but which was applied even more frequently to the poorer citizens. We could say that distinct value judgements and ideological positions lurk behind the employment of such terms in the ancient literature itself. De Ste Croix warns us to stay constantly aware of Thucydides' place in the social hierarchy as we attempt to evaluate how he uses key political terms.

Tensions between the men of property and wealth and 'the many and poor' are for de Ste Croix manifestations of class conflict. This is the theoretical model he has espoused as a Marxist historian. A cautious application of Marx's theory of classes in the ancient world guides and colours his survey of the tensions between oligarchs and democrats in Athens and other Greek city states. It underpins his contention that there was considerable support for the Athenian democratic experiment from the *demos* in allied societies. ◆

Reading associated with Block 4, Part 1, Sub-section 3.3

The first article to be read in conjunction with Block 4 explores vase scenes for their interpretative as well as functional qualities. The author, François Lissarrague, teaches in Paris and is a researcher at the major French Institute, Centre National des Recherches Scientifiques. He is a specialist in Greek iconography and has written various books and articles on this subject. For further reading you may like to look at his book, *The Aesthetics of the Greek Banquet: Images of Wine and Ritual* (tr. Andrew Szegedy-Maszak, Princeton University Press, 1987).

The strength of Lissarrague's approach is its imaginative but not over-prescriptive way of looking at images on painted pottery. (Note that Epictetus is prior to your period, but only just.)

You might want to consider how the author expands our ideas about the artistic function of the vases, and how the artist's statement of self goes beyond the written signature on the pot.

Lissarrague takes us into quite a sophisticated area of visual culture and the 'rules for reading' that culture (p.45). You will gather from the discussion in Section 3.3 of Block 4 that the scenes depicted on Greek vases (Greek drinking-vessels are subsumed under this category) are also part of our evidence for Athenian social life: 'the sheer survival of vases makes them attractive as evidence for all sorts of aspects of Athenian life' (Block 4, Sub-section 3.3).

As you read through the article, you should consider the way in which Lissarrague argues that the artist integrates the spirit of the symposium into his interpretation of the scenes on the symposium vases. The artist achieves this by working at distinct levels of representation. These include:

- the depiction of the social setting

- the choice of a narrative moment for the myth (highlighting tensions between order and disorder)

- the reinforcement of ritual.

Lissarrague is suggesting ways in which the participants in a drinking party might have interacted with both the design (form) and the subject-matter (content) of the scenes on their drinking vessels. He argues that the artist achieved an open play of combinations made through visual associations of various kinds – narrative, metaphoric or purely formal, similar to those one encounters in lyric poetry. The pleasure of the symposium lies in just such variations and in the surprises created both by the exchanges between the guests and the interplay between the various elements present in the symposium – songs, conversation and pictures.

The user of the cup, then, is manipulated by the creator of the cup into becoming not just a spectator of the scenes but a participant in the pictures – in more ways than one – as he drinks from it. This might seem fanciful at first reading, but it adds a further dimension to the section 'Vase-painting as evidence' by introducing another dialogue between art and the representation of 'reality'. You may recall a similar discussion on the tensions between representation and interpretation in the works of Thucydides (Block 3, Part 1, Section 4). Colin Macleod's judgement on Thucydides is applicable to the vase-painter who wishes to make his mark on the historical scene he portrays. Macleod likens Thucydides' technique of reconstructing speeches in the service of historical truth to that of an artist, 'refashioning his subject in order to bring out this significance'.

Glossary of terms

Silenoi, p.45: originally there was one individual, Silenos, a tipsy old 'tutor' of Dionysos; the tutor often rode an ass when accompanying the god. The *Silenoi*, like the Satyrs, are the god's drunken followers, of fairly grotesque appearance.

psychostasia, p.51: 'the weighing of lives', to determine who has the longer to live by fate's decree.

Reading associated with Block 4, Part 2

You will be asked to investigate Athenian social relations further at this point in the block by reading three thought-provoking articles. All three authors focus to a greater or lesser extent on the place of women in Athenian society, but they sift and evaluate the ancient evidence to create a broader picture of Athenian social identity and to highlight contradictions and correspondence between perceptions and realities (both past and present).

This is a good point at which to pause and contextualize the issue of Athenian women within the Athenian ethos. You may remember the broad question in the introduction to Part 2, 'Did the Athenians have a clear and unified picture of themselves?' The statement in the funeral speech about women has inevitably become a keystone in studies of Athenian social values in general and the question of gender construction in particular.

To refresh your memory, it goes like this: 'Great will be your glory in not falling short of your natural character; and greatest will be hers who is least talked of among the men whether for good or for bad' (*WA* p.60, paragraph 45).

Introduction to Walcot, Hardwick and Gould (Block 4, Part 2, Subsection 6.4)

Peter Walcot is professor of Greek in the Classics Department, University of Cardiff. His specialist interests are early Greek society, ancient morals, social values and women in antiquity. His emphasis upon cultural continuity is clearly illustrated by his work on the seclusion and separation of women in Athens. He draws upon and generalizes from studies that deal with patterns of behaviour and gender-roles *in the twentieth century* in the Mediterranean area.

In his article, which takes the Funeral Speech as its starting point, Walcot evaluates prevailing attitudes towards women in Athens to illustrate aspects of male civic identity. He discusses images of masculinity, and the ways in which they are reinforced through the restriction of women's roles. He argues that the seclusion of women is a continuing feature of rural life in some Mediterranean regions and implies that it is reasonable to draw inferences about the ancient world from modern customs.

Lorna Hardwick is a senior lecturer in the Department of Classical Studies at The Open University. As a graduate student she was a pupil of M.I. Finley (see article eight, 'Athenian demagogues', and his biography below). Hardwick's main work has been in the cultural politics of ancient Greece and its relationship with subsequent ideas and literature. This article was written as a result of her interest in examining a specific historical situation in the light of perspectives suggested by recent theoretical developments in social anthropology and feminist theory.

She examines the tensions in loyalties which might have threatened Athenian democracy and which crystallized around the issues of kinship and property transmitted through women. The article focuses sharply on the political realities of Periclean Athens. She demonstrates how essential it is to re-evaluate community history in the light of our investigation of women's history.

It will be important to read both these articles because they expand the concepts raised in Part 2 of Block 4. They will also consolidate your understanding of historiography as source material because, when examining the speech that Thucydides assigns to Pericles, the authors place it in the general context of social and material evidence.

Bear in mind that Hardwick's article was written twenty years after Walcot's. Important analyses of the Funeral Speech, its form and function, had been made by Ziolkowski and Loraux (see Block 4, Part 2, 5.3.1 and 5.3.2) during the intervening period and have to be taken into account by scholars of the 1990s.

John Gould has taught at Christ Church College, Oxford, and University College, Swansea, and has held the H.O. Wills professorship of Greek at the University of Bristol. He has written on Greek poetry and drama and on Greek religious and social institutions. His work on Herodotus brought an important new focus on the value of story-telling historians for a comprehensive interpretation of events and attitudes in the ancient world. His method is characterized by close attention to all the available evidence on the period or theme under study and an openness to data that are underused or dismissed as unreliable. He combines this approach with a critical re-examination of those sources that Classicists have used not wisely but too well.

We have reproduced the Gould article without its extensive footnotes. In the main these notes gave examples and quotations from ancient evidence (Greek and Latin authors) which supported each stage of his argument.

Reading Gould: absorbing and responding

Please now read the first five pages of Gould's 'Law, custom and myth: aspects of the social position of women in Classical Athens'. As you read, consider the following:

(a) *What difficulties does Gould identify in the presentation and representation of women through the classical literature of Athens?*

(b) *How does he suggest we might deal with these difficulties?*

Discussion _____

(a) On p.76 Gould talks about a male-dominated world, a world articulated by men. Perhaps you felt this was rather an obvious point about the exclusively male authors in Athens at this time, but Gould is reminding us that the cultural works of Athens that we study were the artistic endeavours of men, and that we see the women of that society through their eyes.

Gould suggests that even the most careful scholars can be carried away by powerful moments in Greek drama and forget that an emotive speech by a heroine (for instance, an Antigone or a Hecabe) was actually penned by a male playwright who had a largely male audience in view. Even if we cannot be sure about the attendance of women at the drama festival, we do know that the panel of judges was exclusively male.

11

Gould is also prepared to accept that women's value, place and function as represented by men are not necessarily a distortion of – or in constant opposition to – the way in which women themselves saw their role in society at this time. Precisely because Athenian society was male-dominated, we might not receive a radically different picture of Athenian society even if it became possible for us to view it through the works of Athenian women.

(b) Gould does not believe that the methodology for assessing women's social and legal status at Athens has advanced very far: most modern scholars persist in evaluating Athenian women from the male perspective. This not only distorts the way in which we address the issue, but also inevitably creates a uniform set of criteria by which women are judged. For instance, we tend to evaluate women's status negatively in terms of their exclusion from certain male spheres of activity. We should no longer be satisfied with the simple or single construct of 'the Athenian woman' that this produces.

Gould's second point is that previous scholarship tends to privilege one area of 'discourse' over another when it comes to gathering data on Athenian women. I use 'discourse' here in the broader sense of how a society constructs and conveys a sense of identity through its cultural products. Gould warns against selectivity of the texts, and selectivity within those texts that are most often used to yield evidence of trends in Athenian society. ♦

On pp.77–8 Gould deals with Gomme's use of tragedy to gather evidence on Athenian women.

Please now summarize Gomme's use of the evidence, and Gould's principal objections to it. (Note that Gould returns to Gomme on p.79.)

Discussion _____

Gomme argues from examples in tragedy that women in Athens were not secluded but could move about 'at will'. Such a use of tragedy and 'tragic women' assumes that drama is a legitimate source of evidence for social customs prevailing at the time of its production, irrespective of where and when the action of the plays is set.

Gould does not challenge the premise that the legendary, larger-than-life women of tragedy may say something to us about the social existence of women in Athens, even though their situations and status are atypical. Instead he confronts Gomme on his own ground and demonstrates that the same corpus of Greek tragedy can portray women as physically restricted and socially constrained. They are not always 'wild and free'. In any case, when women do move freely and at will in the plays, patterns of conventions are noticeably disturbed.

More than one commentator on tragic women has underlined the point that those women who do violate boundaries and expand their spheres of action are exhibiting consciously abnormal behaviour. For instance, Antigone reinforces an independent spirit and foolhardiness by invading male spaces. Her movement and her words signify rebellion. ♦

Gould's brief introduction to similar misreadings (in his view) of forensic literature reinforces his overall approach: he argues that one has to look at the texts in their totality. He is not concerned at this stage with any literary or rhetorical colouring that legal speeches might contain. As documentary source material these speeches must be methodically cross-referenced and approached as a body of evidence.

Gould's introduction finishes with a statement of intent. He aims to integrate what previous scholarship has regarded as 'mutually exclusive sets of data'. The main body of the article draws material from law, custom and myth –

sources that complement each other because all of these areas will, Gould believes, uncover similarly complex polarities in the portrayal of women.

Please now read the article to the end.

(NB: much of his evidence on pp.80–83 is drawn from the fourth century, which is considerably richer in surviving legal documentation. Don't get too bogged down in the minutiae of these examples but note how they tie in later with his overall conclusions.)

I would like you then to look back at the discussion in Block 4 (Part 1, Sub-section 3.3 and Part 2, Sub-section 6.4), and to reread the section on women in WA, 4.23–28. Is Gould simply substantiating the view that women were regarded with ambivalence in Athens, or do his conclusions go deeper than that?

Discussion

Gould has a healthy respect for the different kinds of data he surveys, and he seeks to evaluate the evidence thoroughly and equitably. His discussion is a sophisticated extension of *WA*'s conclusions at 4.31.

He introduces the term 'liminality' (from *limen*, Latin for 'threshold') into the discussion on women and the attitudes of Athenian men towards them. This idea of women on the margins or thresholds of society is a fruitful one, which can have a general application in our study of women's functions in the areas of law, politics and religion.

It is a useful term to apply in the sphere of property relations: women could be viewed as boundary-crossers from one *oikos* to another, and at the same time as transmitters of property that they neither owned nor controlled.

'Liminality' also identifies tenacious anxieties of the time – that women were close to 'nature in the raw', and were only really kept within the boundaries of society, order and convention by constant constraint and confinement (which would also justify their formal exclusion from politics).

Gould suggests that the images of women in myth and their customary roles in rituals cannot be divorced from their status in law and their place in society in general. This was all part of the defining, demarcating and structuring of women's roles and activities in Athenian society.

Perhaps women in Greek drama continue to come across so powerfully precisely because they challenge the boundaries and reveal their potential for playing many influential roles. For example, in Simon Goldhill's article 'The Great Dionysia and civic ideology' an interesting case is made for the acceptable disturbance of civic norms portrayed on the stage in the performances. Goldhill concludes that all the tensions and polarities that tragedy and comedy set in motion reflect aspects of Dionysus, the divinity associated with illusion and change, paradox and ambiguity, release and transgression (S.D. Goldhill (1987) 'The Great Dionysia and civic ideology', *Journal of Hellenic Studies*, 58–76, p.76). ◆

You may find it an interesting exercise to re-read both Walcot and Hardwick when you have completed your study of Gould. Note down the benefits that Gould's painstaking scholarship on women has brought to subsequent appraisals of Athenian society. Ask yourself, for example: 'Has Gould established criteria for a more comprehensive and, especially, a more objective approach to the data?'

Finley (Block 4, Part 2, Sub-section 6.5.3)

Moses Finley was born in New York in 1912 and died in 1986. He rapidly made his mark as a lecturer, teacher and writer principally in the field of Greek society, economy and politics. He was a victim of McCarthyism and left America in the 1950s to become a lecturer and later Professor of Ancient

History at Cambridge University. He was Master of Darwin College, and received a knighthood. His training in history and law gave him an acuity in the treatment of ancient sources, which he viewed critically and often quite sceptically.

He considered that in conjunction with the critical investigation of the ancient sources, historians of the ancient world should pay equal attention to the nature of the questions they themselves were asking. His work demonstrated how interpretation of the evidence depended not only on analysis of the sources but also on the construction of models which enabled generalizations about the main features of the ancient economy and society.

His highly influential scholarly output includes the well-known books, *The Ancient Economy* (Chatto and Windus, 1973), *Democracy Ancient and Modern* (Chatto and Windus, 1973), *The Use and Abuse of History* (Chatto and Windus, 1975), *Ancient Slavery and Modern Ideology* (Chatto and Windus, 1980), *Economy and Society in Ancient Greece* (Chatto and Windus, 1981) and *Politics in the Ancient World* (Cambridge University Press, 1982).

You are familiar with Finley's style and approach from his introduction and notes to the Penguin Thucydides. In his article 'Athenian demagogues', he provides a lively and wide-ranging survey of the processes of Athenian democracy, and expands the concepts that are raised in Block 4, Part 2, Section 6.4.

There is a great deal of interpretative history in Finley's article – what we could call informed speculation – about how far, in practice, citizens participated in Athenian politics. Subsequent studies have questioned assumptions that Finley espouses on p.99. For instance, he suggests that urban residents were more likely than rural residents to attend the *ekklesia* regularly. However, although it is true that city-dwellers could quite literally be 'roped into' attendance at the assembly (*WA*, p.202), it has been argued that working citizens at Athens would only 'shut up shop' for exceptional assemblies, whereas agricultural life had prolonged periods of enforced seasonal inactivity when farmers could come to town. Of course, this does not tell us who, *at any particular time*, attended the *ekklesia*.

This conflict of interpretation is a good example of differing ways of 'reading' the socio-economic circumstances that are surveyed at the end of Part 1, Block 4.

Finley reconstructs the kind of mutual manipulation that might have occurred between citizens and leaders, and examines checks and balances in the working of Athenian democracy. An interesting premise in the article – and one also open to question – is Finley's statement about the absence of any 'articulated democratic theory' in Athens at that time.

This issue connects Finley's approach with de Ste Croix whose article on Athenian imperalism was discussed earlier. De Ste Croix analysed the character of Athenian imperialism with reference to the concept of democracy, and he also emphasized that those terms conjure up certain features for the modern reader which can distort our perceptions of fifth-century Athens.

Reading associated with Block 5, Sub-section 1.5

The offprints by Muir and Bowie are discussed within the text of Block 5 (see Sections 1.5 and 3.5). Biographical information is given below.

John Muir taught at Kings College London, where he had major responsibility for the training of teachers of classics, and has contributed to the development of Ancient Language teaching in UK schools and universities.

His research interests lie in the field of ancient educational practice and, in particular, the methods and doctrines of the fifth-century Greek sophists: for example, Protagoras.

Angus Bowie is Fellow and Lecturer in Classics at The Queen's College, Oxford. The major book on Aristophanes from which this chapter is taken reflects the author's continuing interest in the relation between myth, ritual and drama. As well as studying ritual stereotypes and comic reversal, he also has explored the function of myth in tragedy, in particular *The Oresteia* of Aeschylus. His interests also extend to Latin literature, notably to studies of allegory in the Virgilian recreation of history.

A final point about The Offprints

To reiterate a point made in the introduction to this guide: the articles have been selected to represent a range of interpretations of the period; they do not constitute the only accepted (or canonical) approach to the areas they tackle. A sensible and relevant use of them will gain you credit in your assignments and in the examination. As you work through the revision tape at the end of the academic year, do come back to this secondary material so that your programme and plan have the depth and breadth of a 60-point course at second level.

A note on the footnotes: with some of the articles that follow, footnotes have been renumbered for ease of reference, and you should bear this in mind if you subsequently refer to the original publication.

THE PLACE OF HERODOTUS IN THE HISTORY OF HISTORIOGRAPHY[1]

Source: *Studies in Historiography*, Weidenfeld & Nicolson, 1966, Chapter 8, pp.127–42.

By A.D. Momigliano

[...] Admittedly, the Greeks and Romans were not apt to kneel in silent adoration before their own classical writers. Historians were especially open to accusations of dishonesty. But no other writer was so severely criticized as Herodotus. His bad reputation in the ancient world is something exceptional that requires explanation. It does so the more because the ancient opinion had a considerable influence on Herodotus' reputation among the students of ancient history from the fifteenth century to our own times. The story of Herodotus' posthumous struggle against his detractors is an important chapter in the history of historical thought: it is also, in my opinion, an important clue to the understanding of Herodotus himself.

Herodotus combined two types of historical research. He enquired about the Persian war – an event of one generation earlier – and he travelled in the East to collect information about present conditions and past events in those countries. The combination of two such tasks would be difficult for any man at any time. It was particularly difficult for a historian who had to work in Greece during the fifth century BC. When Herodotus worked on Greek history, he had very few written documents to rely upon: Greek history was as yet mainly transmitted by oral tradition. When he travelled to the East, he found any amount of written evidence, but he had not been trained to read it.

Let us say immediately that Herodotus was successful in his enterprise. We have now collected enough evidence to be able to say that he can be trusted. Curiously enough we are in a better position to judge him as a historian of the East than as historian of the Persian Wars. In the last century Orientalists have scrutinized Herodotus with the help of archaeology and with the knowledge of languages that he could not understand. They have ascertained that he described truthfully what he saw and reported honestly what he heard. Where he went wrong, either his informants misled him or he had misunderstood in good faith what he was told. We are not so well placed for the history of the Persian Wars because Herodotus himself remains our main source. Wherever we happen to be able to check him with the help of inscriptions or of simple topography, we have no reason to be dissatisfied with him. This, however, does not mean that we are in a position to say how Herodotus wrote his history. We do not yet know exactly how he proceeded in his enquiry, compared different versions, wrote down his notes, gave them their present literary form. Above all we cannot say how much he owed to earlier writers. But we know enough about Herodotus' alleged predecessors – Cadmus of Miletus, Hecataeus, Dionysius of Miletus, Charon of Lampsacus, Xanthus of Sardes – to state confidently that they did not do the work for him. There was no Herodotus before Herodotus.

The almost total loss of the geographical and ethnographical literature that preceded and accompanied Herodotus' work makes it impossible for us to assess exactly how much he owed to earlier and contemporary writers. But any careful reader of his work will agree that his main research must have been done not on written, but on oral tradition. After all, Herodotus himself tells us that he used ὄψις, γνώμη and ἱστορία: his eyes, his judgment and his talent for enquiry. This can be confirmed by an analysis of the main episodes of the Persian Wars. It is easy to see that what he knows about Thermopylae chiefly comes from Sparta, whereas Athenian traditions are behind his accounts of Marathon, Salamis and Plataea.

---

[1] *History* 43 (1958), 1–13. A paper read at the Anglo-American Conference of Historians, July 1957.

In other words Herodotus managed to produce a very respectable history mainly on the basis of sightseeing and oral tradition. He succeeded in putting together a trustworthy account of events he was too young to have witnessed and of countries whose languages he did not understand. We know that his history is respectable because we are now able to check it against independent evidence. But we must admit that if we had to give an *a priori* estimate of the chances of success in writing history by Herodotus' method, we should probably shake our heads in sheer despondency. Herodotus' success in touring the world and handling oral traditions is something exceptional by any standard – something that we are not yet in a position to explain fully. The secrets of his workshop are not yet all out. Therefore we cannot be surprised if the ancients found it difficult to trust an author who had worked on such a basis as Herodotus.

It is only too obvious that Thucydides ultimately determined the verdict of antiquity on his predecessor. He carefully read (or listened to) his Herodotus and decided that the Herodotean approach to history was unsafe. To write serious history, one had to be a contemporary of the events under discussion and one had to be able to understand what people were saying. Serious history – according to Thucydides – was not concerned with the past, but with the present; it could not be concerned with distant countries, but only with those places in which you lived and with those people whose thoughts you could put into your own words without difficulty. Thucydides did not believe that there was a future in Herodotus' attempt to describe events he had not witnessed and to tell the story of men whose language he could not understand. We now know that Thucydides was insensitive to Herodotus' bold attempt to open up the gates of the past and of foreign countries to historical research. But we must recognize that he knew what he was doing in criticizing Herodotus. He was setting up stricter standards of historical reliability, even at the risk of confining history to a narrow patch of contemporary events. Thucydides claimed that a historian must personally vouch for what he tells. He allowed only a limited amount of inferences from present facts to events of the past. He also implied that it is easier to understand political actions than any other type of action. With Thucydides history became primarily political history and was confined to contemporary events.

Now Thucydides certainly did not succeed in imposing his strict standard of historical reliability on other historians, but he succeeded in discouraging the idea that one could do real research about the past. Greek and Roman historians in fact, after Herodotus, did very little research into the past and relatively seldom undertook to collect first-hand evidence about foreign countries. They concentrated on contemporary history or summarized and reinterpreted the work of former historians. Search for unknown facts about the past was left to antiquarians, and the work of the antiquarians hardly influenced the historians. It can be doubted whether Polybius studied Aristotle's constitutions or whether Livy ever read his Varro thoroughly. Indeed, the very existence of the antiquarians was conditioned by the fact that historians interested themselves only in a small sector of what nowadays we should call history. Every generalization of this kind is bound to do violence to a certain number of facts. But on the whole it is apparent that the great historians of antiquity left their mark either on first-hand accounts of contemporary events or on the reinterpretation of facts already collected by previous historians. Xenophon, Theopompus, Hieronymus of Cardia, Polybius, Sallust were pre-eminently historians of their own time. Ephorus, Livy and Tacitus are at different levels to be considered original historians only in so far as they reinterpreted facts which previous historians had collected. The surviving books of Tacitus' *Annals* are the most conspicuous example of a great work of history written with a minimum amount of independent research. And Tacitus himself is an example of what can happen to a historian who relies on interpretation rather than on research: if he is not wrong in his facts, he is liable to be arbitrary in his explanations.[2]

[2] For a different point of view, R. Syme, *Tacitus* (Oxford 1958).

A PERSON WHO TAKES THE THOUGHTS & IDEAS OF ANOTHER AN USES THEM FOR HIMSELF.

Ancient historiography never overcame the limitations imposed by what we can call the paramouncy of contemporary history. The more remote the past, the less likely historians were to contribute anything new to the knowledge of it. Ephorus and Livy were honest men. They were by no means deprived of critical sense. Ephorus decided that it was no use trying to tell the story of the Greeks before the Dorian invasion. Livy was acutely aware of the legendary character of the traditions he was bound to follow about the early history of Rome. But neither of them knew how to go beyond the literary sources for an independent enquiry about the past.

Thus Thucydides imposed the idea that contemporary political history was the only serious history; and Herodotus was cut off from the stream of ancient historiography. He was neither a contemporary nor a political historian. His tales, however attractive, looked oddly unprofessional. Even those who liked him as a patriotic and pleasant writer could hardly defend him as a reliable historian. Herodotus invited awkward questions: how could he tell so much about events he had never seen and about people whose language he did not know and whose countries he had only visited for a short time, if at all? *Either* he had concealed his sources, and was a plagiarist, *or* he had invented his facts and was a liar. The dilemma dominated ancient criticism of Herodotus. There was not a very great choice of predecessors, as we know, from whom he could have stolen his facts, but some could be found. A few were authentic enough: the geographer Hecataeus, the mythographer Acusilaus, the genealogist Pherekydes of Athens, perhaps also Xanthus the historian of Lydia, and Dionysius of Miletus the historian of Persia. Others were late forgers, but were accepted as authentic archaic writers by the majority of ancient critics: for instance the alleged first historian Cadmus of Miletus. Furthermore there were genuine historians whom Hellenistic scholarship placed before Herodotus, whereas some at least of the most authoritative modern scholars incline to take them for his younger contemporaries. To mention only the best instance, F. Jacoby has given very cogent reasons for dating Charon of Lampsacus not in the middle but at the end of the fifth century.[3] All these historians counted in the eyes of ancient scholars as potential sources of Herodotus and were made to contribute to the case for Herodotus' plagiarism. But even with the help of writers who were later than Herodotus and therefore may have used him, rather than having been used by him, the case for plagiarism can never have been a very impressive one. Many of Herodotus' enemies seem to have preferred the alternative line of attack which was to present him as a liar. It was obviously easier to dismiss his evidence than to trace his sources. After all, he could not have been considered the father of history if it had been so evident that he had copied from his predecessors. Though we shall see that there were books on Herodotus as a plagiarist, the final impression left by the ancient criticisms of Herodotus is that he was a story-teller – a liar. Here again we can measure the impact of Thucydides' verdict on his predecessor.

Herodotus had hardly ceased writing his history when Thucydides began to reflect on the mistakes and shortcomings of his predecessor. A few decades after Thucydides, Ctesias launched another attack against Herodotus by questioning his competence both as a student of Greek history and as an historian of the East. Ctesias had all the external qualifications for checking Herodotus' results. He had lived several years at the Persian court and must have understood Persian. He had opportunities of access to Persian records certainly denied to Herodotus. The impact of Ctesias' attack was somewhat reduced by its very violence and extravagance. A historian who puts the battle of Plataea before Salamis in order to impress on his readers his independence from the despised predecessor is likely to get himself into trouble. People were not slow to realize that Ctesias was no less open to suspicion than Herodotus. But, as we know, conflicting suspicions do not cancel each other out. Herodotus' reputation remained tarnished. Paradoxically, he was often associated with Ctesias as an unreliable historian. Even Aristotle went out of his way to denounce

---

[3] *Abhandlungen zur Griechischen Geschichtsschreibung* (1956) p.178.

Herodotus' mistakes over small details of natural history; and he formulated his criticism in such terms as to involve the reliability of the whole of Herodotus' history. He calls Herodotus a 'story-teller'.

The expedition of Alexander the Great, by opening up the East, certainly revealed lacunae in Herodotus' information. Strabo in his *Geography* repeatedly echoes and makes his own the criticisms of Alexandrian scholarship. Meanwhile, the Orientals themselves were being Hellenized. They learnt to read what the Greeks had written about them in former centuries and, not unnaturally, found it unsatisfactory. Manetho, the Egyptian priest who tried to present the history of his people to the Greeks, also wrote a pamphlet against Herodotus. The Greeks themselves became increasingly impatient with Herodotus for patriotic reasons. What may seem to us the wonderful serenity and sense of humour of Herodotus in judging the issues between Greeks and Barbarians was for them evidence that the historian had been 'a friend of the barbarians'. Even the local patriotism of Hellenistic Greeks operated against his reputation. Local historians and antiquarians were glad to show him up: he had not said enough about the glories of their own cities. All the anti-Herodotean literature of the Hellenistic age is unfortunately lost, but Plutarch's *De Herodoti Malignitate* can give us some idea of the complaints that were lodged against the father of history. Plutarch puts together a series of criticisms against Herodotus: excessive sympathy for the barbarians, partiality for Athens, gross unfairness towards the other Greek cities, lack of truthfulness where facts are concerned and lack of balance where judgments are involved. History was a form of encomium to Plutarch, and evidently Herodotus did not fit into the pattern. It is a pity that nobody has yet produced a competent commentary on Plutarch's pamphlet against Herodotus, both because it is typical of the way in which late Greeks looked at their past and because it influenced the judgment about Herodotus of many classical scholars from the fifteenth to the nineteenth century. Plutarch does not seem to have said the worst about Herodotus. To guess from the titles of lost works, even worse was in store for the father of history. Titles such as *On Herodotus' thefts* by Valerius Pollio or *On Herodotus' lies* by Aelius Harpocration – not to speak of the book by Libanius *Against Herodotus* – seem to imply that there was no dishonesty of which he was not capable.[4]

With all that, Herodotus remained a classic. The immaculate grace of his style defied criticism. His information about Oriental countries was more easily criticized than replaced. Notwithstanding Manetho and Berossus, he remained the standard authority on Egypt and Babylonia. His epic tale of the Persian wars was a unique document of the Greek past. The accusation of lack of patriotism could hardly pass unchallenged. We can easily draw up a list of admirers of Herodotus. Theopompus summarized him in two books. No less a critic than Aristarchus wrote a commentary on him. The discovery of a fragment of this commentary has been enough to dispose of the legend that Herodotus was almost forgotten in the Hellenistic age. From the first century BC to the late second century AD Herodotus was in special favour as a model of style. Archaism operated in his favour. Dionysius of Halicarnassus, Arrian and Lucian were his champions. Dionysius says, 'If we take up his book, we are filled with admiration till the last syllable and always seek for more.' What more splendid compliment could Herodotus desire? Lucian is no less enthusiastic: 'If only we could imitate Herodotus – not all his good qualities because this is beyond hope – but at least one of them.'[5]

Yet there are very disturbing features in these apologies for Herodotus. Dionysius does not argue that Herodotus is a reliable historian: he compares him with Thucydides and gives reasons for the superiority of Herodotus that can persuade only those who do not care for reliability in a history. According to Dionysius, Herodotus chose a better subject than Thucydides, because he

[4] Details in W. Schmid, *Geschichte der griech. Literatur* II (1934) pp.665–70.

[5] Dionysius, *Letter to Pompeius*, 3, ed. W. Rhys Roberts; Lucian, *Herodotus* (21), 1.

told the glories and not the misfortunes of the Greeks. He gave his history a better beginning and a better end. He wrote up his subject in a more interesting way and he arranged his materials better. In points of style he can at least compete with Thucydides. If Thucydides is more concise, Herodotus is more vivid; if Thucydides is more robust, Herodotus is more graceful. Herodotus' beauty is 'radiant', where Thucydides' is awe-inspiring. All is in favour of Herodotus – except truth.

In the same way Lucian admires him without ever implying that he is a reliable historian. Indeed Lucian positively denies that Herodotus is trustworthy. At least twice he couples him with Ctesias as one of the historians who are notorious liars. In the pamphlet of 'How to write history' (*Quomodo sit historia conscribenda*) Lucian definitely presents Thucydides as the model of the fearless, incorruptible, free, sincere and truthful historian. He emphasizes the fact that Thucydides developed his rules for the historian after having observed what Herodotus had done (41–2). Those who speak about Dionysius and Lucian as the great champions of Herodotus in antiquity too often forget to add that Dionysius implicitly and Lucian explicitly deny his truthfulness.

It is my submission that all this resulted from the fact that Herodotus had dared to write a kind of history of which Thucydides disapproved and which later historians found remote and uncongenial. The legend of Herodotus the liar is the result of the authentic achievements of Herodotus the historian. But it will have been observed that if Thucydides disapproved of writing on the past, he did not challenge Herodotus' assumption that history can be written from oral tradition. In the circumstances of the fifth century it was hardly possible to think otherwise. At least in Greece there were not enough written documents to make a sufficiently broad basis for history. Thucydides was far from being blind to the possibilities offered by the exploitation of written documents. Indeed he was one of the very few ancient historians to use written diplomatic records. But it could never occur to him that written records were the primary source for history: if he had thought so, he would never have written the history of the Peloponnesian War. More remarkable is the fact that later historians never tried to modify an approach that had originally been dictated by the conditions of fifth-century Greece. In Hellenistic Egypt there would have been an embarrassing wealth of written records to exploit; and written records were certainly not scarce in Rome during the late Republic and the Empire. But the study of written records remained to the end an exceptional occupation for the Greek and Roman historians. If Thucydides dictated the paramouncy of contemporary history, Herodotus determined the paramouncy of oral evidence. This explains why, though discredited, he remained the father of history.

The pre-eminence of personal observation and oral evidence lasted until historians decided to go to the record office. Familiarity with the record office, as we all know, is a recently acquired habit for the historian, hardly older than a century. It is true that the Roman and Greek antiquarians knew something about the use of documents and that the antiquarians of the Renaissance perfected this approach to the past. But this method became really effective and universally accepted only a hundred years ago. The antiquarians began to study systematically the records of the past in the fifteenth century, but only in the eighteenth century did the barriers between antiquarianism and history break down, and only in the nineteenth did it become established practice for the historian to look for new evidence before writing new books of history. The historians continued to compile ancient literary sources and medieval chronicles long after Spanheim, Maffei and Mabillon had worked out the proper method of studying coins, inscriptions and medieval charters. Gibbon was perhaps the first historian concerned with the classical world to pay attention to the results of antiquarian studies: he used the results of antiquarian labour. But even Gibbon made very little independent research in the fields of numismatics, epigraphy and archaeology. The documentary or antiquarian approach to the past is now so integral a part of historical studies that we sometimes forget that Mommsen was the first Roman historian systematically to use inscriptions and coins. Not until Rostovtzeff did archaeology come into its own for the history of the Roman empire. I am old enough to have witnessed the surprise caused by Rostovtzeff's mastery of archaeological data for historical purposes.

The antiquarian or documentary approach to history has been the most effective way of dealing with Thucydides' objection against a history of the past. We may indulge in the illusion that if Thucydides were to come back to life he would not reject our methods with the contempt with which he rejected the method of Herodotus. The labours of the antiquarians between the fifteenth and the nineteenth centuries prepared the way for an approach to the past that effectively undermined the paramouncy of contemporary history. By excavating sites, searching the files of the record office, comparing coins, reading inscriptions and papyri, we have gone into the past with the same confidence with which Thucydides and his informants went about the assembly places of contemporary Sparta and Athens. We can collect reliable facts without being eye-witnesses in the Thucydidean sense. In unguarded moments of pride we may even be tempted to tell Thucydides that we know more about Athenian tribute lists than he ever did.

It would however be a great mistake of historical perspective to believe that the documentary approach to history has been the only way in which modern historiography has overcome the limitations imposed by Thucydides on ancient historiography. Before the study of documentary and archaeological evidence became a generalized practice, there was a revival of the Herodotean attempt to get into the past by way of enquiries founded on travels and the study of oral tradition. Defeated in antiquity, Herodotus triumphed in the sixteenth century. The revival of the Herodotean approach to the past, which happened then, is the first contribution of modern historiography to an independent study of the past.[6]

[... the next section of the article discusses in detail sixteenth-century attitudes to Herodotus.]

The stupendous developments of the study of Greek and Oriental history in the last three centuries would never have happened without Herodotus. Trust in Herodotus has been the first condition for the fruitful exploration of our remote past. The people who went to excavate Egypt and Mesopotamia had primarily Herodotus as their guide. But there is something more to Herodotus than this. It is true that professional historians now mainly work on written evidence. But anthropologists, sociologists and students of folklore are doing on oral evidence what to all intents and purposes is historical work. The modern accounts of explorers, anthropologists and sociologists about primitive populations are ultimately an independent development of Herodotus' *historia*. Thus Herodotus is still with us with the full force of his method of studying not only the present, but also the past, on oral evidence. It is a strange truth that Herodotus has really become the father of history only in modern times.[7]

[6] *Cf.* my paper *Erodoto e la Storiografia Moderna, Aevum* 31 (1957) pp.74–84 for other details.

[7] Compare the excellent paper by H. Strasburger, *Herodots Zeitrechnung, Historia* 5 (1956) pp. 129–61. [W. von Leyden, *Spatium Historicum, Durham University Journal* (1950) 89–104; T. S. Brown, *Herodotus and his Profession, Amer. Hist. Rev.* 69 (1954) 829–43; H. R. Immerwahr, *Aspects of Historical Causation in Herodotus, Trans. Am. Phil. Ass.* 87 (1956) 241–80; F. Mitchel, *Herodotus' Use of Genealogical Chronology, The Phoenix,* 10 (1956) 48–69; R. Lattimore, *The Composition of the History of Herodotus, Classical Philology,* 53 (1958) 9–21; K. Latte, *Histoire et historiens dans l'antiquité* (1958) 3–37.]

ON MISUNDERSTANDING THE *OEDIPUS REX*[1]

Source: *Greece and Rome*, 13, 1966, pp.37–49.

By E.R. Dodds

On the last occasion when I had the misfortune to examine in Honour Moderations at Oxford, I set a question on the *Oedipus Rex*, which was among the books prescribed for general reading. My question was 'In what sense, if in any, does the *Oedipus Rex* attempt to justify the ways of God to man?' It was an optional question; there were plenty of alternatives. But the candidates evidently considered it a gift: nearly all of them attempted it. When I came to sort out the answers I found that they fell into three groups.

The first and biggest group held that the play justifies the gods by showing – or, as many of them said, 'proving' – that we get what we deserve. The arguments of this group turned upon the character of Oedipus. Some considered that Oedipus was a bad man: look how he treated Creon – naturally the gods punished him. Others said 'No, not altogether bad, even in some ways rather noble; but he had one of those fatal ἁμαρτίαι [flaws] that all tragic heroes have, as we know from Aristotle. And since he had a ἁμαρτία [flaw] he could of course expect no mercy: the gods had read the *Poetics*.' Well over half the candidates held views of this general type.

A second substantial group held that the *Oedipus Rex* is 'a tragedy of destiny'. What the play 'proves', they said, is that man has no free will but is a puppet in the hands of the gods who pull the strings that make him dance. Whether Sophocles thought the gods justified in treating their puppet as they did was not always clear from their answers. Most of those who took this view evidently disliked the play; some of them were honest enough to say so.

The third group was much smaller, but included some of the more thoughtful candidates. In their opinion Sophocles was 'a pure artist' and was therefore not interested in justifying the gods. He took the story of Oedipus as he found it, and used it to make an exciting play. The gods are simply part of the machinery of the plot.

Ninety per cent of the answers fell into one or the other of these three groups. The remaining ten per cent had either failed to make up their minds or failed to express themselves intelligibly.

It was a shock to me to discover that all these young persons, supposedly trained in the study of classical literature, could read this great and moving play and so completely miss the point. For all the views I have just summarized are in fact demonstrably false (though some of them, and some ways of stating them, are more crudely and vulgarly false than others). It is true that each of them has been defended by some scholars in the past, but I had hoped that all of them were by now dead and buried. Wilamowitz thought he had killed the lot in an article published in *Hermes* (34 [1899], 55ff.) more than half a century ago; and they have repeatedly been killed since. Yet their unquiet ghosts still haunt the examination-rooms of universities – and also, I would add, the pages of popular handbooks on the history of European drama. Surely that means that we have somehow failed in our duty as teachers?

It was this sense of failure which prompted me to attempt once more to clear up some of these ancient confusions. If the reader feels – as he very well may – that in this paper I am flogging a dead horse, I can only reply that on the evidence I have quoted the animal is unaccountably still alive.

---

[1] A paper read at a 'refresher course' for teachers, London Institute of Education, 24 July 1964.

I shall take Aristotle as my starting point, since he is claimed as the primary witness for the first of the views I have described. From the thirteenth chapter of the *Poetics* we learn that the best sort of tragic hero is a man highly esteemed and prosperous who falls into misfortune because of some serious flaw or error (μεγάλη) ἁμαρτία: examples, Oedipus and Thyestes. In Aristotle's view, then, Oedipus' misfortune was directly occasioned by some serious ἁμαρτία; and since Aristotle was known to be infallible, Victorian critics proceeded at once to look for this ἁμαρτία [flaw]. And so, it appears, do the majority of present-day undergraduates.

What do they find? It depends on what they expect to find. As we all know, the word ἁμαρτία [flaw] is ambiguous: in ordinary usage it is sometimes applied to false moral judgements, sometimes to purely intellectual error – the average Greek did not make our sharp distinction between the two. Since *Poetics* 13 is in general concerned with the moral character of the tragic hero, many scholars have thought in the past (and many undergraduates still think) that the ἁμαρτία of Oedipus must in Aristotle's view be a moral fault. They have accordingly gone over the play with a microscope looking for moral faults in Oedipus, and have duly found them – for neither here nor anywhere else did Sophocles portray that insipid and unlikely character, the man of perfect virtue. Oedipus, they point out, is proud and over-confident; he harbours unjustified suspicions against Teiresias and Creon; in one place (lines 964ff.) he goes so far as to express some uncertainty about the truth of oracles. One may doubt whether this adds up to what Aristotle would consider μεγάλη ἁμαρτία [serious flaw]. But even if it did, it would have no direct relevance to the question at issue. Years before the action of the play begins, Oedipus was already an incestuous parricide; if that was a punishment for his unkind treatment of Creon, then the punishment preceded the crime – which is surely an odd kind of justice.

'Ah,' says the traditionalist critic, 'but Oedipus' behaviour on the stage reveals the man he always was: he was punished for his basically unsound character.' In that case, however, someone on the stage ought to tell us so: Oedipus should repent, as Creon repents in the *Antigone*; or else another speaker should draw the moral. To ask about a character in fiction 'Was he a good man?' is to ask a strictly meaningless question: since Oedipus never lived we can answer neither 'Yes' nor 'No'. The legitimate question is 'Did Sophocles intend us to think of Oedipus as a good man?' This *can* be answered – not by applying some ethical yardstick of our own, but by looking at what the characters in the play say about him. And by that test the answer is 'Yes'. In the eyes of the Priest in the opening scene he is the greatest and noblest of men, the saviour of Thebes who with divine aid rescued the city from the Sphinx. The Chorus has the same view of him: he has proved his wisdom, he is the darling of the city, and never will they believe ill of him (504ff.). And when the catastrophe comes, no one turns round and remarks 'Well, but it was your own fault: it must have been; Aristotle says so.'

In my opinion, and in that of nearly all Aristotelian scholars since Bywater, Aristotle does *not* say so; it is only the perversity of moralizing critics that has misrepresented him as saying so. It is almost certain that Aristotle was using ἁμαρτία here as he uses ἁμάρτημα in the *Nicomachean Ethics* (1135b12) and in the *Rhetoric* (1374b6), to mean an offence committed in ignorance of some material fact and therefore free from πονηρία [wickedness] or κακία [moral defect].[2] These parallels seem decisive; and they are confirmed by Aristotle's second example – Thyestes, the man who ate the flesh of his own children in the belief that it was butcher's meat, and who subsequently begat a child on his own daughter, not knowing who she was. His story has clearly much in common with that of Oedipus, and Plato as well as Aristotle couples the two names as examples of the gravest ἁμαρτία [flaw] (*Laws* 838 c). Thyestes

---

[2] For the full evidence see O. Hey's exhaustive examination of the usage of these words, *Philol.* 83 (1927), 1–17; 137–63. Cf. also K. von Fritz, *Antike und Moderne Tragödie* (Berlin, 1962), 1ff.

and Oedipus are both of them men who violated the most sacred of Nature's laws and thus incurred the most horrible of all pollutions; but they both did so without πονηρία [wickedness], for they knew not what they did – in Aristotle's quasi-legal terminology, it was a ἁμάρτημα [failure, mistake], not an ἀδίκημα [intentional wrong]. That is why they were in his view especially suitable subjects for tragedy. Had they acted knowingly, they would have been inhuman monsters, and we could not have felt for them that pity which tragedy ought to produce. As it is, we feel both pity, for the fragile estate of man, and terror, for a world whose laws we do not understand. The ἁμαρτία [flaw] of Oedipus did not lie in losing his temper with Teiresias; it lay quite simply in parricide and incest – a μεγάλη ἁμαρτία [serious flaw] indeed, the greatest a man can commit.

The theory that the tragic hero must have a grave moral flaw, and its mistaken ascription to Aristotle, has had a long and disastrous history. It was gratifying to Victorian critics, since it appeared to fit certain plays of Shakespeare. But it goes back much further, to the seventeenth-century French critic Dacier, who influenced the practice of the French classical dramatists, especially Corneille, and was himself influenced by the still older nonsense about 'poetic justice' – the notion that the poet has a moral duty to represent the world as a place where the good are always rewarded and the bad are always punished. I need not say that this puerile idea is completely foreign to Aristotle and to the practice of the Greek dramatists; I only mention it because on the evidence of those Honour Mods. papers it would appear that it still lingers on in some youthful minds like a cobweb in an unswept room.

To return to the *Oedipus Rex*, the moralist has still one last card to play. Could not Oedipus, he asks, have escaped his doom if he had been more careful? Knowing that he was in danger of committing parricide and incest, would not a really prudent man have avoided quarrelling, even in self-defence, with men older than himself, and also love-relations with women older than himself? Would he not, in Waldock's ironic phrase, have compiled a handlist of all the things he must not do? In real life I suppose he might. But we are not entitled to blame Oedipus either for carelessness in failing to compile a handlist or for lack of self-control in failing to obey its injunctions. For no such possibilities are mentioned in the play, or even hinted at; and it is an essential critical principle that *what is not mentioned in the play does not exist.* These considerations would be in place if we were examining the conduct of a real person. But we are not: we are examining the intentions of a dramatist, and we are not entitled to ask questions that the dramatist did not intend us to ask. There is only one branch of literature where we *are* entitled to ask such questions about τὰ ἐκτὸς τοῦ δράματος [what is outside the play], namely the modern detective story. And despite certain similarities the *Oedipus Rex* is not a detective story but a dramatized folktale. If we insist on reading it as if it were a law report we must expect to miss the point.[3]

In any case, Sophocles has provided a conclusive answer to those who suggest that Oedipus could, and therefore should, have avoided his fate. The oracle was *unconditional* (line 790): it did not say 'If you do so-and-so you will kill your father'; it simply said 'You will kill your father, you will sleep with your

[3] The danger is exemplified by Mr. P.H. Vellacott's article, 'The Guilt of Oedipus', which appeared in this journal (vol. xi [1964], 137–48) shortly after my talk was delivered. By treating Oedipus as an historical personage and examining his career from the 'common-sense' standpoint of a prosecuting counsel Mr. Vellacott has no difficulty in showing that Oedipus must have guessed the true story of his birth long before the point at which the play opens – and guiltily done nothing about it. Sophocles, according to Mr. Vellacott, realized this, but unfortunately could not present the situation in these terms because 'such a conception was impossible to express in the conventional forms of tragedy'; so for most of the time he reluctantly fell back on 'the popular concept of an innocent Oedipus lured by Fate into a disastrous trap'. We are left to conclude either that the play is a botched compromise or else that the common sense of the law-courts is not after all the best yardstick by which to measure myth.

mother'. And what an oracle predicts is bound to happen. Oedipus does what he can to evade his destiny: he resolves never to see his supposed parents again. But it is quite certain from the first that his best efforts will be unavailing. Equally unconditional was the original oracle given to Laius (711ff.): Apollo said that he *must* (χρῆναι) die at the hands of Jocasta's child; there is no saving clause. Here there is a significant difference between Sophocles and Aeschylus. Of Aeschylus' trilogy on the House of Laius only the last play, the *Septem*, survives. Little is known of the others, but we do know, from *Septem* 742ff., that according to Aeschylus the oracle given to Laius *was* conditional: 'Do not beget a child; for *if* you do, that child will kill you.' In Aeschylus the disaster could have been avoided, but Laius sinfully disobeyed and his sin brought ruin to his descendants. In Aeschylus the story was, like the *Oresteia*, a tale of crime and punishment; but Sophocles chose otherwise – that is why he altered the form of the oracle. There is no suggestion in the *Oedipus Rex* that Laius sinned or that Oedipus was the victim of an hereditary curse, and the critic must not assume what the poet has abstained from suggesting. Nor should we leap to the conclusion that Sophocles left out the hereditary curse because he thought the doctrine immoral; apparently he did not think so, since he used it both in the *Antigone* (583ff.) and in the *Oedipus at Colonus* (964ff.). What his motive may have been for ignoring it in the *Oedipus Rex* we shall see in a moment.

I hope I have now disposed of the moralizing interpretation, which has been rightly abandoned by the great majority of contemporary scholars. To mention only recent works in English, the books of Whitman, Waldock, Letters, Ehrenberg, Knox, and Kirkwood, however much they differ on other points, all agree about the essential moral innocence of Oedipus.

But what is the alternative? If Oedipus is the innocent victim of a doom which he cannot avoid, does this not reduce him to a mere puppet? Is not the whole play a 'tragedy of destiny' which denies human freedom? This is the second of the heresies which I set out to refute. Many readers have fallen into it, Sigmund Freud among them;[4] and you can find it confidently asserted in various popular handbooks, some of which even extend the assertion to Greek tragedy in general – thus providing themselves with a convenient label for distinguishing Greek from 'Christian' tragedy. But the whole notion is in fact anachronistic. The modern reader slips into it easily because *we* think of two clear-cut alternative views – either we believe in free will or else we are determinists. But fifth-century Greeks did not think in these terms any more than Homer did: the debate about determinism is a creation of Hellenistic thought. Homeric heroes have their predetermined 'portion of life' (μοῖρα); they must die on their 'appointed day' (αἴσμον ἦμαρ); but it never occurs to the poet or his audience that this prevents them from being free agents. Nor did Sophocles intend that it should occur to readers of the *Oedipus Rex*. Neither in Homer nor in Sophocles does divine foreknowledge of certain events imply that all human actions are predetermined. If explicit confirmation of this is required, we have only to turn to lines 1230ff., where the Messenger emphatically distinguishes Oedipus' self-blinding as 'voluntary' and 'self-chosen' from the 'involuntary' parricide and incest. Certain of Oedipus' past actions were fate-bound; but everything that he does on the stage from first to last he does as a free agent.

Even in calling the parricide and the incest 'fate-bound' I have perhaps implied more than the average Athenian of Sophocles' day would have recognized. As A.W. Gomme put it, 'the gods know the future, but they do not order it: they know who will win the next Scotland and England football match, but that does not alter the fact that the victory will depend on the skill, the determination, the fitness of the players, and a little on luck'.[5] That may not satisfy the analytical philosopher, but it seems to have satisfied the ordinary man at all periods.

[4] Sigmund Freud, *The Interpretation of Dreams* (London, Modern Library, 1938), 108.

[5] A.W. Gomme, *More Essays in Greek History and Literature* (Oxford, 1962), 211.

Bernard Knox aptly quotes the prophecy of Jesus to St. Peter, 'Before the cock crow, thou shalt deny me thrice.' The Evangelists clearly did not intend to imply that Peter's subsequent action was 'fate-bound' in the sense that he could not have chosen otherwise; Peter fulfilled the prediction, but he did so by an act of free choice.[6]

In any case I cannot understand Sir Maurice Bowra's[7] idea that the gods *force* on Oedipus the knowledge of what he has done. They do nothing of the kind; on the contrary, what fascinates us is the spectacle of a man freely choosing, from the highest motives, a series of actions which lead to his own ruin. Oedipus might have left the plague to take its course; but pity for the sufferings of his people compelled him to consult Delphi. When Apollo's word came back, he might still have left the murder of Laius uninvestigated; but piety and justice required him to act. He need not have forced the truth from the reluctant Theban herdsman; but because he cannot rest content with a lie, he must tear away the last veil from the illusion in which he has lived so long. Teiresias, Jocasta, the herdsman, each in turn tries to stop him, but in vain: he must read the last riddle, the riddle of his own life. The immediate cause of Oedipus' ruin is not 'Fate' or 'the gods' – no oracle said that he must discover the truth – and still less does it lie in his own weakness; what causes his ruin is his own strength and courage, his loyalty to Thebes, and his loyalty to the truth. In all this we are to see him as a free agent: hence the suppression of the hereditary curse. And his self-mutilation and self-banishment are equally free acts of choice.

Why does Oedipus blind himself? He tells us the reason (1369ff.): he has done it in order to cut himself off from all contact with humanity; if he could choke the channels of his other senses he would do so. Suicide would not serve his purpose: in the next world he would have to meet his dead parents. Oedipus mutilates himself because he can face neither the living nor the dead. But why, if he is morally innocent? Once again, we must look at the play through Greek eyes. The doctrine that nothing matters except the agent's intention is a peculiarity of Christian and especially of post-Kantian thought. It is true that the Athenian law courts took account of intention: they distinguished as ours do between murder and accidental homicide or homicide committed in the course of self-defence. If Oedipus had been tried before an Athenian court he would have been acquitted – of murdering his father. But no human court could acquit him of pollution; for pollution inhered in the act itself, irrespective of motive. Of that burden Thebes could not acquit Oedipus, and least of all could its bearer acquit himself.

The nearest parallel to the situation of Oedipus is in the tale which Herodotus tells about Adrastus, son of Gordies. Adrastus was the involuntary slayer of his own brother, and then of Atys, the son of his benefactor Croesus; the latter act, like the killing of Laius, fulfilled an oracle. Croesus forgave Adrastus because the killing was unintended (ἀέκων), and because the oracle showed that it was the will of 'some god'. But Adrastus did not forgive himself: he committed suicide, 'conscious' says Herodotus, 'that of all men known to him he bore the heaviest burden of disaster'.[8] It is for the same reason that Oedipus blinds himself. Morally innocent though he is and knows himself to be, the objective horror of his actions remains with him and he feels that he has no longer any place in human society. Is that simply archaic superstition? I think it is something more. Suppose a motorist runs down a man and kills him, I think he *ought* to feel that he has done a terrible thing, even if the accident is no fault of his: he has destroyed a human life, which nothing can restore. In the objective order it is acts that count, not intentions. A man who has violated that order may well feel a sense of guilt, however blameless his driving.

[6] B.M.W. Knox, *Oedipus at Thebes* (Yale, 1957), 39.

[7] C.M. Bowra, *Sophoclean Tragedy* (Oxford, 1944), ch. v.

[8] Herodotus I.45. Cf. H. Funke, *Die sogenannte tragische Schuld* (Diss. Köln, 1963), 105 ff.

But my analogy is very imperfect, and even the case of Adrastus is not fully comparable. Oedipus is no ordinary homicide: he has committed the two crimes which above all others fill us with instinctive horror. Sophocles had not read Freud, but he knew how people *feel* about these things – better than some of his critics appear to do. And in the strongly patriarchal society of ancient Greece the revulsion would be even more intense than it is in our own. We have only to read Plato's prescription for the treatment to be given to parricides (*Laws* 872 c ff.). For this deed, he says, there can be no purification: the parricide shall be killed, his body shall be laid naked at a cross-roads outside the city, each officer of the State shall cast a stone upon it and curse it, and then the bloody remnant shall be flung outside the city's territory and left unburied. In all this he is probably following actual Greek practice. And if that is how Greek justice treated parricides, is it surprising that Oedipus treats himself as he does, when the great king, 'the first of men', the man whose intuitive genius had saved Thebes, is suddenly revealed to himself as a thing so unclean that 'neither the earth can receive it, nor the holy rain nor the sunshine endure its presence' (1426)?

At this point I am brought back to the original question I asked the undergraduates: does Sophocles in this play attempt to justify the ways of God to man? If 'to justify' means 'to explain in terms of *human* justice', the answer is surely 'No'. If human justice is the standard, then, as Waldock bluntly expressed it, 'Nothing can excuse the gods, and Sophocles knew it perfectly well'. Waldock does not, however, suggest that the poet intended any attack on the gods. He goes on to say that it is futile to look for any 'message' or 'meaning' in this play: 'there is no meaning', he tells us, 'in the *Oedipus Rex*; there is merely the terror of coincidence'.[9] Kirkwood seems to take a rather similar line: 'Sophocles', he says, 'has no theological pronouncements to make and no points of criticism to score.'[10] These opinions come rather close to, if they do not actually involve, the view adopted by my third and last group of undergraduates – the view that the gods are merely agents in a traditional story which Sophocles, a 'pure artist', exploits for dramatic purposes without raising the religious issue or drawing any moral whatever.

This account seems to me insufficient; but I have more sympathy with it than I have with either of the other heresies. It reflects a healthy reaction against the old moralizing school of critics; and the text of the play appears at first sight to support it. It is a striking fact that after the catastrophe no one on the stage says a word either in justification of the gods or in criticism of them. Oedipus says 'These things were Apollo' – and that is all. If the poet has charged him with a 'message' about divine justice or injustice, he fails to deliver it. And I fully agree that there is no reason at all why we should require a dramatist – even a Greek dramatist – to be for ever running about delivering banal 'messages'. It is true that when a Greek dramatic poet had something he passionately wanted to say to his fellow citizens he felt entitled to say it. Aeschylus in the *Oresteia*, Aristophanes in the *Frogs*, had something to say to their people and used the opportunity of saying it on the stage. But these are exceptional cases – both these works were produced at a time of grave crisis in public affairs – and even here the 'message' appears to me to be incidental to the true function of the artist, which I should be disposed to define, with Dr. Johnson, as 'the enlargement of our sensibility'. It is unwise to generalize from special cases. (And, incidentally, I wish undergraduates would stop writing essays which begin with the words 'This play *proves* that...' Surely no work of art can ever 'prove' anything: what value could there be in a 'proof' whose premisses are manufactured by the artist?)

Nevertheless, I cannot accept the view that the *Oedipus Rex* conveys *no* intelligible meaning and that Sophocles' plays tell us nothing of his opinions concern-

[9] A.J.A. Waldock, *Sophocles the Dramatist* (Cambridge, 1951), 158, 168.

[10] G.M. Kirkwood, *A Study of Sophoclean Drama* (Ithaca, 1958), 271.

E.R. Dodds

ing the gods. Certainly it is always dangerous to use dramatic works as evidence of their author's opinions, and especially of their religious convictions: we can legitimately discuss religion *in* Shakespeare, but do we know anything at all about the religion *of* Shakespeare? Still, I think I should venture to assert two things about Sophocles' opinions:

First, he did not believe (or did not always believe) that the gods are in any human sense 'just';

Secondly, he did always believe that the gods exist and that man should revere them.

The first of these propositions is supported not only by the implicit evidence of the *Oedipus Rex* but by the explicit evidence of another play which is generally thought to be close in date to it. The closing lines of the *Trachiniae* contain a denunciation in violent terms of divine injustice. No one answers it. I can only suppose that the poet had no answer to give.

For the second of my two propositions we have quite strong *external* evidence – which is important, since it is independent of our subjective impressions. We know that Sophocles held various priesthoods; that when the cult of Asclepius was introduced to Athens he acted as the god's host and wrote a hymn in his honour; and that he was himself worshipped as a 'hero' after his death, which seems to imply that he accepted the religion of the State and was accepted by it. But the external evidence does not stand alone: it is strongly supported by at least one passage in the *Oedipus Rex*. The celebrated choral ode about the decline of prophecy and the threat to religion (lines 863–910) was of course suggested by the scene with Creon which precedes it; but it contains generalizations which have little apparent relevance either to Oedipus or to Creon. Is the piety of this ode purely conventional, as Whitman maintained in a vigorous but sometimes perverse book?[11] One phrase in particular seems to forbid this interpretation. If men are to lose all respect for the gods, in that case, the Chorus asks, τί δεῖ με χορεύειν (895). If by this they mean merely 'Why should I, a Theban elder, dance?', the question is irrelevant and even slightly ludicrous; the meaning is surely 'Why should I, an Athenian citizen, continue to serve in a chorus?' In speaking of themselves as a chorus they step out of the play into the contemporary world, as Aristophanes' choruses do in the *parabasis*. And in effect the question they are asking seems to be this: 'If Athens loses faith in religion, if the views of the Enlightenment prevail, what significance is there in tragic drama, which exists as part of the service of the gods? To that question the rapid decay of tragedy in the fourth century may be said to have provided an answer.

In saying this, I am not suggesting with Ehrenberg that the character of Oedipus reflects that of Pericles,[12] or with Knox that he is intended to be a symbol of Athens:[13] allegory of that sort seems to me wholly alien to Greek tragedy. I am only claiming that at one point in this play Sophocles took occasion to say to his fellow citizens something which he felt to be important. And it *was* important, particularly in the period of the Archidamian War, to which the *Oedipus Rex* probably belongs. Delphi was known to be pro-Spartan: that is why Euripides was given a free hand to criticize Apollo. But if Delphi could not be trusted, the whole fabric of traditional belief was threatened with collapse. In our society religious faith is no longer tied up with belief in prophecy; but for the ancient world, both pagan and Christian, it was. And in the years of the Archidamian War belief in prophecy was at a low ebb; Thucydides is our witness to that.

[11] C.H. Whitman, *Sophocles* (Cambridge, Mass., 1951), 133–5.

[12] V. Ehrenberg, *Sophocles and Pericles* (Oxford, 1954), 141ff.

[13] B.M.W. Knox, op. cit., ch. ii.

I take it, then, as reasonably certain that while Sophocles did not pretend that the gods are in any human sense just, he nevertheless held that they are entitled to our worship. Are these two opinions incompatible? Here once more we cannot hope to understand Greek literature if we persist in looking at it through Christian spectacles. To the Christian it is a necessary part of piety to believe that God is just. And so it was to Plato and to the Stoics. But the older world saw no such necessity. If you doubt this, take down the *Iliad* and read Achilles' opinion of what divine justice amounts to (xxiv. 525–33); or take down the Bible and read the Book of Job. Disbelief in divine justice as measured by human yardsticks can perfectly well be associated with deep religious feeling. 'Men', said Heraclitus, 'find some things unjust, other things just; but in the eyes of God all things are beautiful and good and just.'[14] I think that Sophocles would have agreed. For him, as for Heraclitus, there is an objective world-order which man must respect, but which he cannot hope fully to understand.

Some readers of the *Oedipus Rex* have told me that they find its atmosphere stifling and oppressive: they miss the tragic exaltation that one gets from the *Antigone* or the *Prometheus Vinctus*. And I fear that what I have said here has done nothing to remove that feeling. Yet it is not a feeling which I share myself. Certainly the *Oedipus Rex* is a play about the blindness of man and the desperate insecurity of the human condition: in a sense every man must grope in the dark as Oedipus gropes, not knowing who he is or what he has to suffer; we all live in a world of appearance which hides from us who-knows-what dreadful reality. But surely the *Oedipus Rex* is also a play about human greatness. Oedipus is great, not in virtue of a great worldly position – for his worldly position is an illusion which will vanish like a dream – but in virtue of his inner strength: strength to pursue the truth at whatever personal cost, and strength to accept and endure it when found. 'This horror is mine,' he cries, 'and none but I is *strong* enough to bear it' (1414). Oedipus is great because he accepts the responsibility for *all* his acts, including those which are objectively most horrible, though subjectively innocent.

To me personally Oedipus is a kind of symbol of the human intelligence which cannot rest until it has solved all the riddles – even the last riddle, to which the answer is that human happiness is built on an illusion. I do not know how far Sophocles intended that. But certainly in the last lines of the play (which I firmly believe to be genuine) he does generalize the case, does appear to suggest that in some sense Oedipus is every man and every man is potentially Oedipus. Freud felt this (he was not insensitive to poetry), but as we all know he understood it in a specific psychological sense. 'Oedipus' fate', he says, 'moves us only because it might have been our own, because the oracle laid upon us before birth the very curse which rested upon him. It may be that we were all destined to direct our first sexual impulses towards our mothers, and our first impulses of hatred and violence towards our fathers; our dreams convince us that we were.'[15] Perhaps they do; but Freud did not ascribe his interpretation of the myth to Sophocles, and it is not the interpretation I have in mind. Is there not in the poet's view a much wider sense in which every man is Oedipus? If every man could tear away the last veils of illusion, if he could see human life as time and the gods see it, would he not see that against that tremendous background all the generations of men are as if they had not been, ἴσα καὶ τὸ μηδὲν ζώσας (1187)? That was how Odysseus saw it when he had conversed with Athena, the embodiment of divine wisdom. 'In Ajax' condition', he says, 'I recognize my own: I perceive that all men living are but appearance or unsubstantial shadow.'

[14] Heraclitus, fragm. 102.

[15] Sigmund Freud, op. cit., 109.

ὁρῶ γὰρ ἡμᾶς οὐδὲν ὄντας ἄλλο πλὴν
εἴδωλ᾽, ὅσοιπερ ζῶμεν, ἢ κούφην σκιάν.[16]

So far as I can judge, on this matter Sophocles' deepest feelings did not change. The same view of the human condition which is made explicit in his earliest extant play is implicit not only in the *Oedipus Rex* but in the *Oedipus Coloneus*, in the great speech where Oedipus draws the bitter conclusion from his life's experience and in the famous ode on old age.[17] Whether this vision of man's estate is true or false I do not know, but it ought to be comprehensible to a generation which relishes the plays of Samuel Beckett. I do not wish to describe it as a 'message'. But I find in it an enlargement of sensibility. And that is all I ask of any dramatist.

[16] *Ajax* 124–6.

[17] *O. C.* 607–15; 1211–49.

THE CHARACTER OF THE ATHENIAN EMPIRE[1]

Source: *Historia III*, 1954–5, pp.1–41; only the first sixteen pages of the article are included here.

By G.E.M. de Ste Croix

Was the Athenian empire[2] a selfish despotism, detested by the subject whom it oppressed and exploited? The ancient sources, and modern scholars, are almost unanimous that it was, and the few voices (such as those of Grote, Freeman, Greenidge and Marsh) raised in opposition to this harsh verdict – which will here be called 'the traditional view' – have not succeeded in modifying or even explaining its dominance. Characteristic of the attitude of many historians is the severe judgment of Last,[3] who, contrasting Athens as the 'tyrant city' with Rome as *'communis nostra patria'* [our shared native land], can see nothing more significant in Athenian imperial government than that 'warning which gives some slight value to even the worst of failures'.

The real basis of the traditional view, with which that view must stand or fall, is the belief that the Athenian empire was hated by its subjects – a belief for which there is explicit and weighty support in the sources (above all Thucydides), but which nevertheless is demonstrably false. The first section of this paper will therefore be devoted to showing that whether or not the Athenian empire was politically oppressive or economically predatory, the general mass of the population of the allied (or subject) states, far from being hostile to Athens, actually welcomed her dominance and wished to remain within the empire, even – and perhaps more particularly – during the last thirty years of the fifth century, when the ὕβρις [violent pride] of Athens, which bulks so large in the traditional view, is supposed to have been at its height.

I   The alleged unpopularity of the Empire

By far the most important witness for the prosecution, in any arraignment of Athenian imperialism, is of course Thucydides; but it is precisely Thucydides who, under cross-examination, can be made to yield the most valuable pieces of detailed evidence of the falsity of his own generalizations. Before we examine his evidence, it will be well to make clear the conception of his speeches upon which some of the interpretations given here are based. Whatever Thucydides may have meant by the much discussed expression τὰ δέοντα,[4] whatever purpose he may originally have intended the speeches to serve, there can surely be no doubt that some of the speeches[5] in fact represent what the

Some detailed discussion of textual points has been omitted from the footnotes; such omissions are indicated by '[...]'.

[1] Historia III, I. Much of this article is based on a paper on 'The Alleged Unpopularity of the Athenian Empire', read to the London Classical Society on 14 June 1950. I have to thank Mr R. Meiggs, Dr V. Ehrenberg, Prof. A. Andrewes and Mr P.A. Brunt for making valuable criticisms. I am specially grateful to Prof. A.H.M. Jones for his help and encouragement at every stage. This article, although written earlier (1950–51), may be regarded as a supplement to his 'Athenian Democracy and its Critics,' in Camb. Hist. Journ. XI (1953) 126. Among publications, I owe most to A.W. Gomme, Historical Commentary on Thucydides, Vol. I (hereafter referred to as HCT I), and B.D. Meritt, H.T. Wade-Gery and M.F. McGregor, The Athenian Tribute Lists (ATL).

[2] The word 'empire' (which often has a very different connotation) is used here, in most cases, simply as a convenient translation of ἀρχῆ.

[3] In Camb. Anc. Hist. XI 435–6.

[4] I 22.1. I would translate, 'what was most appropriate' (cf. I 138.3; II 60.5).

[5] Above all that of the Athenians at Sparta in 432 (1 73–8).

speakers would have said if they had expressed *with perfect frankness* the sentiments which the historian himself attributed to them,[6] and hence may sometimes depart very far from what was actually said, above all because political and diplomatic speeches are seldom entirely candid.

Now Thucydides harps constantly on the unpopularity of imperial Athens, at least during the Peloponnesian War. He makes no fewer than eight of his speakers[7] accuse the Athenians of 'enslaving' their allies or of wishing to 'enslave' other states, and he also uses the same expression in his own person.[8] His Corinthian envoys at Sparta, summarizing the historian's own view in a couple of words, call Athens the 'tyrant city'.[9] Thucydides even represents the Athenians themselves as fully conscious that their rule was a tyranny: he makes not only Cleon but also Pericles admit that the empire had this character.[10] It must be allowed that in such political contexts both 'enslavement' and 'tyranny' – δουλεία and τυραννίς, and their cognates – are often used in a highly technical sense: any infringement of the ἐλευθερία [freedom] of a city, however slight, might be described as 'enslavement';[11] and terms such as τύραννος πόλις do not necessarily imply (as the corresponding English expressions would [tyrant city]) that Athens was an oppressive or unpopular ruler. However, it will hardly be denied that Thucydides regarded the dominance of Athens over her allies as indeed oppressive and unpopular. The speech he puts into the mouths of the Athenians at Sparta in 432 admits that their rule is 'much detested by the Hellenes' and that Athens has become 'hateful to most people'.[12] At the outbreak of the war, says Thucydides,[13] 'people in general were strongly in favour of Sparta, especially as she professed herself the liberator of Hellas.[14] Every individual and every city was eager to help her by word and deed, to the extent of feeling that personal participation was necessary if her cause were not to suffer. So general was the indignation felt against Athens, some desiring to be liberated from her rule, others dreading to pass under it'. In the winter of 413–12, when the news of the Athenian disaster in Sicily had become known, Thucydides[15] would have us believe that all Hellas was astir, neutrals feeling that they ought to attack Athens spontaneously, and the subjects of Athens showing themselves ready to revolt 'even beyond their capacity to do so', feeling passionately on the subject and refusing even to hear of the Athenians being able to last out the summer.

This is what Thucydides wanted his readers to believe. It is undoubtedly the conception he himself honestly held. Nevertheless, his own detailed narrative proves that it is certainly false. Thucydides was such a remarkably objective historian that he himself has provided sufficient material for his own refu-

---

[6] Cf. J.H. Finley, Thucydides (1947) 96: the speeches expound 'what Thucydides thought would have seemed to him the factors in a given situation had he stood in the place of his speakers'. This is almost the same thing. And see Jones, op. cit. (n.1) 20–21.

[7] The Corinthians (I 68.3; 69.1; 121.5; 122.2; 124.3), the Mytileneans (III 10.3, 4, 5; 13.6), the Thebans (III 63.3), Brasidas (IV 86.1; 87.3; V 9.9), Pagondas (IV 92.4), the Melians (V 86; 92; 100), Hermocrates (VI 76.2, 4; 77.1; 80.5; cf. 82.3), Gylippus and the Syracusan generals (VII 66.2; 68.2). And see III 70.3; 71.1 (Corcyra). All occurrences of the words for political

[8] I 98.4; VII 75.7. See also Ps.-Xen., Ath. Pol. I 18 (cf. I 8, 9; III 11; and Thuc. IV 86.4–5, for δουλεία [enslavement] as subjection to the opposite political party); Plut., Cim. 11.3; Isocr. XII 97; cf. the repudiation in IV 109.

[9] I 122.3; 124.3.

[10] III 37.2; II 63.2. Cf. VI 85.1.

[11] See Thuc. I 141.1.

[12] I 75.1, 4. Cf. I 76.1; II 11.2 Isocr. VIII 79, 105; XII 57; Dem. IX 24.

[13] II 8.4–5.

[14] Cf. Thuc. I 69.1; II 72.1; III 13.7; 32.2; 59.4; IV 85.1; 86.1; 87.4; 108.2; 121.1; VIII 46.3; 52; Isocr. IV 122 etc.

[15] VIII 2.1–2; cf. IV 108.3–6.

tation. The news columns in Thucydides, so to speak, contradict the editorial Thucydides, and the editor himself does not always speak with the same voice.

In the 'Mytilenean Debate' at Athens in 427, Thucydides[16] makes Diodotus tell the assembled Athenians that in all the cities the demos is their friend, and either does not join the Few, the ὀλίγοι, when they revolt, or, if constrained to do so, at once turns on the rebels, so that in fighting the refractory state the Athenians have the mass of the citizens (τὸ πλῆθος) on their side. (The precise meaning of these expressions – δῆμος, πλῆθος, ὀλίγοι and the like [the people, the many, the few] – will be considered in the third section of this paper). It is impossible to explain away the whole passage on the ground that Diodotus is just saying the kind of thing that might be expected to appeal to an Athenian audience. Not only do we have Thucydides' general statement[17] that throughout the Greek world, after the Corcyraean revolution of 427, the leaders of the popular parties tried to bring in the Athenians, as οἱ ὀλίγοι [the few] the Spartans; there is a great deal of evidence relating to individual cities, which we must now consider. Of course, the mere fact that a city did not revolt from Athens does not of itself necessarily imply fidelity: considerations of expediency, short-term or long-term, may often have been decisive – the fear of immediate Athenian counter-action, or the belief that Athens would ultimately become supreme.[18] But that does not alter the fact that in almost every case in which we do have detailed information about the attitude of an allied city, we find only the Few hostile; scarcely ever is there reason to think that the demos was not mainly loyal. The evidence falls into two groups: for the 450s and 440s BC it is largely epigraphic, for the period of the Peloponnesian War it is mainly literary. We shall begin with the later period, for which the evidence is much more abundant.

The revolt of Lesbos in 428–7, in which Mytilene was the ringleader, is particularly interesting, because it is only at the very end of Thucydides' account that we gain any inkling of the real situation. At first, Thucydides implies that the Mytileneans were wholehearted and that only a few factious citizens, who were proxenoi of Athens, cared to inform the Athenians of the preparations for revolt.[19] We hear much of the determined resistance of the Mytileneans and of their appeal to Sparta, and we may well be astonished when we suddenly discover from Thucydides[20] that 'the Mytileneans' who had organized and conducted the revolt were not the main body of the Mytileneans at all, but only the governing oligarchy, for no sooner had the Spartan commander Salaethus distributed hoplite equipment to the formerly light-armed demos, with the intention of making a *sortie en masse* [mass break-out] against the besieging Athenian force, than the demos immediately mutinied and the government had to surrender to Athens.

In describing the activities of Brasidas in the 'Thraceward region' in 424–3, Thucydides occasionally gives us a glimpse of the internal situation in the cities. First, it is worth mentioning that in recording the northward march of Brasidas through Thessaly, Thucydides says[21] that the mass of the population there had always been friendly to Athens, and that Brasidas would never have

[16] III 47.2. Diodotus just afterwards lets fall a remark which is a valuable clue to Thucydides' mentality: he advocates the acquittal of the δῆμος [demos, people] of a revolting city [...]. It is 'only the mass of the people' in an allied state which is likely to be loyal.

[17] III 82.1.

[18] Any such considerations must have become much weaker after the Sicilian disaster in 413 and the offer of Persian financial support for Peloponnesian operations in the Aegean during the ensuing winter: see e.g. Thuc. VIII 2.1–2; 5.5; 24.5.

[19] III 2.3.

[20] III 27–28 [...]. And note the mercenaries who appear in III 2.2; 18.1, 2.

[21] IV 78.2–3.

been allowed to pass if ἰσονομία [equality of rights, democracy] instead of the traditional δυναστεία [upper-class rule] had existed in Thessaly. When Brasidas arrived in the 'Thraceward district,' probably in September 424, there seem to have been few if any Athenian garrisons there, for Thucydides mentions none, except that at Amphipolis, and represents the Athenians as sending out garrisons at the end of that year, 'as far as they could at such short notice and in winter'.[22] Brasidas made his first attempt on Acanthus. The inhabitants were divided, the common people being faithful to Athens; but eventually the citizens gave way and opened their gates, influenced not only by an able speech from Brasidas, a judicious blend of threats and promises, but also by 'fear for their fruit', for it was just before vintage, and Brasidas had threatened to ravage.[23] When the Spartan invited the surrender of Amphipolis, he at first found little support within that town.[24] However, the combined effect of his military success in occupying the surrounding country, the advantageous terms he offered, and the efforts of his partisans within, was sufficient to procure the surrender of the city.[25]

Thucydides[26] declares now categorically that there was general enthusiasm for revolt among the Athenian subject cities of the district, which sent secret messages to Brasidas, begging him to come to them, each wishing to lead the way in revolting. They had the additional inducement, as Thucydides points out, of the recent Athenian defeat at Delium. On the face of it, Thucydides' account is plausible enough. There is good reason to suppose, however, that when he speaks of the 'cities' that were subject to Athens, he is thinking merely of the propertied classes. When Brasidas marched into the peninsula of Acte, most of the towns (which were insignificant) naturally surrendered at once, but Sane and Dium, small as they were, and surrounded by cities now in alliance with Brasidas, held out, even when their lands were ravaged.[27] Turning his attention to the Sithonian peninsula, Brasidas captured Torone, though it was held by an Athenian garrison (probably just arrived); but this was done only through the treachery of a few, to the dismay of the majority, some of whom joined the Athenian garrison when it shut itself up in the fort of Lecythus,[28] only to be driven out to Pallene. A Spartan commander was subsequently put in charge of the town.[29] In 423, after Scione had revolted spontaneously, its neighbour Mende was betrayed to Brasidas by a few.[30] Later, when the Athenian army arrived, there were disturbances at Mende, and soon the common people fell upon the mixed Scionean and Peloponnesian garrison of seven hundred. After plundering the town, which had not made terms of surrender, the Athenians wisely told the Mendeans that they could keep their civic rights and themselves deal with their own traitors. In the case of Acanthus, Sane, Dium, Torone and Mende, then, we have positive evidence that the bulk of the citizens were loyal

---

[22] IV 108.6. It appears from IV 104.4 that apart from Eucles and his garrison in Amphipolis there were no reinforcements available except the seven ships of Thucydides at Thasos, half a day's sail distant. Thuc. IV 105.1 shows that Amphipolis could hope for no reinforcements from Chalcidice, but only ἐκ θαλάσσης καὶ ἀπὸ τῆς Θράκης [from the sea and from Thrace]. In Thuc. IV 7 (425 BC), Simonides collects a few Athenians ἐκ τῶν φρουρίων [from the garrisons], which may have been almost anywhere in the N. Aegean. Part of the evidence on the subject of garrisons in the Athenian empire is given by A.S. Nease in The Phoenix III (1949) 102–11.

[23] Thuc. IV 84.1–2; 87.2; 88.1; cf. Diod. XII 67.2.

[24] Thuc. IV 104.3–4. Although an Athenian colony, it contained few citizens of Athenian origin (IV 106.1).

[25] Thuc. IV 103–106.

[26] IV 108.3–6; cf. 80.1; Diod. XII 72.1.

[27] Thuc. IV 109.5.

[28] Thuc. IV 110–113; cf. Diod. XII 68.6.

[29] Thuc. IV 132.3.

[30] Thuc. IV 121.2; 123.1–2; 129–30.

to Athens, in circumstances which were anything but propitious. In Aristophanes' *Peace*,[31] produced in 421, it is οἱ παχεῖς καὶ πλούσιοι [rich and wealthy] whom the Athenians are said to have pursued with charges of favouring Brasidas. It would be simple-minded to suppose that this happened just because the richest citizens were the most worth despoiling. It may be that some of the other towns went over to Brasidas with the free consent of the demos, but only in regard to Scione,[32] and possibly Argilus (whose citizens apparently hoped to gain control over Amphipolis by backing Brasidas),[33] does the narrative of Thucydides provide any grounds for this assumption; and even at Scione, which did not revolt until 423, some at first 'disapproved of what was being done'.[34]

We now have to examine the movements in the Ionian cities after the Sicilian catastrophe, in 412 and the years following, when Thucydides, in the statement quoted earlier, attributes to the subjects of Athens a passionate desire to revolt, even beyond their capacity to fulfil. Jacqueline de Romilly, in her recent book, *Thucydide et l'impérialisme athénien*[35] [Thucydides and Athenian imperialism], asserts that although 'l'opposition oligarchie–démocratie' [opposition between oligarchy and democracy] played an important role until the time of Brasidas, thereafter 'l'opposition maître–sujets balaye tout' [opposition between rulers and subjects sweeps everything away], and 'on verra les Athéniens incapables de retenir leurs sujets par l'appui d'aucun parti: le désir d'indépendance aura pris le pas sur toutes les autres querelles' [it will be seen that the Athenians were incapable of holding on to their subjects by the support of either side. Desire for independence will have taken priority over all the other quarrels]. This statement is not borne out by the evidence. In only a few cases have we sufficient information about the internal situation in a given city. Again we find, in all these cases, with perhaps one or two exceptions, that it was only the Few who had any desire to revolt. The events at Samos are particularly interesting: the Samian demos, after at least two if not three 'purges' of δυνατοί or γνώριμοι[36] [powerful or notable], remained faithful to Athens to the bitter end, and were rewarded with the grant of Athenian citizenship.[37] At Chios, although Thucydides speaks in several places[38] of 'the Chians' as planning to revolt from Athens early in 412, it is perfectly clear from two passages[39] that it was only the Few who were disaffected, and that they did not even dare to disclose their plans to the demos until Alcibiades and a Spartan force arrived. The leaders of the pro-Athenian faction were then executed and an oligarchy was imposed by force, under the supervision of the Spartan commander Pedaritus;[40] but this had no good results. When the Athenians invested the city, some of the Chians plotted to surrender it to them,[41] but the blockade eventually had to be abandoned. At Rhodes, again, it was the δυνατώτατοι ἄνδρες [most powerful men] who called in the Spartans.[42] When ninety-four Peloponnesian ships arrived at

---

[31] 639–40. Cf. Ar., Vesp. 288–9, also 474–6, 626–7.

[32] Thuc. IV 120–1.

[33] Thuc. IV 103.4.

[34] IV 121.1.

[35] pp. 77–8, 263 n.4.

[36] Thuc. VIII 21 (412 BC); 73 (411); Xen., Hell. II 2.6 (405 – but this may be a reference back to the earlier purges). See also IG i² 101/102.

[37] Tod 96 (= IG i² 126 = ii² 1).

[38] VIII 5.4; 6.1, 3–4; 7.1; cf. 2.2.

[39] VIII 9.3; 14.2.

[40] Thuc. VIII 38.3. Until now Chios may have been a moderate oligarchy rather than a democracy.

[41] Thuc. VIII 24.6.

[42] Thuc., VIII 44.1.

unfortified Camirus, οἱ πολλοί [the many] fled in terror; but they were later got together by the Spartans (with the people of Lindus and Ialysus, the other two Rhodian cities) and 'persuaded' to revolt from Athens.[43] (With the terror of the Rhodians at the sight of the Peloponnesian fleet we may usefully contrast the friendliness of the Ionians in 427[44] towards ships which they took to be Athenian but which were in fact a Peloponnesian squadron – a friendliness which had fatal consequences.) About a year later there was an attempted revolution at Rhodes, which was suppressed by Dorieus.[45]

When Astyochus the Spartan, with twenty ships, made an expedition to the mainland cities opposite Chios, with the intention of winning them away from Athens, he first failed to take so small a town as Pteleum, which must have put up a stout resistance, and then failed again in his assault on Clazomenae, though it too was unwalled.[46] Clazomenae had revolted a little earlier, but this seems to have been the work of a small party of oligarchs, and the movement had easily been suppressed.[47] At Thasos, the extreme oligarchs in exile were delighted when the Athenian Dieitrephes set up a moderate oligarchy, for this, according to Thucydides, was exactly what they wanted, namely, 'the abolition of the democracy which would have opposed them' in their design of making Thasos an oligarchy independent of Athens.[48] The demos was not easily crushed, however, and the island remained in a very disturbed condition until Thrasybulus brought it back into the Athenian alliance in 407.[49] That the Thasian demos should have been friendly to Athens is all the more remarkable when we remember that the island had revolted,[50] about 465, as the result of a dispute with Athens about its ἐμπόρια [commerce] and gold mine in Thrace, had stood a siege of over two years, and upon surrendering had been given terms which have been described as 'terribly severe'[51] – a sequence of events which has often been cited as an example of 'Athenian aggression'.[52] After describing what happened at Thasos in 411, Thucydides[53] makes the very significant comment that what occurred there was just the sort of thing that did happen in the subject states: 'once the cities had achieved σωφροσύνη' [moderation] – he means, of course, oligarchies of a moderate type – 'and impunity of action, they went on to full independence'. We must not fail to notice that Neapolis on the mainland opposite, apparently a colony of Thasos, refused to join the island in its revolt, stood a siege, and finally co-operated in force in the reduction of Thasos, earning the thanks of the imperial city, expressed in decrees recorded in an inscription which has survived.[54]

---

[43] Thuc. VIII 44. The Spartans then raised a levy of no less than 32 talents from the Rhodians (VIII 44.4).

[44] Thuc. III 32.1–3.

[45] Diod. XIII 38.5; 45.1.

[46] Thuc. VIII 31.2–3.

[47] Thuc. VIII 14.3; 23.6; cf. Diod. XIII 71.1.

[48] Thuc. VIII 64.2–5; Hell. Oxy. II 4. Of course the demos would oppose the destruction of the democracy [...].

[49] Xen., Hell. I 4.9; Diod. XIII 72.1; cf. Corn. Nep., Lys. II 2. And see Dem. XX 59 for the grant of privileges to the pro-Athenian party [...].

[50] Thuc. I 100.2; 101.3; Diod. XI 70.1; Plut., Cim. 14. For the date, see Gomme, HCT I 391.

[51] E.M. Walker in Camb. Anc. Hist. V 59.

[52] E.g. by Meiggs in JHS LXIII (1943) 21.

[53] VIII 64.5. (The participial clause has been deliberately ignored here, since the text is uncertain.)

[54] Tod 84 (= IG i² 108), lines 39–55, re-edited by Meritt and Andrewes in BSA XLVI (1951) at pp.201–3, lines 48–64. The date of this part of the inscription must be 407/6. As to whether Neapolis was a Thasian colony, see ATL II 86.

There is reason to think that in Lesbos[55] also there was little enthusiasm for revolt, except among the leading citizens. Although a Chian force of thirteen ships procured the defection of Methymna and Mytilene in 412, an Athenian expedition of twenty-five ships was able to recover Mytilene virtually without striking a blow (αὐτοβοεί) [at the first war-cry], and when the Spartan admiral Astyochus arrived, in the hope of at least encouraging Methymna to persevere, 'everything went against him'. In the following year, 411,[56] a party of Methymnaean exiles – evidently rich men, since they were able to hire two hundred and fifty mercenaries – failed to get possession of their city. In 406 Methymna,[57] which then had an Athenian garrison (probably at its own request), was faithful to Athens and, refusing to surrender to Callicratidas the Spartan commander, was captured (with the aid of traitors within) and plundered. Mytilene[58] remained even longer on the Athenian side, only submitting to Lysander after Aegospotami. Other cities also refused to desert Athens, even when confronted with a formidable Peloponnesian armament. In 405, Cedreae in Caria[59] resisted Lysander's attack but was stormed and the inhabitants (whom Xenophon describes as μιζοβάρβαροι [semi-barbarians]) were sold into slavery; and soon afterwards Lampsacus,[60] which also resisted Lysander, was taken and plundered. Most remarkable of all in this group is Carian Iasus.[61] Although it had paid heavily for its alliance with Athens by being sacked by the Peloponnesians in 412, and garrisoned after that, we find it loyal to Athens seven years later, for according to Diodorus, Lysander now took it by storm, massacred the eight hundred male citizens, sold the women and children as slaves, and destroyed the city – a procedure which suggests that resistance had been vigorous. So much for the alleged enthusiasm of the allies of Athens for 'liberation'.

Only at Ephesus,[62] and perhaps (during the Ionian War) Miletus,[63] among the cities about which we have any information, is there no visible trace of a pro-Athenian party. We may remember that Ephesus was always a centre of Persian influence: for example, its large donation in gold to the Spartan war-chest, probably in 427, recorded in an inscription found near Sparta,[64] consisted of a thousand darics, the equivalent of four Attic silver talents or a little more.

We can now go back to the 450s and 440s BC, a period for which, as mentioned above, the evidence on the questions under discussion is pre-dominantly epi-

---

[55] Thuc. VIII 22–23; 32. The events of 427 (even the cleruchy) had evidently not created general hostility to Athens in Lesbos.

[56] Thuc. VIII 100.3. Athenian φρουροί [members of the garrison] from Mytilene joined in the defence.

[57] Xen., Hell. I 6.12–15 (specifically recording that those in control of affairs at Methymna were pro-Athenian); Diod. XIII 76.5.

[58] Xen., Hell. I 6.16, 38; II 2.5; Diod. XIII 76.6 to 79.7; 97.2; 100.1–6. It is true that Mytilene was a main Athenian base, but the Mytileneans seem to have been friendly: see Diod. XIII 78.5; 79.2.

[59] Xen., Hell. II 1.15.

[60] Xen., Hell. II 1.18–19; Diod. XIII 104.8.

[61] Thuc. VIII 28.2–3 (the attack was a surprise) and 36.1; 29.1; Diod. XIII 104.7; perhaps Xen., Hell. I 1.32.

[62] Ephesus was in revolt by 412 (Thuc. VIII 19.3) and seems to have been in Persian hands (VIII 109.1: Xen., Hell. 1 2.6). It remained an important Persian-Peloponnesian base for the rest of the war (Xen., Hell. I 5.1, 10; II 1.6, etc.).

[63] For the earlier history of Miletus, see below and n. 66. For Miletus in the Ionian War, see esp. Thuc. VIII 17.1–3 (cf. Ar., Lysistr. 108–9); 25.1–3; 28–29; 33.1; 36.1; 84.4–5; Xen., Hell. I 2.2–3; 6.8–12. Cf. Diod. XIII 104.5–6 and Plut., Lys. 8; 19.

[64] Tod 62 (= IG V i 1), lines 22–23. For the date, see p.41 below.

graphic. The revolt of Erythrae,[65] from 454 or earlier to 452, was almost certainly due to the seizure of power by a Persian-backed tyranny. Miletus[66] was also in revolt from at least 454 until 452/1; but during this period she was apparently under the control of a close oligarchy or tyranny, which seems to have driven out an important section of the citizen body (perhaps with Persian support), and was sentenced in its turn to perpetual and hereditary outlawry about 452, when the exiles returned and the city was brought back into the Athenian empire. The probable absence of Colophon[67] from the tribute quota-lists of the second assessment period (450/49 to 447/6), and the Athenian decree relating to that city of (probably) 446, certainly point to a revolt about 450; but the known Persian associations of this inland city, the fact that it was handed over to the Persian Itamenes in 430 by one of two parties in a στάσις (presumably of the usual character – oligarchs against democrats), and the Colophonian oath to preserve democracy – perhaps newly introduced, or at any rate restored – in the treaty made with Athens in 446 or thereabouts, strongly suggest that the revolt was the work of oligarchs receiving Persian support. The revolt of Euboea in 446 may well have been mainly the work of the Hippobotae, the aristocrats of Chalcis, for the Athenians drove them out on the reduction of the island and probably gave their lands to cleruchs,[68] but inflicted no punishment beyond the taking of hostages,[69] as far as we know, on the other Euboeans, except that they expelled the Hestiaeans (who had massacred the crew of an Athenian ship) and settled an Athenian colony on their lands.[70] The revolt of Samos in 440/39,[71] after certain Samians who 'wished to revolutionize the constitution' had induced the Athenians to set up a democracy, was certainly brought about by exiled oligarchs, who allied themselves with the Persian satrap Pissuthnes, employed a force of seven hundred mercenaries, and worked in conjunction with the δυνατώτατοι [most powerful men] remaining in the city. Here again there is no evidence of general hostility to Athens among the Samians, although once the oligarchs had got a firm grip on the city, and had captured and expelled the democratic leaders,[72] they put up a stout resistance to Athens and were no doubt able to enforce the adherence of a considerable number of the common folk.

It is significant that in this early period, whenever we do have information about the circumstances of a revolt, we find good reason for attributing it to oligarchs or tyrants, who could evidently rely on Persian assistance wherever the situation of the city permitted. This is precisely the state of affairs we have already seen to exist later, during the Peloponnesian War. In some cases, both early and late, the bare fact of a revolt is recorded, without detail. Some of these revolts may have been wholehearted, but we certainly cannot assume so just because we have no evidence. Surely the reverse is true: surely we may assume that the situation we find in virtually all the towns for which we do have sufficient information existed in most of the remainder. The mere fact of

[65] See Tod 29 (= SEG X 11 = D 10 in ATL II 38, 54–57) and the very probable reconstruction of events in ATL III 252–5.

[66] See the admirable account by Meiggs in JHS LXIII (1943) 25–27; cf. ATL III 257. (For IG i² 22, with later additions, see now D 11 in ATL II 57–60; SEG X 14.)

[67] See Meiggs, op. cit. 28; ATL III 282–3. For IG i² 14/15 (probably 447/6), see now D 15 in ATL II 68–69; SEG X 17. For the events of 430 and later, see p.39 below.

[68] Plut., Per. 23; Ael., VH VI1 (2000 κλῆροι [cleruchs]). See the highly ingenious arguments of ATL III 294–7, where the other evidence is cited. For the Hippobotae, see also Hdts. V 77.2; Strab. X 1.8, p.447.

[69] For the hostages, see Tod 42 (= IG i² 39), lines 47–52 (Chalcis, 446/5); IG i² p.284 (Eretria, 442/1: note the reference to the πλουσιώτατοι [richest men]). Examination of the quota-lists shows that almost certainly none of the Euboean cities suffered any increase in tribute.

[70] Thuc. I 114.3; Plut., Per. 23 etc.

[71] Thuc. I 115.2 to 117.3 (cf. VIII 76.4); Diod. XII 27–28; Plut., Per. 24–28 etc.

[72] Thuc. I 115.5; Diod. XII 27.3.

the coming to power of an oligarchy in an allied city immediately upon a revolt from Athens, as evidently at Eretria in 411,[73] tends to confirm that the democratic party in that city was pro-Athenian.

It is not difficult to find other examples of loyalty to Athens on the part of her allies, or pro-Athenian movements inside cities in revolt. When the Athenian armament in Sicily was at its last gasp, the division under Demosthenes being on the very point of surrender, the Syracusans made a proclamation offering freedom to any of the islanders (the Athenian allies) who were willing to come over to them. Further resistance was now quite hopeless, and nothing could have restrained the allies from deserting except the strongest sense of loyalty. Yet Thucydides tells us that 'not many cities went over'.[74] The majority remained, to undergo a fate which they must have well known could only be death or enslavement. In 428 Methymna[75] refused to follow the rest of the Lesbian cities in their revolt. In 430 there was a στάσις [stasis, civil strife] at Colophon:[76] one faction called in the Persians and expelled the other, which removed to Notium but itself split into two factions, one of which gained control of the new settlement by employing mercenaries and allied itself with the medising citizens remaining in Colophon. In 427 the defeated party, no doubt democratic in character, called in the Athenians, who founded a new colony at Notium for the exiled Colophonians. The capture of Selymbria[77] and Byzantium[78] by the Athenians in 408–7 was brought about in each case by the treachery of a faction inside the city.

In the light of all the evidence which has been cited above, we can understand and accept Plato's explanation of the long life of the Athenian empire: the Athenians, he says, kept their ἀρχή [power, empire] for seventy years 'because they had friends in each of the cities'.[79]

---

[73] Tod 82 (= IG XII 9, 187), the prescript of which refers to the βουλή [Council] but not to the δῆμος (*demos*, people).

[74] Thuc. VII 82.1.

[75] Thuc. III 2.1, 3; 5.1; 18.1–2; 50.2.

[76] Thuc. III 34.

[77] Diod. XIII 66.4; Plut., Alc. 30.

[78] Xen., Hell. I 3.16–20; II 2.1; Diod. XIII 66.6; 67; Plut., Alc. 31.

[79] Epist. VII 332c. Since Plato gives this as the one sufficient reason, it will hardly be maintained that he is merely referring to a handful of pro-Athenian individuals of note, such as those who received Athenian proxenia and were evidently expected (see Thuc. III 2.3) to act as Athenian watchdogs.

On many occasions we find support given to Athens by states, or democratic parties within states, outside the Athenian 'empire' proper. The bulk of the Plataeans, of course, were always faithful to Athens; it was only a few wealthy aristocrats who called in the Thebans in 431.[80] The Athenians had democratic supporters at Corcyra[81] and Argos,[82] and in the Boeotian cities,[83] especially Thespiae, Chaeronea and Siphae. In 424 the leading democrats at Megara[84] plotted to betray the city to Athens. Here we find the popular party, in a state which had been specially harassed by the Athenians, by a stringent trade embargo (the 'Megarian Decree', of c.432 BC) and two ravaging expeditions a year,[85] prepared to take desperate risks to re-enter the Athenian alliance. There were pro-Athenian parties at Thurii and Messana;[86] and three other Sicilian towns (Egesta, Naxos and Catana), as well as certain Sicel communities, were on Athens' side. It would be unsafe to draw any general conclusions from the existence of pro-Athenian elements in the Sicilian states, since fear of Syracuse[87] may well have been the decisive factor in most cases. In his comment on the first naval defeat of Athens by Syracuse, however, Thucydides[88] clearly implies that the Athenians were used to creating dissension among their opponents by holding out the prospect of constitutional changes – in the direction of democracy, needless to say. And indeed, apart from the examples already mentioned, there are several recorded attempts, successful or unsuccessful, by parties inside cities, especially besieged cities, to betray them to the

[80] Thuc. II 2.2; 3.2; III 65.2.

[81] See esp. Thuc. III 70.1 (cf. I 55.1) to 81; 85; IV 2.3; 46–48; Diod. XIII 48.1–6.

[82] See esp. Thuc. I 102.4; V 29.1; 76.1–2; 78; 81.2; 82; 83.1–2; 116.1; VIII 86.8–9; Diod. XII 81.2–5.

[83] Thuc. III 62.5 and IV 92.6 (458/7–447/6); IV 76.2–3 and 89 (424, specifically mentioning Siphae and Chaeronea); Diod. XII 69.1 (also 424); Thuc. IV 133.1 (Thespiae, 423); VI 95.2 (Thespiae, 414). IG i² 36, of c.447/6 (SEG X 33 gives a new fragment), is an Athenian proxeny decree in favour of four named Thespians, one of whom is called, significantly, Athenaios. SEG X 81 (= IG i² 68/69, with a new fragment) may refer to the settlement of the Thespian and other Boeotian exiles in 424/3. Thuc. III 62.5 (cf. IV 92.6) makes the Thebans say that before Coronea (447/6) the Athenians had already made themselves masters of most of Boeotia κατὰ στάσιν [through civil strife]. The στάσις [civil strife] may well have involved pro- and anti-Athenian factions in the other towns (cf. Xen., Mem. III 5.2), but in view of Thuc. IV 76.2; VI 95.2, can we doubt that the strife took the usual social form, even if the question of Theban supremacy also entered into it? As for that well known puzzle, Ps.-Xen., Ath. Pol. III 11, there seems to be no certain evidence that Athens set up democracies in 458/7 in the Boeotian cities, other than Thebes (Ar., Pol. 1302b 29–30), and it is possible she may have accepted the existing oligarchies for a time, only to be compelled to remove or exile them for oppressive conduct (ὁ δῆμος ἐδούλευσεν [the people were enslaved]: Ps.-Xen.) before 447/6, when they made their come-back. For an equally possible alternative, see Gomme, HCT I 318.

[84] Thuc. IV 66–74; Diod. XII 66–67.

[85] Thuc. IV 66.1; cf. Plut., Per. 30.

[86] Thuc. VII 33.5–6 (Thurii); VI 74.1 (cf. 50.1) and Plut., Alc. 22 (Messana). Cf. Thuc. VI 52.1; 88.1 (Camarina).

[87] See e.g. Thuc. VI 88.1.

[88] VII 55.2.

Athenians, notably at Syracuse,[89] and also at Spartolus,[90] Eion in Thrace,[91] Anactorium,[92] Cythera,[93] Tegea,[94] and even Melos.[95]

Now Melos is, for most people, the characteristic example of Athenian brutality. The cruel treatment of the conquered island was certainly indefensible. There are, however, certain features in the affair, often overlooked, which may at least help us to see the whole incident in better proportion. Although we have no record of any recent hostilities between the two states, we know that earlier the Melians had not remained neutral in the war, as so many people, obsessed by the Melian Dialogue,[96] seem to think. Doubtless in 416 the Melians, when confronted with a large Athenian armament, said they would like to be regarded henceforth as neutrals.[97] In the Dialogue,[98] Thucydides appears to make the Athenians concede that they are committing what would nowadays be called 'unprovoked aggression'. Just before he begins the Dialogue, however, Thucydides[99] tells us that during the war the Melians had at first remained neutral, but that when the Athenians used violence towards them and plundered their lands, ἐς πόλεμον φανερὸν κατέστησαν [they were in an open state of war]. Epigraphic evidence allows us to go further still: it puts the original Athenian attack on Melos in quite a different light. The inscription found near Sparta, to which reference has already been made, records[100] two separate donations by Melos to the Spartan war-funds, one of twenty Aeginetan minae (roughly half an Attic talent) [...]. This shows that the Melian subscription was an official one. According to a speech of Brasidas, in Thucydides,[101] the payment of tribute to Athens by Acanthus was regarded by Sparta as a hostile act; and the same interpretation would not unreasonably be placed by Athens, *a fortiori*, on a voluntary donation to Sparta. Now Adcock[102] showed a few years ago that there is good reason to think these gifts to Sparta were made in the spring of 427, during Alcidas's expedition, when the Melians very probably gave aid and comfort to Alcidas. The Athenian ravaging expedition, which did not take place until the following year (and was led, incidentally, by Nicias),[103] was doubtless sent in retaliation for the assistance the Melians had given to Sparta. At any rate, Thucydides says expressly that after this the Melians ἐς πόλεμον φανερὸν κατέστησαν. Diodorus[104] describes Melos as the

---

[89] Thuc. VII 48.2; 49.1; 73.3; Plut., Nic. 21; 22; 26. There were Syracusan exiles with the Athenian army in 415 (Thuc. VI 64.1). Thuc. VII 55.2 conveys the impression that in 415 Syracuse was a full democracy, just like Athens; but in view of Thuc. VI 41; Ar., Pol. 1304a 27–29; Diod. XIII 34.6; 35, it seems certain that its constitution was distinctly less democratic than that of Athens.

[90] Thuc. II 79.2.

[91] Thuc. IV 7.

[92] Thuc. IV 49.

[93] Thuc. IV 54.3.

[94] Thuc. V 62.2; 64.1.

[95] Thuc. V 116.3.

[96] Thuc. V 85–113. This is not to be treated as an historical record: see H. Ll. Hudson-Williams in AJP LXXI (1950) 156ff., esp. 167–9. Cf. now M. Treu in Historia II 253 ff.

[97] As in V 94; 112.3.

[98] See V 89: [...].

[99] V 84.2 [...].

[100] Tod 62 (= IG V i 1), lines 24–30, 36–41. The Chian donation is recorded in lines 8–10.

[101] IV 87.3. Cf. SEG X 89 (= Tod 68 = IG i² 90), lines 19–20.

[102] In Mélanges Glotz I 1–6.

[103] Thuc. III 91.1–3. A command would seldom be entrusted to a general not in sympathy with its objectives.

[104] XII 65.2. Probably this statement is technically incorrect.

one firm ally of Sparta among the Cycladic islands in 426. It is particularly interesting to observe that in 416 the Athenian envoys were not permitted by the Melian authorities to address the assembled people but were made to state their case 'before the magistrates and the few'[105] – a circumstance upon which Thucydides allows the Athenians to make scornful comment. Melos put up a stout resistance to Athens, it is true, but so at first did Mytilene, where, as we have seen, the majority had no great desire to fight Athens. As we learn from Thucydides that at the end of the siege there was treachery inside Melos, it seems likely that the Melian commons did not entirely share the passion for neutral autonomy so eloquently expressed by their oligarchs.[106]

On the question of atrocities in general, it should be emphasized that very few acts of brutality are recorded against the Athenians during the war: the only serious ones[107] are those at Melos and Scione[108] and those (less shocking) at Torone[109] and Thyrea.[110] All these were to a greater or less extent sanctioned by the Greek laws of war,[111] even if they shocked some of the more humane Greeks of the time. The essential point is that the Athenians were certainly no more brutal, on the whole, in their treatment of the conquered than were other Greek states of their day; and the behaviour of the demos (in striking contrast with that of their own oligarchs) under the greatest test of all, civil strife, was exemplary: Aristotle's reference[112] to the 'habitual clemency of the demos' was well deserved, in particular by their conduct in 403, to which Aristotle and others pay tribute.[113] The Argives enslaved the whole population of Mycenae and destroyed the town on capturing it about 465 BC.[114] In the Peloponnesian War, we are told by Thucydides,[115] the Spartans began the practice of butchering all the traders they caught at sea – Athenians and their allies and, in the early part of the war, even neutrals. The Spartan admiral Alcidas slaughtered most of the prisoners he had taken from the Ionian states during his expedition in 427,[116] although apparently they were not in arms. The Spartans in the same

[105] Thuc. V 84.3; 85.

[106] Some problems remain. Melos was evidently a prosperous island in 416: it was assessed for tribute in 425 at 15 talents (the same assessment as that of e.g. Andros, Naxos, Eretria), and shortly before the siege it seems to have issued a plentiful new coinage (see J.G. Milne, 'The Melos Hoard of 1907' = Amer. Num. Soc. Notes and Monographs no. 62, 1934); yet the Athenian cleruchy sent to Melos was of 500 men only. Thuc. (V 116.4) tells us that the Athenians put to death Μηλίων ὅσους ἡβῶντας ἔλαβον [the Melians they captured who were in the prime of life]. But surely the traitors at least were spared? Were they perhaps very numerous? And who were the Melians restored by Lysander in 405 (Xen., Hell. II 2.9; Plut., Lys. 14)?

[107] Even minor acts of cruelty seem to have been rare: the massacre of the crews of two captured ships in 405, by order of Philocles (Xen., Hell. II 1.31–32), was remembered as an isolated atrocity. The decree mentioned by Xen. (ibid.) and Plut., Lys. 9; 13 may or may not be historical (Grote rejected it), and certainly never took effect.

[108] Thuc. V 116.4 etc. (Melos); V 32.1 and Diod. XII 76.3–4 (Scione). These two massacres were evidently a favourite theme of anti-Athenian propaganda: see e.g. Xen., Hell. II 2.3; Isocr. IV 100; XII 63.

[109] Thuc. V 3–4; Diod. XII 73.3. Here the men were spared.

[110] Thuc. IV 56.2 (cf. II 27.2); 57.3–4. But these men were in the position of the garrison of a fort and hence were liable to be slaughtered on capture.

[111] Xen., Cyrop. VII 5–73; cf. Xen., Mem. IV 2.15.

[112] Ath. Pol. 22.4.

[113] Ath. Pol. 40.3; Ps.-Lys. II 63–66; Xen., Hell. II 4.43; Isocr. XVIII 31–32, 44, 46, 68; Epist. VIII 3; Plat., Menex. 243e; Epist. VII 325b; Cic. I Phil. I 1.

[114] Diod. XI 65.5.

[115] II 67.4.

[116] Thuc. III 32.1–2.

year, to gratify their implacable Theban allies, killed every one of the surviving defenders of Plataea in cold blood and enslaved their women.[117] When the Helots were felt to be specially dangerous, apparently in 424, the Spartans secretly and treacherously murdered two thousand of the best of them.[118] The Spartans massacred all the free men they captured on the fall of Argive Hysiae in 417.[119] The men of Byzantium and Chalcedon slaughtered the whole multitude of prisoners (men, women and children) they had taken on their expedition into Bithynia in c.416/5.[120] After Aegospotami, in 405, all the Athenian prisoners, perhaps three or four thousand in number,[121] were put to death by the Peloponnesians under Lysander, who during the same campaign killed all the men and enslaved the women and children of at least one city he took by storm, and enslaved all the inhabitants of at least one other.[122] The close oligarchies which Lysander installed at this time in the Aegean and Asiatic cities executed their political opponents wholesale, as did Lysander's *protégés* the Thirty at Athens, and the victorious revolutionaries and counter-revolutionaries at Corcyra, Argos and elsewhere. It is necessary to emphasize all this, because isolated Athenian acts of cruelty have been remembered while the many other contemporary atrocities have been largely forgotten, and the quite misleading impression has come to prevail that the Athenians, increasingly corrupted by power, became ever harsher and more vindictive as the war progressed. In reality, this impression is probably due mainly to the Mytilenean Debate and the Melian Dialogue, in both of which our attention is strongly focused upon the character of Athenian imperialism, as Thucydides conceived it. In the Mytilenean Debate,[123] by the nature of the arguments he presents, Thucydides conveys the impression that the Athenians were swayed only by considerations of expediency. As Finley puts it,[124] 'the advocate of simple decency had no other course than to talk in terms of calculation'. But mark how Thucydides explains the holding of the second assembly on the very next day after that on which the cruel sentence was pronounced. On the following day, he says, μετάνοιά τις εὐθὺς ἦν αὐτοῖς καὶ ἀναλογισμὸς ὠμὸν τὸ βούλευμα καὶ μέγα ἐγνῶσθαι, πόλιν ὅλην διαφθεῖραι μᾶλλον ἢ οὐ τοὺς αἰτίους [there was a sudden change of feeling and people began to think how cruel and how unprecedented such a decision was – to destroy not only the guilty but the entire population of a state – tr. Warner] – no mere prudence here, but the moral emotion of remorse. Arguments from expediency may have predominated in the second assembly,[125] but in view of the passage just quoted it is difficult to accept Thucydides' implication that what really changed the minds of the Athenians was nothing but a callous consideration of self-interest.

---

[117] Thuc. III 68.1–2, 4; Diod. XII 56.4–6; cf. Isocr. XIV 62; XII 93. Some may feel that Thuc. is over-anxious to extenuate the *Spartan* share in the massacre: notice, in § 1, the apologetic clauses and the placing of ultimate responsibility on the Thebans in § 4.

[118] Thuc. IV 80.3–4 seems to put this event in 424, as does Diod. XII 67.3–4, no doubt following Thuc. For another Spartan killing of Helots, apparently in the early 460s BC, see Thuc. I 128.1 (cf. Paus. IV 24.5).

[119] Thuc. V 83.2; Diod. XII 81.1.

[120] Diod. XII 82.2.

[121] Xen., Hell. II 1.31 (no figure); Plut. Lys. 11 (3000); 13; Paus. IX 32.6 (4000). Cf. the massacre of prisoners after the battles of Leucimme and Sybota (Thuc. I 30.1; 50.1).

[122] Iasus and Cedreae (see pp. 37ff. above).

[123] Thuc. III 36–49. One may well wonder how fully the Athenian Assembly was

[124] Thuc. 177.

[125] What precisely does Thuc. III 49.1 mean by ῥηθεισῶν δὲ τῶν γνωμῶν τούτων μάλιστα ἀντιπάλων πρὸς ἀλλήλας? 'After the delivery of these two opinions, directly contradicting each other?' Or something like 'The two opinions thus expressed were the ones that most directly contradicted each other' (Crawley), suggesting that there were other opinions too? At any rate, it is quite impossible to believe that on such an occasion only two speeches were made.

An overwhelming body of evidence has now been produced to show that the mass of the citizens in the allied or subject states were loyal to Athens throughout the whole period of the empire, until the final collapse in the Ionian War, and could on occasion give proof of a deep devotion to the imperial city, which can only be compared with the similar devotion of contemporary oligarchs to Sparta.[126] This judgment holds, whatever the character of Athenian imperialism may have been and whatever verdict we ourselves may wish to pass upon it. The evidence is all the more impressive in that it comes mainly from Thucydides, who, whenever he is generalizing, or interpreting the facts rather than stating them, depicts the subjects of Athens as groaning under her tyrannous rule. A subsidiary conclusion of no small importance which has emerged from this survey is that Thucydides, generally (and rightly) considered the most trustworthy of all ancient historians, is guilty of serious misrepresentation in his judgments on the Athenian empire. He was quite entitled to disapprove of the later empire, and to express this disapproval. What we may reasonably object to is his representing that the majority of its subjects detested it. At the same time, it must be laid to Thucydides' credit that we are able to convict him of this distortion precisely because he himself is scrupulously accurate in presenting the detailed evidence. The partiality of Thucydides could scarcely have been exposed but for the honesty of Thucydides.

---

[126] Cf. Xen., Hell. II 3.25; Thuc. VI 11.7 [...]. This situation tended to reassert itself during the first half of the 4th century: see e.g. Xen., Hell. IV 8.20, 27; VI 3.14; Isocr. IV 16; VI 63.

EPIKTETOS EGRAPHSEN: THE WRITING ON THE CUP

Source: Goldhill, S. and Osborne, R. (eds) (1994) *Art and Text in Ancient Greek Culture*, Cambridge University Press, Chapter 1, pp.12–27 and 285–6.

By François Lissarrague

When Alcibiades describes Socrates in Plato's *Symposium*, he decides to do so 'using images (*di' eikonōn*)'.[1] There then follows the famous description of the Silenoi whom the philosopher resembles not only physically but also by reason of his inner wealth. We should not be surprised at Alcibiades' decision, nor should we imagine it to have been a mere jest, prompted by the effects of wine. On the contrary, it is altogether in line with all the elements that went to make up such a moment of sociability: in the course of the symposium, poetic song circulated amongst the guests, as did conversation – whether of a philosophic, political or erudite nature – and also the wine that had been mixed in a krater and was then poured from jugs into the guests' cups. A whole specialised set of utensils was used, either metal or earthenware, frequently ornamented with pictorial representations. The users of those utensils may or may not have scrutinised the engraved or painted images carefully, according to their deliberate choice. The present paper sets out to examine this question of the images at a symposium: how the drinkers may have reacted to them and the role that they played in the visual culture of the Athenians. I take as my point of departure a specific example, one that is quite unusual, indeed probably exceptional, but which will allow us to perceive a number of 'rules for reading'. It is a cup that bears the signature of the painter Epiktetos. I shall attempt to analyse first the meaning of each of the three images displayed on this pot, then their interrelationships and the role of the inscriptions and writing on the pot. Finally, I shall try to formulate some reflections of a more general nature on the cups that were used in banquets and the attitude of the symposiasts to them.

Fig. 3a

I have not chosen this particular cup at random. It is a cup that bears two signatures: that of the painter – EPIKTETOS EGRAPHSEN [Epiktetos drew it] – and that of the potter – PYTHON EPOISEN [Python made it]. It was discovered in the excavations at Vulci and is now to be found in the British Museum.[2]

The shape of this cup is very unusual: its base is not made up, as is usual, of a stem that connects the cup to a round, flat foot; instead, it takes the form of a

[1] Plato, *Symp.* 215a.

[2] London E38; *ARV* 72.16.

wide-based cone of a type more frequently encountered in so-called 'Chalcidian' products and which seems to be inspired by models from metal-ware.[3] This extremely stable foot gives the cup a massive air and reminds one that much of the luxury-ware used in Athens was indeed fashioned from metal: bronze, silver or gold. Although this particular cup seems to us exceptional, it does not in truth belong to the top category of luxury objects. Our modern impression is distorted by the fact that ancient pottery has survived while the metal artefacts have disappeared; and those who point out that the idea that pottery represented the apex of Greek art should be revised are quite right to do so.[4] However, the pots produced by the Greeks still testify eloquently to the richness of a Greek symposium and, where figurative art is concerned, they remain a source of information of the greatest importance.[5]

The London cup bears three images, two on the outside and a tondo within (figs. 3a, b, c). When a drinker held the cup, looking into the picture at the bottom, a symposium scene (fig. 3a) would be facing his chest while his fellow-drinkers would be presented with a scene depicting one of Herakles' exploits (fig. 3b). To analyse this object, we must undertake at least a minimal ecphrasis.

Image A, on the outside of the cup, presents the eyes of the drinker with a symposium scene (fig. 3a): three couches are set out, side by side, each of which is occupied by a guest. Two of these are depicted reclining, while the third, to the right, at a right angle to the others, is seen from the back. On the left, a woman is playing a double *aulos* [flute], standing before a drinker who has set his cup down on the floor. No tables are placed by the couches, and this is unusual. The first guest tilts his head backwards, supports the nape of his neck with his right hand, and opens his mouth: he is singing, to the accompaniment of the *aulos*.[6] In the centre a naked young boy is pouring the contents of his jug into the cup proffered by the second guest. The third guest, on the right, is seen from the back. His head is incomplete, but his gesture is clear: he is drinking from the cup that is raised to his lips.

In this relatively commonplace scene, two elements stand out as remarkable. The positioning of the couches is unusual: normally, they are depicted side by side, all on the same level, in a single row regularly disposed across the surface of the pot, whether it be around a circle, as on the bottom of a cup, or round a cylinder, as on larger pots such as kraters or amphoras. Here, the painter has disrupted that pattern, creating a different kind of space, one that is presented to the eyes of the beholder not as a flat surface but as a space that incorporates a dimension of depth, in which the beholder is himself involved, as one side of the square formed by the guests at the banquet.

The sophistication of this graphic transposition of space – which does not amount to true perspective, as the painted figures are simply juxtaposed with no effort made to create a spatial homogeneity and continuity between all the elements in the picture – results from what has been called the 'corporeal space'. The figure of the drinker seen from the back and foreshortened, repre-

---

[3] See Bloesch (1940) 28, pl. 7 and Beazley (1933) 7 on pl. 1, 1–2.

[4] Vickers (1987).

[5] See Fehr (1971) and Lissarrague (1990a).

[6] For this gesture see the examples collected by Vermeule (1965).

sented a novelty in Attic imagery, one that was becoming fashionable around 510–500, under the influence of the pioneers of red-figure painting.[7] A cup painted by Douris, which seems to be close to this one by Epiktetos, uses the same spatial device.[8] The effect of depth that is thus created is all the more forceful given that the image is reflexive: the person drinking from this cup is himself reclining at the banquet, on a couch placed along one side of the square room. The arrangement of the couches around him is identical to that in the image displayed to him on his cup.

The other remarkable factor is the positioning of the painter's signature. The inscription EPIKTE TOS EGRAPH SE(N) is written between the depicted figures. The formula in itself is unexceptional and the fact that it spreads round the whole outer surface of the cup is in no way unusual. But in this case, instead of writing round the rim of the cup, as he does elsewhere,[9] the painter has chosen to place the letters lower, at the level of his drinkers' faces. Thus, the first letters of the name, EPIKTE, are positioned before the open mouth of the singer, while the rest of the signature is to be read in between the other faces, which are in this way all linked together by a long chain of letters which the spectator's eye is forced to follow from left to right, if he wishes to read it. The writing in the picture accordingly plays a double role: in the first place, it has a linguistic meaning in that it states the name of the painter; but at the same time, it produces a visual impact, possessing a graphic effect in that it unites the drinkers as if to convey that song and speech are circulating among those present at the banquet. So it is that both senses of the term *graphein* – to write and to draw – are simultaneously present in the plastic disposition of the letters.[10]

This representation of a banquet clearly constructs an image in which the space of the spectator and the space of the picture interfere with each other in an example of the mirror-play that was characteristic of the Greek symposium. An analogous reflexive interplay is developed in lyric poetry, which also frequently sets up a scene within the space of a banquet – the space which it uses as peculiarly its own in which to make its statement and create its effect. And it is precisely that poetic activity that is called to mind by the integration of the letters into the picture. The long chain of graphic signs, which as it were imparts sound to what is visual, stretches from one drinker to the next, like the drinking-song that each takes over from the other. We might indeed, at this point, have expected to read the actual words of the drinking-song, as they are sometimes to be found on other pots.[11] However, that equation of form and meaning, which seems essential to our modern eyes, was not an overriding consideration for the Attic painters, who were content to let what is visual take priority. But in truth, we are not particularly surprised to read the painter's signature in this position: just as Anacreon, in his banquet poems, introduces himself into the banquet scene, similarly here the image makes manifest the condition for its own production, by stating the name of its painter. That

---

[7] On the representation of the body and graphic experimentations in that period see Williams (1991). Here is a list (which could probably be augmented) of foreshortened beds or symposiasts seen from behind: *ARV* 72.16 (Epiktetos); 97.2 (Euergidean); 105.4 (Group of Acropolis); 139.23 to 141.63 (Pithos Painter; cf. Lissarrague, forthcoming); Basle, Cahn HC 680 (Hegesiboulos; cf. Williams (1991) 292 and fig. 8); 241.56 bis, 1638 (Myson); 275.47 (Harrow Painter); 355.35 (Colmar Painter); 402.12 (Foundry Painter); 432.52, 55 and 443.227 (Douris); London 95.10–27.2 (imitation of Douris; cf. Csapo and Miller 1991); 525.38 (Orchard Painter). In the early classic period, the Painter of Bologna 417 uses this motif almost routinely; cf. *ARV* 911.68, 71, 73–5, 77–9 and 918.214. Note that Epiktetos draws also symposiasts leaning with their heads on the left (instead of the usual position, head on the right): *ARV* 72.14 bis; 72.17; 75.56; 76.83 ter.

[8] See Robertson (1976) 37 suggesting that Epiktetos is influenced by Douris in that case; against this idea, Williams (1991) 292.

[9] For example on *ARV* 70.3; 71.8; 72.24. See Immerwahr (1990) 61–3 and, for other aspects of Epiktetos' signatures, Cohen (1991) 58–9 and n.63.

[10] See Lissarrague (1985, 1992), and Hurwit (1990).

[11] Examples in Lissarrague (1990a), Csapo and Miller (1991).

analogy is a limited one, however, for the image does not represent Epiktetos himself nor is the drinker engaged in hymning the praises of the painter. The image cannot be reduced to the text, nor the text to the image: the way the one functions does not make the other redundant.

Human banquets and mythical banquets

As has been noted, the other side of this cup is signed by the potter Python. The inscription is positioned just beneath the rim, to the side of the picture and, in this case, unlike on the other side, no attempt is made to produce an effect of the words being spoken. On this side of the cup (fig. 3b), which is turned towards the other guests when the drinker tips the inner tondo towards his face, the picture evokes a quite different set of connotations. The scene, full of action, is organized in a symmetrical fashion around a central axis constituted, in the background, by a cubic construction: an altar. In the foreground, to the left, Herakles is recognizable from the lion-skin in which he is draped and the quiver that hangs from his waist. With his club, he is felling a figure whom he grasps by the throat and who is bleeding from skull and jaw. The figure is clothed in a fine *chiton* [tunic], as are all his companions. He has a shaven head[12] and a negroid profile, indicating that he is an Egyptian. The picture represents the episode of Herakles' visit to Busiris:[13] Egypt was afflicted by drought at the time and the pharaoh Busiris was sacrificing to the gods all foreigners who happened to be passing through his land. On his arrival, Herakles at first believed that he was being fêted as a guest, as the Greek rules of hospitality to strangers dictated. He was led to the altar in procession, and it was only at the moment of sacrifice that he realized his mistake: he himself was the intended victim and the feast that was to follow was to be a cannibalistic meal in which his own role was simply to constitute the main dish. At this point the Theban hero struggled free, putting the Egyptian priests to flight and upsetting the whole monstrous ritual in which he was supposed to be the sacrificial victim. This is the moment that Epiktetos seized upon, as did most of the artists who represented this episode. Normally in Attic iconography, a sacrifice would always be represented as a moment of peace; the picture would concentrate upon either the stately procession making its way to the altar, or else the scene once it arrived there, in which each person would occupy a particular place and would be seen proffering one of the ritual objects necessary for the correct sequence of events to unfold.[14] In contrast, the representation of Herakles being led to the sacrifice always takes on the air of an explosion of violence in which the correct sacrificial order is destroyed and all its elements are scattered. The barbarian and monstrous practices of the impious pharaoh, which reverse the Greek customs of hospitality, are matched by an iconography which, equally, turns the order of Greek sacrifice upside down. Also noticeable, in the case of Epiktetos' cup, is the fact that the four people who, instead of converging upon the altar, are fleeing away from it, are each connected with a particular object. On the extreme left, one of the Egyptians holds a knife, *machaira*. This instrument, which is used to cut the throat of the victim and is a symbol of murder and violence, is normally concealed in the three-cornered basket, *kanoun*, which in this instance has fallen at the feet of the sacrificer. The disarray of the procession makes manifest that which the ritual usually seeks to conceal: the act of cutting the victim's throat. The second Egyptian is a musician, an *aulos*-player. On his left shoulder he carries his *aulos*-case and his mouth is still swathed in the band, *phorbeia*, which serves to control the inflation of his cheeks. On the right, the first Egyptian, close to the altar, holds the *oenochoe* used for libations, whilst his companion has dropped his *cithara* [lyre] in its sling. This symmetrical image of flight thus interweaves in subtle chiasmus

[12] Cf. Williams (1985) 275–6.

[13] Durand and Lissarrague (1983).

[14] Durand (1986).

Fig. 3b

sacrificial implements (knife, basket, jug) and musical instruments (*aulos*, *cithara*), objects that are held (knife, *aulos*-case, jug) and objects that fall to the ground (basket, *cithara*).

The remarkable precision of this arrangement cannot be due to chance, nor can the connection that links the two sides of the cup. The two scenes are at once opposed and complementary: opposed in that the one refers to a mythical context while the other evokes an ordinary, even humdrum activity; the one is animated by the movement scattering the Egyptians in divergent directions, the other is organized as a stable circle of drinking companions. But at the same time these two images are complementary, for they revolve around the theme of hospitality and conviviality:[15] sacrifice, when carried out in the normal fashion, implies a sharing of meat and harmony between men and gods, through a meal, *deipnon,* which is followed by a symposium. The two stages are here presented first in a positive form (the symposium), then in a negative one (the cannibalistic sacrifice), on a cup which thus counterbalances a model with an anti-model, the Greek world with the barbarian world, order with disorder, in the matter of table manners.

The complementarity of the two sides of the cup might be thought to be somewhat tenuous, no more than a coincidence, were it not for the fact that the tondo inside the cup reinforces the impression, by also harping on the symposium theme.

The centre of the cup shows two figures (fig. 3c): on the left, a young, naked man, with his head wreathed and a *chiton* thrown over one shoulder, is stepping forward, playing a double *aulos*. On the right, a woman is dancing to the rhythm produced by this music and the *crotala* (clappers) that she holds in her hands. Her costume is striking: her head bears a *sakkos* [snood, cap] and she is adorned with a necklace and ear-rings. She wears a dappled animal pelt, a fawn-skin, which leaves her breast bare, for she wears no *chiton,* only some kind of shorts, the hem of which can be glimpsed on her upper thigh. This heterogeneous attire combines a number of models of feminine costume: the *sakkos* and jewellery, which are those of an ordinary Greek woman, the short skirt of an athlete or dancer, the fawn-skin of a woman who has become wild and turned into a maenad. This woman is a dancer, a *hetaira,* the kind whose services would be hired for the occasion of a symposium.[16] She is not a maenad, but

---

[15] On this aspect see Lissarrague and Schmitt-Pantel (1988).

[16] Peschel (1987) 117.

Fig. 3c

her costume in part evokes a Dionysiac woman of that type and her dancing imitates the frenzy of the maenads. There is a close connection between the symposium scene on the side of the cup and this dancing scene: the tondo of the cup evokes the kind of spectacle that would sometimes be laid on for the occasion of a symposium, spectacles of which Xenophon's *Symposium*, admittedly at a much later date, provides an excellent example.[17]

So this image completes the other two. It falls within the same frame of reference as the symposium scene on side A of the cup in that it represents a dancing scene of the kind that might be witnessed at a symposium. But the dancer is imitating a maenad, and the model that her dance evokes reminds one of the Dionysiac world, a mythical frame of reference that is shared by side B, which represents the figure of Herakles. The image displayed by the tondo inside the cup conveys a double interplay of representations: before the drinker's eyes, within his cup, is the equivalent of a spectacle which can sometimes be viewed by the guests in the room where a symposium takes place. However, this is not a mirror-image as is the one on side A, which refers the user of the cup to a representation of himself; instead, it is a representation of a representation, a second-degree image, a reproduction of a spectacle to be seen at a symposium in which the woman, an accessory to the symposium, becomes an instrument of visual pleasure.

The three pictures can be perceived to be linked not just on the visual plane but on the aural plane also. We know that Greek culture was a musical one and the three scenes depicted on this cup can all be interpreted musically. In the symposium picture, the female *aulos*-player provides an accompaniment for the guest who is singing as he reclines on his couch. In contrast, in the tondo, a male *aulos*-player provides the music for a female dancer. Finally, at the sacrifice, the *aulos* and the *cithara* are certainly present, but the fact that they have been dropped indicates that this monstrous ritual has come to grief. The singing, the dancing and the procession – those three musical modalities – reinforce the coherence of the three pictures displayed on the cup and suggest that we should regard them as a complementary whole, organized in three tiers:

the mirror-image, with the self-representation of the drinker and the couches;

the spectacle-image, in which feminine models are transposed in the dance;

the mythical image, in which sacrificial values are turned upside down.

[17] Xenophon, *Symposium* 2.

By setting up an interchange between the fields of reference involved, the three scenes on this pot make it possible for us to explore the various modalities of representation which reach out from the drinker himself to one who is other, from a Greek man, the same as himself, to a woman, who is other than a man, and to a barbarian, here represented as the opposite of the Greek model.

Variants, combinations, agenda

What significance should we attach to the above remarks? Supposing that it is possible to detect a coherence in the composition of this cup as a whole, may we generalize from those remarks and expect to find in every cup a similar interplay of images? Or is this particular example simply an isolated – if interesting – exception?

In truth, there is no easy answer to that question and it is impossible to generalize without introducing qualifications. Let us first compare the London cup with another, in the Museum of the Villa Giulia, which is signed by the same painter, Epiktetos (fig. 4).[18] It is probably somewhat earlier in date and on one side it displays the same subject: the confrontation between Herakles and Busiris. The theme is the same, but there are many variations in details. On this pot too, we find the altar in the central position, but the general composition of the picture is different. Here, the basket has fallen to the ground in the centre of the picture, before the altar, while the *machaira* can be seen in the grasp of a fleeing Egyptian on the left. The *aulos* is the only musical instrument represented, here brandished by an Egyptian on the right, whose *phorbeia* has slipped down his neck. This picture thus contains fewer ritual instruments than the one on the London cup, but they are scattered in a similar fashion and the violence of Herakles is equally evident: here he is grasping two Egyptians at once. The two cups do not repeat each other, then; each of the pictures uses the same iconographical elements in such a way as to produce a unique work of art.

But that is not all. Whereas on the London cup, the episode of the sacrifice of Herakles is, as we have seen, accompanied by a simple symposium scene and a picture representing a dance, the cup in the Villa Giulia presents a very different combination: side B carries representations of the duel between Achilles and Memnon, the *psychostasia* [the weighing of lives] effected by Hermes, and Thetis and Eos, the divine mothers of the heroes, appealing to Zeus. In the tondo of the cup, a naked woman is riding a phallus in the form of a bird. The two pictures on the outside of the bowl evoke the world of the heroes, the exploit of Herakles and post-Homeric episodes, while the tondo presents the drinker with a picture of a fantastical *hetaira*.

In two separate works whose signatures explicitly credit them to the same painter, we thus find that the two pictures devoted to the same theme do not repeat one another sign for sign, and that one and the same theme may be incorporated into very different combinations of images. In other words, nothing predetermines how particular images should be combined with others on Greek pots. That does not mean to say that there is no connection between the images that appear on the same pot—as I hope to have demonstrated above – but simply that the choice of combinations is an open one. Various connections are possible, but none of them essential, so each cup is a particular case. And therein lies the charm of these cups: the user is invited, as he turns the cup in his hands, to discover for himself the associations suggested by the painter. Many different combinations are possible: on one cup, in Ferrara, the Busiris theme occupies not only both sides but the inner medallion as well; the

[18] Rome, Villa Giulia 57912; *ARV* 72.24.

Fig. 4

whole pot is devoted to the same subject.[19] That is also frequently the case with the symposium theme, which can occupy the whole cup,[20] but not invariably; for it may, instead, be complemented by images of the *kōmos* [band of revellers, often in honour of the gods] or a mythical scene depicting a *thiasos,* a Dionysiac parade of satyrs and maenads.

The way in which these images are combined on a pot depends primarily upon the imagination and whim of the painter; and the degree of coherence in his selection of images may vary: the criteria for his choice may be iconographical, but may instead be purely determined by considerations of shape. The logic behind the grouping is not always clear and in some cases there may simply be no obvious logic; but the same could be said of the manner in which a symposium might develop. It was impossible to know in advance what would be said or done; the pleasure of the symposium lay precisely in the unforeseeable interconnections in the conversation and the interrelations that would develop within a particular mix of guests.

The same goes, it seems, for the images that are combined in ways that vary not only from cup to cup but also from one set of cups to another; for the interplay between the images may extend to the whole collection of pots used in the course of the symposium. Of course, it would be possible not to look at the pictures, to leave them as it were dormant,[21] simply using the pots as useful objects; but on the other hand, the guest was free to choose to pay attention to the pictures displayed on them and to make his own associations between the images, passing from one cup to another.

There is no way for the modern interpreter to verify those associations: they seem to escape us entirely. However, it is possible to detect one or two hints which seem to suggest that the Greeks did relate the pictures, not just on a single pot, but passing from one pot to another. Consider the case of a pair of cups which are today to be found in the Vienna Museum.[22] They are not of the same date, but were discovered together in a tomb at Caere and seem to have been chosen by the purchaser to be contemplated at the same time.[23] These two pots are signed both by the painter – DOURIS EGRAPHSEN – in each case in

---

[19] Ferrara T499; *ARV* 415.2.

[20] For example on the following cups: *ARV* 317.16 (Onesimos); 348.7 (Cage Painter); 371.24 and 372.28 (Brygos Painter); 401.11 and 402.12 (Foundry Painter); 427.2, 432.55, 57, 58 and 438.140 (Douris); 467.119, 122, 127 (Macron).

[21] This notion of 'sleeping image' has been recently used by Veyne (1991) 341.

[22] Vienna 3694 and 3695; *ARV* 427.3 and 429.26.

[23] According to Beazley's chronology, these two cups belong to different phases (early and early middle); their association is a choice made by the user, not by the producer.

the tondo, and also by the potter, Python, the craftsman who also made the London cup painted by Epiktetos. Python's two signatures are set out in a striking way: the name appears on the side of the foot of each cup, in letters widely spaced apart and clearly intended to be ornamental. On one of the cups the name reads from left to right, as is usual for writing at this date; on the other cup, it reads from right to left, which is very unusual for this date and produces an effect of convergence when the cups are set side by side.

The way that the writing is organized, so that it guides the spectator's eye, draws attention to the way in which the two cups clearly complement one another – a complementarity which is confirmed by their iconography. The first cup is entirely devoted to the story of Achilles' weapons: on side A, Odysseus and Ajax are arguing over them; on side B, the Greeks are voting on the matter, with Athena presiding; in the tondo, Odysseus, who won the vote, is handing over Achilles' arms to his son, Neoptolemos. The three pictures complement one another, telling the story in the correct order and so, as it were, forming a trilogy.[24] The outside of the other cup shows a group of warriors donning their arms, while a woman and an old man look on; in the inner tondo, a woman is pouring a libation for a warrior. The three images develop the theme of warriors arming themselves for battle and then departing.[25] One sees clearly that the two cups are designed to treat the warrior panoply as an object of great importance, whether it be a matter of passing on a hero's weapons or that of ordinary warriors preparing for battle. Each cup is coherent in itself, and constitutes a homogeneous, self-sufficient entity; but at the same time, taken together, the pair of cups is complementary and they correspond to one another, not in a symmetrical and repetitive fashion, but with the one taking up and extending the theme of the other, passing from the context of the ordinary life of warriors and their families to a mythical context where the gods are present. As a pair these cups spell out the epic reference which, for an ancient Greek, was always present behind the image of warfare.

To understand how the pictures on the cups function at a symposium, we may thus envisage the hypothesis of an open play of combinations made through visual associations of various kinds: narrative, metaphoric or purely formal, similar to those that one encounters in lyric poetry. The pleasure of the symposium lies in just such variations and in the surprises created both by the exchanges between the guests and the interplay between the various elements present in the symposium – songs, conversation and pictures.

Finally, to strengthen that last point, let me cite a fragment from the *Anacreontea*, often attributed to Anacreon himself, which certainly enjoyed great popularity.[26] The poem testifies to the interplay that is possible between song and image, the way that the one can refer to the other. Playing with the idea of a deliberate iconographic selection, it implies a conscious choice of images on the part of the drinker, in an order passed not, in this instance, to a painter, but to a goldsmith, to the artisan *par excellence*, Hephaistos himself:

> Take your tools, but make for me,
>
> Vulcan, no silver panoply;
>
> For what care I for war's array?
>
> Make me the deepest cup you may.
>
> No stars upon it, if you please,
>
> Arcturus or the Pleiades,
>
> Nor yet the wain; Orion grim,

[24] Cf. Williams (1980).

[25] On this see Lissarrague (1990).

[26] *Anacreontea* 4; see also *Anthology* 11.48 and Gellius, *Noct. Att.* 19.9.6.

What have I to do with him?

But grave me on't the clambering vine

And the laughing clusters fine,

And, gathering them, a Maenad crew;

And make a winepress on it too,

And three gold figures treading there,

Love, Bacchus and my fairest fair.[27]

This brief poem of course refers to the ecphrasis *par excellence*, a quasi-cosmological ecphrasis, which is connected with the origins of the genre and founds it within the poetic tradition, namely Homer's description of the shield of Achilles.[28] We know that it was not simply a matter of describing a particular object, for a double work of creation was involved: before the very eyes of the listener, Homer describes Hephaistos at work fashioning the shield which is a universe in itself. The song of the poet is thus in a position to rival the work of the craftsman-god: it can create an object with words, just as the blacksmith fashions it.

In the poem from the *Anacreontea*, a different world is conjured up: not the starry heavens which adorn the shield but the world of vines and the god who presented them to men as a gift. Dionysus is the figure most frequently to be found represented on drinking-cups, and scenes of satyrs, rather than men, working at the vintage, are also common.[29] The poet thus passes from one cosmos to another, turning the cup set before us by his poem into the focal point in the arrangement of the space of the symposium.

The cup by Epiktetos which we have chosen to analyse operates in exactly the same way. It illustrates how it is itself used and the various ways in which it may be included within the context of a symposium. As we have seen, this cup is unique in the way that it associates three themes which are not found in combination on any other pot known to us. But at the same time it remains a model in as far as the very principle of a symposium is that each occasion must be distinct, true to the principle of live performance, which turns each performance into a unique event. Within a given visual and poetic framework, each poem, and each image, plays freely with the organizational rules suggested by the symposium.

Epiktetos' cup thus appears as just one of many possible combinations of themes and images, but a particularly richly elaborated one.[30]

[Abbreviations]

AK *Antike Kunst*

ARV J.D. Beazley, *Attic Red Figure Vase-Painters*, Oxford, 1963, 2nd edition.

[27] Translation by J. M. Edmonds, *Greek Elegy and Iambus II, Anacreontea*, p. 23, no. 4 (Loeb Classical Library) London and Cambridge, MA, 1961.

[28] *Iliad* 18.483—9.

[29] Sparkes (1976).

[30] This paper was presented at Oxford and Princeton in 1991. I wish to thank R. Osborne and F. Zeitlin for their invitation and comments as well as others who participated in the discussions. Thanks also to J. Lloyd who translated my text; and to I. Jenkins for his help in the British Museum.

Shortened bibliography

Beazley, J.D., *Campana Fragments in Florence*, Oxford, 1933.

Bloesch, H., *Formen attischer Schalen: von Exekias bis zum eine des strengens Stils*, Berne, 1940.

Cohen, B., 'The literate potter: a tradition of incised signatures on Attic Vases', *Metropolitan Museum Journal*, 26: 4–95, 1991.

Csapo, E. and Miller, M.C., 'The "kottobos toast" and an inscribed red-figure cup', *Hesperia* 60.3: 367–82, 1991.

Durand, J., *Sacrifice et labour en Grèce ancienne*, Paris, 1986.

Durand, J. and Lissarrague, F., 'Héros cru ou hôte cuit: histoire quasi-cannibale d'Héraklès chez Busiris' in *Image et céramique grecque*, eds F. Lissarrague and F. Thelamon, Rouen, 1983.

Fehr, B., *Orientalische und griechische Gelage*, Bonn, 1971.

Hurwit, J., 'The words in the image: orality, literacy, and early Greek art', *Word and Image*, 6.2: 180–97, 1990.

Immerwahr, H., *Attic Script: A Survey*, Oxford, 1990.

Lissarrague, F., 'Paroles d'images' in *Ecritures II*, ed. A.M. Christin, Paris, 1985.

Lissarrague, F., *The Aesthetics of the Greek Banquet*, trans by A. Szegedy-Maszak, Princeton, 1990.

Lissarrague, F. and Schmitt-Pantel, P., 'Spartizione e communità nei banchetti greci' in *Sacrificio e società nel mondo antico*, Rome and Bari, 1988.

Peschel, I., *Die Hetäre bei Symposion und Komos*, Frankfurt, 1987.

Robertson, M., 'Beazley and After', *Münchener Jahrbuch der bildenen Künst* 27: 29–46.

Sparkes, B., 'Treading the Grapes', *Bulletin Antieke Beschaving* 51: 47–64, 1976.

Vermeule, E., 'Fragments of a Symposium by Euphronios', AK 8: 34–9, 1965.

Veyne, P., *La Société romaine*, Paris, 1991.

Vickers, M., 'Value and simplicity: eighteenth-century taste and the study of Greek Vases', *Past and Present* 116: 98–137, 1987.

Williams, D.J.R., 'Ajax, Odysseus and The arms of Achilles', *AK* 23: 137–45, 1980.

Williams, D.J.R., 'Close Shaves' in *Ancient Greek and Related Pottery*, ed. H. Brijder, Amsterdam, 1985.

Williams, D.J.R., 'The drawing of the human figure on early red-figure vases' in *New Perspectives in Early Greek Art*, Washington, 1991.

Cup signed by Epiktetos Egraphsen and Python Epoisen, from Vulci. British Museum E.38. Reproduced by permission of the Trustees of the British Museum.

THE FUNERAL SPEECH: A STUDY OF VALUES

Source: *Greece and Rome*, 20, 1973, pp.111–21.

By P. Walcot

Since no one doubts the pre-eminence of Socrates as a teacher, there is much, presumably, to be said in favour of his method of instruction. The picture of Socrates to be gained from the earlier dialogues of Plato is one of a man who consistently challenged orthodox opinions. In the same way, but, of course, with nothing like the Athenian's skill, I propose in what follows to react against a commonly accepted view; to be precise, I wish to scrutinize the opinion that the Funeral Speech, delivered by Pericles at the end of the first year of the Peloponnesian War and known to us from Thucydides, presents the reader with a splendid portrait of fifth-century Athens, and that, in stressing the spirit rather than the forms of Athenian democracy, it qualifies as the ancient equivalent of Lincoln's Gettysburg Address.[1] We all idealize the ancient Greeks; we ignore the harsh realities and prefer to concentrate our attention on what we see as the grandeur of Aeschylus, the splendour of the Parthenon, and the vision of Pericles; and it is the Funeral Speech, beyond everything else in Greek literature, which allows us to indulge in this type of escapism. That the Funeral Speech does have a 'glorious' reputation is a fact. Does it deserve so uncritical a fame? If this question is posed, I ask it not from any perverted desire to debunk its reputation, but simply in order to gain a deeper understanding not only of the speech but also of the Greeks to whom it was addressed and of the particular statesman who delivered it.

Towards the end of his speech (ii. 44) Pericles offers consolation to the parents of the dead: you must bear up in the hope of other children, he says, those of you whose age yet allows you to have them (καρτερεῖ δὲ χρὴ καὶ ἄλλων παίδων ἐλπίδι, οἷς ἔτι ἡλικία τέκνωσιν ποιεῖσθαι, 44.3), for more children will mean that you will forget those you have lost as well as it being a benefit to the state; if you are too old to have children, consider it gain that your happy years were more in number and what is left is short (τόν τε πλέονα κέρδος ὃν ηὐτυχεῖτε βίον ἡγεῖσθε καὶ τόνδε βραχὺν ἔσεσθαι, 44.4); in other words, 'you'll soon be dead'. Such a consolation is horribly bleak, and Gomme notes a marked contrast 'to the warmth and splendour of all the rest of the speech in which the greatness of the city and the opportunities and qualities of the citizens are lauded', while Ehrenberg finds Pericles' exhortations 'rather hollow and empty'.[2] The sentiments voiced by Pericles may be very Greek in their stark realism, but they are none the less depressing for all that. However, something yet more devastating is still to come, the brief word of advice which Pericles goes on to inflict on the wives of Athens (45.2): your great glory is not to be inferior to the nature that is in you (τῆς ὑπαρχούσης φύσεως), to be least spoken about among men whether they are praising you or criticizing you (ἐπ᾽ ἐλάχιστον ἀρετῆς πέρι ἢ ψόγου ἐν τοῖς ἄρσεσι κλέος). Apparently Pericles believed that the less said about a woman the better. Men must not blame women, and this, I suppose, is a fair enough comment, but they also must not praise women, and so we find what seems to be complete anonymity recommended as an ideal for half the human species. One does not need to sympathize with any female liberation movement before one is shattered by this casual dismissal of so large a proportion of the Athenian population. Why does Pericles say what he does? What does he mean when he speaks of 'the nature that is in you'? The meaning of the second part of his statement is clear, and it is as embarrassing as it is clear, for it is hardly the kind of sentiment which adds lustre to the reputation of the Funeral Speech. Yet I believe that if Pericles' advice to the wives is under-

[1] Such a comparison is made, for example, by J. H. Finley, *Thucydides* (Cambridge, Mass., 1942), 144.

[2] A.W. Gomme, *A Historical Commentary on Thucydides*, ii (Oxford, 1956), 143; Victor Ehrenberg, *From Solon to Socrates* (London, 1968), 263.

stood, we are in possession of a key to the values embodied in the Funeral Speech in its entirety. Thus, by discussing a particular problem, we shall perhaps throw light over a much wider area of study.

It is possible to deny the existence of our problem by arguing that the Funeral Speech is Thucydides' own invention, and those who hold to such an opinion often also believe that the speech was compiled after Athens' defeat and was intended to be a comment by a historian who was looking back over his city's record of initial triumph but ultimate defeat.[3] Yet Thucydides said that his method in giving the contents of a speech was to keep as near as possible to the general purport of what was delivered (i. 22. I). The problem is disposed of most easily by the minority of scholars who still today cling to the view that the women of fifth-century Athens were kept in a state of 'oriental seclusion', a peculiar phrase which seems to signify that women were repressed, tightly restrained, and treated at the best with indifference and frequently with contempt. The remark attributed to Pericles is simply confirmation of the correctness of this assessment of the position of women in Athenian society.[4] Few would now subscribe to the view that husband and wife were 'natural enemies', and it is Gomme, Kitto, and others whom we must thank for a more enlightened approach.[5] A parallel drawn from architecture is helpful at this point. Public life in the *polis* was centred in the agora of each city, and the agora comprised an open, level area occupying some commanding position. In its openness the agora symbolized the openness of Greek public life, but the agora was an exclusively male haunt, for only men participated in the affairs of the state. The Greek house offers a strong contrast, being even more of a castle than that proverbially associated with the Englishman: it would have few exterior windows, a small and unobtrusive front-door, and the house would look inwards on a courtyard and not outwards on the public street. Far from being suppressed, women could and did exercise considerable power within the confines of their homes, but private life among the Greeks was intensely private and we hear little of it. And so we get a false impression of the influence, or rather the lack of influence, of the Greek woman. Women did not fight in the state's army, and as a result were not entitled to the privilege of the vote. But what of their position otherwise? 'Women were probably as well protected by the law as in any century before our own, and, granted a reasonable husband or father, enjoyed a life not much narrower and not much less interesting than women in comparable classes of society elsewhere.'[6]

But, if we accept that women were not kept in oriental seclusion, how are we to explain Pericles' recommendation of anonymity? We may argue that the statesman is not expressing an opinion typical of all fifth-century Athenians, although this argument may quickly be countered: a speech delivered on a solemn public occasion by a leading politician hardly affords scope for the expression of individual, eccentric *obiter dicta*. Great play has been made of the personality and circumstances of Pericles himself. His age and, above all else, his association with Aspasia, the Milesian 'courtesan', have been heavily stressed, and it is true that the affair with Aspasia was most irregular. Characteristic of the approach is a comment passed by Bowra: 'whatever might be said about Aspasia, nobody could claim that she was not talked about. So

---

[3] This opinion has become less and less fashionable with the passage of time; note the change of mind registered by F.E. Adcock, *Thucydides and his History* (Cambridge, 1963), 36–7.

[4] Thus, in commenting on the speech, A.R. Burn, *Pericles and Athens* (London, 1948), 223, claims that Athenian and Ionian women were kept 'almost in "purdah" '.

[5] Full details of the controversy, together with bibliography, are to be found in T.M. de Wit-Tak, *Lysistrata, Vrede, Vrouw en Obsceniteit bij Aristophanes* (Groningen, 1967), 29ff. Some indication of the course of the discussion may be gained by comparing F.A. Wright, *Feminism in Greek Literature from Homer to Aristotle* (London, 1923), the article on the position of women by Wright in the first edition of the *Oxford Classical Dictionary* (1949), and the new article by W. K. Lacey in the second edition (1970).

[6] Lacey, *The Family in Classical Greece* (London, 1968), 176.

P. Walcot

these words are a little mysterious. If they are the correct record of what Pericles said, did he say them knowing about current gossip, and mean to defy it, claiming implicitly that Aspasia was in fact a quiet woman who kept to her home?'[7] Bowra reads deeply between the lines, but he is following, admittedly in an extreme form, a lead established by others. Kitto has suggested that Pericles is to be compared to Gladstone and further that Pericles' words imply 'an old-fashioned deference and courtesy' rather than disdain.[8] But, by our own standards, Pericles is surely being offensive when he would deny women the right to be praised and his statement cannot possibly be regarded as an example of courtesy, whether old-fashioned or new-fangled. What we must do is to ask ourselves if we can imagine a situation when we find it objectionable that a woman, say a person's wife, is praised, and there is one obvious example, though my illustration may be thought crude in more than one way. Imagine a husband and wife going to a party. It is a good party and wine flows freely. At a good party a husband and wife should not cling together but mingle separately with the other guests. Imagine now that the husband is approached by a stranger who knows neither husband nor wife. He begins to chat with the husband and points to the wife on the other side of the room. 'That's a nice-looking girl', he says, and at first the husband is pleased, for every man enjoys his wife being praised provided that, and the stipulation is very important, she is praised in moderation. But if the unwitting stranger then goes on to comment too personally on the charms, especially the physical charms, of the wife, the husband will become progressively more and more annoyed, however flattering to the wife the stranger's remarks. Why does the husband become furious? Why was Achilles furious when Agamemnon removed Briseis? Why is a jury in a modern court inclined to deal sympathetically with a crime of passion? Why did Athenian law regard homicide as justified if the victim were caught in the act with the wife, mother, sister, or daughter of the murderer?

A threat (and excessive praise constitutes a threat) to a person's womenfolk, be it wife, mother, sister, or daughter, has a special emotive force, for it calls into question a man's virility and it poses a danger to our sense of personal honour. We are all of us men of honour and concerned by any potential loss of face, less frequently so and less consciously so perhaps in Western Europe or North America than elsewhere – among the Japanese, for example, or much nearer home around the Mediterranean coast where one encounters the hot-blooded Andalusian, the Southern Italian, Sicilian, or contemporary Greek.[9] And man's honour is at its most sensitive when his womenfolk and their protection are at stake, and this is why in medieval romances knights, that epitome of honour, are always rescuing damsels in distress and why it remains the deadliest insult to pass disparaging remarks about a person's mother. The man of honour must demonstrate his honour and be aggressive in its defence, but he requires his womenfolk to display different virtues, to be passive rather than aggressive and to avoid any situation in which they are liable to incur dishonour. It is already difficult enough for a man to uphold his honour without the added complication of a woman within the family group who indulges in dubious behaviour. The role in life of a woman is different from that of a man and what is expected of a woman is different from what is expected of a man; their 'nature' is different, and it is to this distinct nature of a woman that Pericles refers when he speaks of a woman not being inferior to the φύσις which is in her, and this is why the following two lines can be spoken in Aristophanes' Lysistrata:

εἰ δ᾽ ἐγὼ γυνὴ πέφυκα, τοῦτο μὴ φθονεῖτέ μοι,
ἢν ἀμείνω γ᾽ εἰσενέγκω τῶν παρόντων πραγμάτων.

[7] C.M. Bowra, *Periclean Athens* (London, 1971), 193.

[8] H.D.F. Kitto, *The Greeks* (Pelican Book), 224.

[9] See especially the essays published in J.G. Peristiany (ed.), *Honour and Shame, the Values of Mediterranean Society* (London, 1965).

It's true that I was born a woman but don't envy me
if I can contribute better in the current situation.

(verses 649–50; cf. also *Antigone*, verses 61–2)

To urge a woman not to be inferior to her nature, that is, to live up to the standard of behaviour expected of a woman, is not a gratuitous insult, for it assumes the existence of a standard and a high standard at that. It is not the same standard of excellence as that to which men must aspire, but this in no way makes it any the less of a target at which a woman must aim.

The aggressive male must practise love of honour (φιλοτιμία), while the passive female needs to exhibit shame (αἰδώς); one must be positive in his behaviour and the other negative in her behaviour. As Aeschylus' Agamemnon remarks, οὔτοι γυναικός ἐστιν ἱμείρειν μάχης [this desire for conflict is not womanly] (verse 940). The man of honour instinctively thinks of the threat to his prestige posed by a woman; woman, in his opinion, is fundamentally bad and likely to corrupt—they are all, in his eyes, Eves or Pandoras and are going to cause man trouble, and abundant proof of this 'fact' could be found by the fifth-century Athenian in the writings of Thucydides' predecessor as historian, Herodotus. Women threaten your honour, but you may safeguard yourself in two ways, first by the strength of your right arm, and secondly by keeping the women under your protection out of the way of other men, by dressing them in clothes so shapeless as to make them to all intents and purposes sexless, and by formulating the rule that the less said about a woman the better, and this is what the Greeks did. To this extent women were tightly restrained, though not for the reason advanced by the proponents of the oriental seclusion argument; they may have been mistrusted but they were not the objects of contempt; indeed the Greek entertained a healthy respect for their power. If honour is mentioned, a Greek thinks immediately of women, and this is what Pericles appears to do. What has Pericles said just before he addresses his advice to the Athenian wives? 'Love of honour (τὸ φιλότιμον) alone grows not old, and when one is old and helpless it is not money, as some claim, which gives the greater pleasure but τὸ τιμᾶσθαι, being held in honour' (44.4). A chain-reaction has been set in motion and a reference to honour leads on to advice addressed to the female sex.

The moral values exemplified throughout the Funeral Speech are those of a society obsessed with personal honour. Such a society does not believe in the equality of mankind, for some men are clearly more honourable than others and each member of that society will exert himself to gain more honour and so to stand higher in the esteem of his fellows. To win the grudging approval of others, to enhance one's reputation is the goal of life for the man of honour. Yet Athens, as Pericles tells us, qualified as a democracy (37.1), although, of course, it was a democracy in which citizenship was restricted and women, slaves, and many free men had no vote in the assembly. Even when allowance is made for such restrictions, how democratic was Athenian government? Having called Athens a democracy, Pericles carried on with a sentence in which three things are said: (1) 'in their private disputes all share equality according to the laws'; (2) 'but in public esteem when a man is distinguished in any way, he is more highly honoured in public life, not as a matter of privilege but in recognition of merit'; (3) 'on the other hand any one who can benefit the city is not debarred by poverty or by the obscurity of his position'.[10] The first of these statements, the fact that all citizens as individuals are equal before the law, muffles the ominous note struck by the second statement, the distinguished man is more highly honoured in public life, although the occurrence of words such as ἀξίωσιν [held in awe], εὐδοκιμεῖ [esteemed], ἀρετῆς [excellence], and προτιμᾶται [honoured before others] should put us on our guard. Is the final remark, that poverty is no handicap, little more than the expression of a pious hope? Something said later by Pericles is certainly likely to arouse the anger of a person with a social conscience: 'It is no disgrace for a man to admit his

---

[10] I quote the translation by A.H.M. Jones, *Athenian Democracy* (Oxford, 1957), 45 and 48.

poverty; the real shame is not trying to escape it' (τὸ πένεσθαι οὐχ ὁμολογεῖν τινὶ αἰσχρόν, ἀλλὰ μὴ διαφεύγειν ἔργῳ αἴσχιον, 40.I). The present generation is acutely aware of the duty which society owes its 'lame ducks', whether they be private individuals or industrial giants, and it is freely recognized that circumstances rather than any lack of effort may conspire to keep the poor in a state of poverty. 'The needy are greedy' doctrine is considered reactionary and meets little favour.

Throughout the Funeral Speech, as was noted above, sentiments are voiced which reflect the honour code. In his first words (35.1) Pericles refers to 'the glories' (τὰς τιμάς) of the dead and warns his audience of the dangers of envy (διὰ φθόνον and φθονοῦντες) and envy is characteristic of the Greeks and of all honour societies,[11] since the man of honour is anxious to promote his own honour at the expense of the honour of others. There is only a limited amount of honour at hand, and one resents and envies the possession of it by other people. Honour demands that others should acknowledge it, and, therefore, visible evidence of honour, in the form of battle trophies or public recognition, must be available for display. In the Funeral Speech Pericles can claim (41.4) that Athens has provided such evidence as will incite admiration for the future as well as for the present; Athens has no need of a Homer to sing her praises, but everywhere has left everlasting memorials of her achievements. When Pericles turns to the actual dead, the statesman says that by their death on the field of battle (42.3) they have cancelled any debt they might owe their country. The supreme standard of excellence for the man of honour is martial valour (see chapter 39 of the Funeral Speech), and in giving their lives for Athens the dead won an undying renown (43.2) and the most magnificent memorial, and by this Pericles does not mean the grave in which they lie buried but the memorial engraved on man's heart. What Pericles desires is that the citizens should fall in love with the city (ἐραστὰς γιγνομένους αὐτῆς, 43.1) or, in other words, they should regard the city as the equivalent of one of their women and be as staunch in their defence of the city as they would be if one of their womenfolk were exposed to danger. Obligation towards the city is made comparable to obligation towards a woman, and this is the greatest obligation recognized by the honour code.

When Pericles speaks of equality, is his concept of equality based on any splendid principle? Certainly no Greek at this date would believe in the principle of one man (or woman), one vote. At first sight the honour code, inasmuch as it assumes that all are not equal but vary in the degree of honour which they command, and democracy as a political form seem incompatible. But a society dominated by a passion for honour is intensely competitive, for each man strives to increase his own honour and to curtail that of his fellows, and a highly competitive society is subject to constant stress and strain. The Greeks appreciated, as we ourselves do, that prevention is often better than cure, and, in consequence, we find a number of what may be called 'safety-valves' or protective devices functioning in Greek society, and these devices were designed to curb the excessive effects of the competitive element. One of the devices was the maintenance of an appearance of equality.

The case of women will illustrate more clearly the character of the safety-valves. When women are involved, a man defends his honour, as we have already seen, in two ways; by the strength of his right arm and by removing women from the notice of other men. The second method represents a safety-valve, and it was not the only one available, since the dowry system operated in a similar fashion. We tend to think of a dowry as an equivalent of our own wedding presents, but it is more than a device which allows a newly formed family to set itself up in life. If a father can offer potential suitors a lavish dowry, the daughter will stand every chance of an excellent marriage and so will not behave in any way likely to prejudice that chance. A poor parent, however, who

[11] See Gomme, op. cit. 103–4, and Walcot, *Greek Peasants, Ancient and Modern, a Comparison of Social and Moral Values* (Manchester, 1970), 82ff. For envy in general see G.M. Foster, *Current Anthropology* xiii (1972), 165–202.

is in a position where he can offer little or nothing as a dowry, will need to watch his daughter much more carefully, for a negligible dowry means small hope of marriage and no reason, therefore, why a girl should pay undue attention to her reputation—in other words, the girl has nothing to lose. The dowry then is also a device which acts on the principle of prevention being better than cure. A girl is discouraged from acquiring an ill repute if the dowry offered by her father leads her to expect a good marriage.

Pericles was being less idealistic than we imagine when he praises Athenian democracy and the idea of equality. An appearance of equality may function as a stabilizing factor, the best example from the ancient world being provided by the Spartan state, as it was reorganized by 'Lycurgus'. The existence of the Helot population required that all sources of friction likely to arise among the citizens had to be eliminated at Sparta, and as a result apparent equality was called into being. The conquest of Messenia was followed by a new distribution of land based on the principle of equal allotments; the Spartan citizens were actually designated 'Equals' and all in theory possessed an equality of political power. They lived in isolation from the world outside Sparta and received a common education; personal luxury was forbidden, cumbersome iron currency, for example, being retained. More details would serve only to confirm the same picture of Sparta as a self-contained association of equals. Such a state, however, was created not because the Spartans accepted, as we do, the idea of one man, one vote, but because their very survival in the midst of a subject people depended upon the elimination of internal strife among the Spartiates. I am not suggesting that democracy at Athens was developed to fulfil the same purpose, but I do think that we must recognize and acknowledge how socially convenient it was to emphasize the equality of opportunity enjoyed by each and every male citizen.

The devices by which an appearance of equality was maintained among the Athenians are standard ones, for they are far from being peculiar to Athens or to just the ancient world; they can be observed in operation even today in regions where the honour code prevails.[12] Pericles opens his speech with a reference to the ancestors of the Athenians (36.1), and what he mentions is that the Athenians have always occupied their country without change. Continuity of tradition and a tradition, moreover, stretching far back into the dim past, fosters a sense of solidarity, which is further strengthened when Pericles proceeds to claim for Athens complete self-sufficiency both for war and for peace (36.3). The people of Athens are supposed to have sprung from the soil of Attica and, therefore, shared a common kinship, and kin are social equals; they were a race of small-holders and the wide-spread ownership of land meant that the individual as much as the state was self-sufficient and could assert his equality because he depended on no one else for his livelihood. As his speech is developed, Pericles paints a picture of an Athens (chapters 37ff.) whose inhabitants share in a common culture quite distinct from the cultures of others and most obviously distinct from the Spartan pattern of life (e.g. chapter 39), and this is the main burden of the contents of the Funeral Speech. It is the idea of the common, distinct culture, I suggest, which, beyond everything else, promotes a feeling of sameness, of equality within a community, and such an idea has a special force within the framework of the Greek city-state, which tried not only to satisfy the political aspirations of its citizens but also to cater for their every need. Every citizen had an equal share in the national honour of the state, a common stake in Athens' future. The parents of the dead, for instance, can be urged to have more children in the interests of the state, for 'it is not possible that those should offer "equal" and just advice who do not run a comparable risk hazarding the lives of their children' (44.3). At Athens you cannot even drop out – 'we consider the man who does not participate not of insufficient interest but of insufficient use' (40.2). An appearance of equality is a useful

---

[12] Especially relevant is the study of social ranking in a French Alpine community by Susan Hutson, and of reputation in an Austrian village by M. A. Heppenstall, both of which appear in F.G. Bailey (ed.), *Gifts and Poison, the Politics of Reputation* (Oxford, 1971), 41ff. and 139ff.

mechanism to compel everybody to participate. The world of the *polis* was intensely personal, and, given an ideal situation, every citizen should know every other citizen. A citizen may at different times find himself fulfilling a different role—one year he may be just a private citizen but the next year may see him selected for high office. If one is likely to be now in and then out of office, it is a wise tactic to accept and to emphasize the equality of others. It pays always to be polite and a reputation for haughtiness, something even Pericles failed to avoid, is a political liability. The career of Alcibiades, chequered as it was, illustrates the dangers which face a politician who turns his back on so elementary a rule.[13]

The ways in which an appearance of equality is maintained in a French Alpine village and in an Austrian village have recently been discussed, and these are very much the same ways as in Periclean Athens. We shall be able to return to the point at which this discussion commenced if we note the attitude towards women adopted by the two groups of villagers. In the first of these studies it is remarked that 'women do little visiting outside the family' and 'in a society where the sexes are frequently segregated, different standards are applied to their behaviour. A man can build up a good reputation on his openness, friendliness and ability to joke. Women, however, are expected to keep to themselves and to refrain from gossiping. A woman who has friends and is frequently seen out of the house is suspected of telling family secrets and gossiping maliciously.'[14] In the other we read 'ideally the woman's place is in the home. Her meetings with others are therefore more tightly circumscribed than are those of her husband who can spend some of his time in the inn'.[15] Earlier I mentioned the agora of the Greek city as the centre of public life and exclusively a male haunt. The author of a new study of rural society in contemporary Portugal writes as follows:

> *A mulher em casa, o homem na praça* ('the woman at home, the man in the square'), a traditional saying runs. The square immediately evokes cafés, taverns, administrative offices, business transactions, working agreements – the whole outside world with which a man must come into contact in order to guarantee the family's material survival and which should ideally be only the husband's province. The wife should remain secluded at home.[16]

We all resent the label 'dead language' attached to Greek and argue vigorously that the Greeks of antiquity were human beings with the feelings of all human beings. The Greeks are just like us, we are tempted to argue. In fact the ancient Greeks were not just like us, if by 'us' we are referring to the inhabitants of sophisticated Western Europe or North America. Whether or not we are practising Christians, our attitudes have been conditioned by centuries of Lutheran

[13] Compare John Hutson's account of the career of a politician in the village in the French Alps referred to in the preceding note (Bailey, op. cit. 69–96). If a person appears to be superior to others because of his personal wealth or political influence, equality may be restored because of what Susan Hutson terms 'the diversity of ranking criteria', a man's moral character most commonly being cited to minimize the prestige conferred by his material attributes (see Bailey, op. cit. 47–9). One thinks at once of the treatment of politicians in the comedies of Aristophanes and a comment by K.J. Dover, *Aristophanic Comedy* (London, 1972), 35: 'It seems to be the business of comedy to grumble and slander, and to speak fair of a politician or general would have been discordant with its function as a means by which the ordinary man asserts himself against his political or military superiors.' See also Foster, *American Anthropologist* lxvii (1965), 305, who, speaking of the 'peasant', says: 'The ideal man strives for moderation and equality in his behavior. Should he attempt to better his comparative standing, thereby threatening village stability, the informal and usually unorganized sanctions appear ... and it takes the form of gossip, slander, back-biting, character assassination, witchcraft or the threat of witchcraft, and sometimes actual physical aggression.' Compare Foster, *Current Anthropology* xiii (1972), 185.

[14] Bailey, op. cit. 42 and 46.

[15] Ibid. 150–1. See also the various cases cited by Heppenstall, 155, 160–6.

[16] José Cutileiro, *A Portuguese Rural Society* (Oxford, 1971), 107.

Christianity; our society has more recently become industrialized and on the land the peasant has been replaced by the commercially minded farmer. Such developments have yet to touch wide areas, including the coastal regions of the Mediterranean and the remoter corners of Europe. It is in these regions that we find values and attitudes of mind which are much more like those of the ancient Greeks. Our own values are not universal values, and we are foolish to impose our own standards of excellence upon others. The Greek attitude towards women may well seem barbaric to us in the twentieth century, but surely we must understand it before we denounce it. Again we must not idealize the Greeks, praising them because we think we detect echoes of values dear to us. Democracy is only one of the several forms of government current in the modern world and a type of élitism is very much in vogue at present. One does neither the Greeks in general nor Pericles in particular any disservice by attempting to understand the Funeral Speech in terms of Greek values, and that has been the intention of this paper.[17]

[17] The author wishes to acknowledge with gratitude the helpful comments and criticisms made by three colleagues, Dr John Percival, D.E. Hill, and N.R.E. Fisher, while his article was in preparation.

PHILOMEL AND PERICLES: SILENCE IN THE FUNERAL SPEECH

Source: *Greece and Rome*, 51(2), 1993, pp.147–62.

By Lorna Hardwick

'Great will be your glory in not falling short of your natural character; and greatest will be hers who is least talked of among the men whether for good or for bad.' – Pericles in Thucydides 2.45[1]

This comment occurs in the closing sequence of the *epitaphios* of 431/0 attributed to Pericles. The speech was delivered at the public funeral held for Athenian casualties in the first year of the Archidamian War. The earlier part of the speech was devoted to praise of the characteristics, practices, and values of the Athenians as a democratic and imperial community. The features which Pericles is reported as stressing were those which 'made Athens great', those by which her dominance was shown. From these is derived the glory achieved by those who died 'as became Athenians' (2.43).

Therefore, according to Pericles, the occasion is one for comfort to be offered to the bereaved, but not for undue grief. Only from 2.44 onwards does Pericles address the relatives of the dead. The sense of loss felt by bereaved parents is recognized and there is a back-handed expression of sympathy to sons and brothers (largely on the basis that it is difficult to compete with the heroic dead). The difference between the words addressed to the other relatives and those addressed to the women is that Pericles speaks, apparently, about the *feelings* of the parents and male relatives but about the *behaviour* of the women. I shall leave aside the question of whether the sentiments are those of the historical Pericles or of Thucydides (Thuc. 1.22 applies) and will assume without arguing it that the speech was a late composition. However, the essential argument of this article would not be affected if a lesser or greater degree of hindsight is attributed to Thucydides. The essential point is that the words relate to a particular stage in the relations between Pericles and the Athenians and shed light on the political situation in the first year of the war.

Although the advice was initially directed towards widows, all wives were potential widows and all women potential wives. Thus, the lines have sometimes been abstracted and used by social historians in studies of the position of women in classical Athens. For example, A.W. Gomme attributed to the Athenians a quasi-Victorian respect for 'respectable' women while conversely, the lines have been described by Pomeroy as 'an embarrassment to those who argue for the high status of women'. R. Just interprets the words as the expression of a social paradigm and D.C. Richter, despite a review of much of the evidence, gets sidetracked into a discussion of the character of Pericles and regards a little 'healthy misogyny' as 'a good thing' (although he stops short of saying that this is 'what made Athens great'). F.D. Harvey's is perhaps the best detailed discussion of both ancient and modern approaches. Ø. Anderson also makes a telling point by noting the lack of comparability with other *epitaphioi*

---

[1] All quotations from Thucydides are from the translation by R. Crawley (1910), *Thucydides: The History of the Peloponnesian War* (London).

and concluding that therefore 'we are not dealing with a *topos* and Pericles has something special to say'.2

The phases through which discussion of the position of women has gone are an interesting subject in themselves, but I shall resist the temptation to address them or to speculate about whether the Funeral Speech was composed by Aspasia (Plato, *Menexenus* 235E) and if she did write it, whether the closing sequence is her own attempt at black humour or a despairing postscript by Pericles himself. However, it is reasonable to generalize that until quite recently the consensus seemed to be that the words indicate the exclusion of women from the public domain and that they construct a citizens' ideal of female behaviour (separate or oppressed according to one's viewpoint but certainly not held in contempt according to Athenian values).

However, some broader critical insights have been developed. For example, P. Walcot has pointed out that Pericles' comment recognizes the fact that discussion of women could be part of a display of *time* and that competition for honour leads to envy.3 Walcot's main point relates to a general theory of male psychology which identifies women as an extension of property but there are also implications for the historical context of the Funeral Speech, suggesting a narrowing of the gap between private and public attitudes and behaviour. Certainly, over-rigid distinction between public and private spheres has obscured the importance of the lines. Analysis of the context within which they occur reveals a more complex state of affairs, which both sheds light on the social and political aspects of the role of women *and* assists us in interpreting the historical situation to which the Funeral Speech refers. Methodologically, therefore, I take issue with approaches which assume that themes such as the role of women involve study of private life only. The author of a recent study of Athenian citizenship states in his preface – 'If every generation studies the past on the basis of its own concerns, it is understandable that citizenship in Athens might not have received the same treatment as some other themes of greater contemporary interest, such as the role of women in ancient society, Greek homosexuality, or other aspects of *ancient private life*'.4 On the contrary the *public* role of women is central to understanding Pericles' comment.

A second methodological aim is to demonstrate that social anthropology and history can work together. While the valuable insights established by the work of scholars such as Nicole Loraux must be acknowledged, it is true to say that much of the recent work inspired by concepts drawn from anthropology has diverted attention from detailed study of historical context.5 This discussion seeks in a small way to redress that balance.

It is necessary to start by asking apparently straightforward questions. To whom was Pericles' comment *addressed*? To whom does he *refer*? Then it is possible to consider why he made the comment.

---

2 A.W. Gomme (1925), 'The Position of Women in Athens', *CPh* 1–25, reprinted in (1937) *Essays in History and Literature*; S. Pomeroy (1984), 'Selected Bibliography on Women in Antiquity' in (eds) J. Peradotto and J.P. Sullivan, *Women in the Ancient World: The Arethusa Papers* (New York); R. Just (1989), *Women in Athenian Law and Life* (London); D.C. Richter (1971), 'The position of Women in Classical Athens', *CJ* 67, 1–8; F.D. Harvey (1985), 'Women in Thucydides', *Arethusa* 18, 67–90; H.P. Foley (1981) (ed), *Reflections of Women in Antiquity* (New York) contains articles from a variety of standpoints; D.M. Schapps (1977), 'The Women Least Mentioned: Etiquette and Women's Names', *CQ* 27, 323–330 uses mainly fourth-century evidence to argue that defining women by reference to their male relations was a mark of respectability. Ø. Anderson (1987), 'The Widows, the City, and Thucydides (11.45.2)', *SO* 62, 33–50. The literature on *epitaphioi logoi* is reviewed in S. Hornblower (1991), *A Commentary on Thucydides*, Vol. I (Oxford), pp. 294–6.

3 P. Walcot (1973) 'The Funeral Speech, A Study of Values', *G & R*, 11, 1–2 1.

4 P. Brook Manville (1990), *The Origins of Citizenship in Ancient Athens* (Princeton).

5 N. Loraux (1981), 'Marathon ou l'histoire idéologique', *REA* 75, 13–42; (1978), 'Mourir devant Troie, tomber pour Athènes. De la gloire du héros a l'idée de la cité', *Information sur les sciences sociales* 17(6), 801–17; (1986), *The Invention of Athens* (tr. A. Sheridan, Boston).

Pericles spoke directly to the bereaved women but they were part of a wider audience. Then he generalized to a paradigm for female conduct. (Not that adherence to the ideal preserved women from notice if fate was unkind, as Andromache discovered – 'It seems reports of me reached the Greek camp and this was my undoing' (Euripides, *The Women of Troy* 648–658).) However, the important point is – whose talking is to be discouraged? By moving away from the passive mood to the responsible *active* we can focus attention on who was talking and why. If we can discover why men were talking about women in the context of a public funeral this will reveal something of the situation at Athens in the first year of the war. There are several possible reasons why men were talking about bereaved women.

1 Were the female mourners conspicuous, emphasizing the magnitude of the loss of male citizens? The question then becomes, whose widows were they?

2 Were the women perhaps young, eligible, and well dowered so that the men at the funeral were 'looking for their chance'? (In a comparable situation the surplus of potential brides after the 1914–18 war enabled men to be highly selective.)

3 Were the women directly or indirectly perceived as peace agents?

4 What was the women's role at the Funeral? Was this a focus of debate?

1. *Whose widows?* Thucydides says (2.34) 'In the same winter the Athenians gave a funeral at the public cost for those who had first fallen in the war'. The point about a public funeral is that it concentrates awareness of loss. Commemorative inscriptions show that it was the custom to group the names of the fallen by tribe.[6] Although the list of names has not survived, the Potidaia inscription referring to the dead of 432 is an important example relating to one engagement because the epitaph shows an emphasis on the honour of Athens which is comparable to the Funeral Speech – 'placing their lives as a counterpoise, they received glory in exchange and brought honour to their native land'.[7] Thucydides states (1.62–3) that at Potidaia 150 were lost, including the *strategos* Callias. A later battle at Potidaia in 429 saw 450 killed, including all three generals. It is Thucydides' habit not to itemize casualties unless they were particularly heavy but we can see from these and other inscriptions that war losses were by no means trivial.[8]

The difference between 432 and the period to which the Funeral Speech refers is that war was official and that it was affecting Attica itself. The countryside of Attica had been evacuated and Thucydides refers to over-crowding in Athens (2.17). In 2.13 he documents Pericles' reassurance to the Athenians about the number of troops available when Archidamus advanced into Attica.[9] According to Thucydides, the Spartan was hoping to entice the young Athenian troops into battle (2.20).

To address the question 'whose widows?' it is therefore necessary to consider the war strategy of the Athenians. Thucydides 2.31 refers to the biggest Athenian army which had ever taken the field (in the autumn preceding the funeral speech, for the invasion of the Megarid), 2.33 refers to losses at Cephallenia. 2.25 refers to an engagement on Spartan territory with Brasidas and to various other expeditions which must have entailed some casualties.

[6] D.W. Bradeen (1969), 'The Athenian Casualty Lists', *CQ* 19, 145–59 presents conclusions based on about one half of the public monuments erected in the fifth century.

[7] BM GR 1816.6–10.348, discussed in B. Cook (1987), *Greek Inscriptions* (London), pp.33–4.

[8] C.W. Clairmont (1983), *Patrios Nomos* (public burial in Athens during the fifth and fourth centuries BC), BAR International Series 161(i), reviews the evidence from the polyandria in the *demosion sema* and specifically denies that the casualties in 430 at least were 'relatively light' (Vol. 1 p.183).

[9] For discussion about the numbers see M.H. Hansen (1981), 'The Number of Athenian Hoplites in 431 BC', *SO* 56, 19–32.

2.22 refers to an Athenian and Thessalian interest at Phrygia (against Boeotian cavalry and hoplites), leaving dead who were later recovered. The context of Thucydides' discussion of this engagement is important (Phrygia is in the *deme* of the Athmoneis a few miles north-east of Athens). Thucydides says that despite his defensive policy, Pericles 'constantly sent out cavalry to prevent raids on the lands near the city'. Yet Pericles' strategy as set out by Thucydides in 2.13 was to rely on the Athenians' resources and strength by sea, to utilize the protection of the Long Walls, stay inside the city and guard it and not to engage the enemy in land battle outside it. One aspect of Spartan strategy was to use the 'conventional' forms of warfare, ravaging the countryside in order to provoke a decisive land battle or make the Athenians negotiate. Thucydides says that Athenians did sue for peace in the summer of 430, which suggests that Sparta's strategy was effective and that Pericles' policy was challenged (2.59).[10]

Thus, in spite of Pericles' defensive strategy there was action and there were casualties. Significantly, there was anxiety about the ravaging of the countryside. This arose both from material interest and from considerations of honour. 'Knots were formed in the streets and engaged in hot discussions ... Foremost in pressing for the sally were the Acharnians, as it was their land that was being ravaged ... Pericles was the object of general indignation' (2.21). Thucydides suggests that Pericles *had* to use troops, including cavalry, to at least contain the damage to the *chora* and to satisfy public opinion.

I.G. Spence has argued that 'the damage caused by the annual invasions was considerably reduced by using cavalry in a mobile defence role (a minor aspect of strategy but good for morale) and that *in 431* this was the best option facing Pericles.[11] The essential point is that the role of mobile cavalry could be of use in limiting damage in the countryside.[12] If, as Spence asserts, Attica was invaded annually by two-thirds of the total forces of the Peloponnesian league, Pericles clearly had to do something. He may even have had to promise at least to defend the *chora* by cavalry in order to ensure acceptance of his defensive strategy.[13] Given that Thucydides records the determination of the Spartans to provoke action, the eagerness of the young men of Athens, the concern of the rural landowners (2.16 asserts that most of the population lived in rural areas up to the outbreak of war) and the disgrace attached to inaction, it seems likely that at least some defence of the *chora* was forced on Pericles. Certainly, passages in the fourth-century orators show that the ravaging which resulted from Pericles' strategy was sufficiently etched in the Athenian consciousness to become a *topos* (Andocides 3.8 and Aeschines 2.175). After the débacle at the end of the fifth century the Athenians rejected the principle of *city* defence in favour of *border* defence, intending to protect Attica from the ravages of invading land armies. It may be inferred that the psychological impact of invasion had been great and we can see this in the account by Thucydides of the first year of the war.[14]

All this suggests that it was likely that the rich and the citizens of the countryside took the view that, whether or not they had wanted war in the first place, they nevertheless wanted their land to be defended. (Isocrates *Areop. 52* shows that the richness of Athenian country life in the fifth century became a *topos*.) Their political threat to Pericles' position and to his defensive strategy could have been considerable and he had to accommodate them. Pericles' main de-

---

[10] Discussed by G. Cawkwell (1975), 'Thucydides' Judgement of Periclean Strategy', *YCS* 53–70.

[11] I.G. Spence (1990), 'Pericles and the defence of Attica during the Peloponnesian War', *JHS* 110, 91–109.

[12] For the inadequacy of cavalry in controlling mountain passes see G.E.M. de Ste Croix (1972), *Origins of the Peloponnesian War* (London), pp.171–97.

[13] Discussed by J. Ober (1985), 'Thucydides, Pericles and the Strategy of Defence' in (eds) J.W. Eadie and J. Ober, *The Craft of the Ancient Historian* (Montana), pp.171–97.

[14] For full treatment see J. Ober (1985), *Fortress Attica* (Leiden).

fensive weapon in Attica was cavalry, which if not entirely aristocratic was at least by definition, drawn from the wealthier citizens.[15] The inference, therefore, is that some of the casualties were cavalry from prosperous families and perhaps young. If the dead were young they were either unmarried or recently married (if we take 30 as the approximate marriage age for men). Their widows or potential wives were probably well born and from well-off families. Their mothers and sisters would be relatively young also. This leads to my second question:

2. *Were the men therefore talking about the women because they were eligible?* Was remarriage of widows expected? There is circumstantial internal and external evidence to show that expectation of remarriage may have been the case in the historical context of the Funeral Speech.[16] In addressing the bereaved parents Pericles urged them to have more children (2.14). This may seem over-hopeful if mothers were old enough to have already reared sons to adulthood. However, given young marriage for girls these mothers need only have been in their early thirties and this strengthens the inference that some of the casualties were young. Other casualties were old enough to have married or left disappointed potential brides. Pericles' words suggest an urgent need for new births and could imply additional pressure on widows to remarry. (Pericles' citizenship law of 451/0 required mothers as well as fathers of Athenian citizens to be from citizen families. The loss of sons to inherit wealth is a recurrent theme in Greek disaster topoi, e.g. *Iliad* 5.152.)

We do not know how much choice widows had over remarriage, although evidence from the fourth century suggests that they had some say in the matter. In any case, the conventions of Athenian society required that a man should arrange marriage for his daughters and if necessary sisters.[17] What could be more likely to result in talk among men, ranging from discreet enquiries to speculation, gossip, and *rivalry,* especially if there was an (incidental) public display of potential brides and some were upper-class and rich? The propensity of Greek men to use women to enhance their reputation and wealth could have produced tensions which Pericles found it necessary to suppress, since the overall purpose of the speech is clearly to promote a sense of civic identity and unity and to channel aggression and competition outwards against the enemy.

So the fact that women were seen as transmitters of property has direct relevance to the likelihood of gossip and rivalry among men in the context of the Public Funeral. It demonstrates the other side of the habit of not referring to respectable women by their own name but as X's daughter.[18]

The dowry was of course an important expression of male self-esteem (fathers *and* husbands). Since the dowry was the woman's share of the paternal estate, it returned with her if she was childless when her husband died and as a widow she was dowered on remarriage. Also to be noted is the different position of the *epikleros*, who if her father died sonless was used as a means of transmitting his property and was assigned to the nearest male heir in fixed order of precedence. There is an irony that although the reputation of the *epikleros* had to

[15] See G.R. Bugh (1988), *The Horsemen of Athens* (Princeton), ch. 3.

[16] F.D. Harvey, op. cit. and W.E. Thompson (1972), 'Athenian Marriage Patterns: Remarriage', *CaSCA* 5 211–25, although S. Isager (1981–2) 'The Marriage Pattern in Classical Athens', *Class.* and *Med* 33, provides another view. P. Walcot (1991), 'On Widows and their reputation in Antiquity', *SO* 66, 5–26 argues that the ideal of non-remarriage for widows persisted throughout antiquity.

[17] W.A.K. Lacey (1968), *The Family in Classical Greece* (London), pp 104–8.

[18] Schapps, op. cit.; J. Gardner (1989) has shown how the values and structure of the *oikos* fostered male anxiety, 'Aristophanes and Male Anxiety – The Defence of the *oikos*', *G & R*, 51–62.

be closely guarded since she (or rather her prospective husband) had everything to lose, her position may have made her more likely to be the subject of talk, since existing marriages were no impediment. There is also fourth-century evidence that husbands could dispose of widows-to-be in prospect of their own deaths.[19]

Therefore, we have circumstantial evidence to suggest that the occasion of the reception of casualties, the Funeral and *epitaphios* could also be a time of speculation about future marriage and transmission of property and that this could involve social stress, rivalry, and envy between competing males and between *oikoi* and factions seeking desirable social, economic, and political alliances. The political implications would be greater if a significant portion of the casualties were upper-class and if there was the opportunity for negotiation of new alliances among those who were or might be Pericles' opponents because they were opposed to his war policy or his defensive strategy, or both.

3. Were the female relatives of the dead perceived as peace agents, i.e. as protesters in grief?

In favour of this we might speculate that it is the *first* casualties of war which tend to have the greatest impact. They mark a kind of *rite de passage* in the acceptance that the state is at war. However, an attempt to apply this generalization to the Athenians looks anachronistic since war was endemic among the *poleis* and there were casualties in most years. Nevertheless, the potential of women to develop a peace movement is explored later by Aristophanes (in the illogical plot of *Lysistrata*).

However, it would be a serious mistake to suggest that direct public expression by women in wartime is necessarily peaceful. We all know of the White Feathers of the First World War. Herodotus says (3.87–88) that after the Aeginetan defeat the solitary survivor was surrounded by the widows of his colleagues and stabbed to death with their brooch pins, while in 480 when a member of the exiled council of Salamis suggested acceptance of Persian terms he was stoned and Athenian women went to his home and killed his wife and children in the same way (9.5). Even if the historicity of such anecdotes may be dubious, they attest to a certain mental outlook and moreover an outlook and tradition current in the *mid*-fifth century, when Herodotus was writing. Furthermore, there is a tradition preserved by Plutarch which suggests that Pericles' *epitaphios* performance attracted 'groupies'.

> When Pericles returned home after subduing Samos he had burial honours paid to all those Athenians who had lost their lives in the campaign, and he won special praise for the speech he delivered over their tombs, according to the usual custom. As he stepped down from the rostrum, many of the women of Athens clasped his hand and crowned him with garlands and fillets like a victorious athlete. Elpinike, however, came up to him and said: 'This was a noble action, Pericles, and you deserve all these garlands for it. You have thrown away the lives of these brave citizens of ours, not in a war against the Persians or the Phoenicians, such as my brother Kimon fought, but in destroying a Greek city which is one of our allies.'[20]

Even allowing for the difficulty of reconstructing historical accuracy from such a late passage, two points emerge. The first is the highly charged atmosphere on such occasions. The second is the inference that older and aristocratic women were more likely to find war between Greeks and Greeks offensive, perhaps because of their closeness to the coalition against the Persians and its subsequent eulogy and perhaps because the inter-*polis* relationships of the aristocracy were part of their outlook (cults, *proxenoi*, and other diplomatic contacts

---

[19] See J.P. Gould (1980), 'Law, Custom and Myth: Aspects of the Social Position of Women in Classical Athens', *JHS* 100, 38–59.

[20] Plutarch, *Pericles 28*, tr. I. Scott-Kilvert and modified R. Just (op. cit., p.109).

and perhaps, too, intermarriage before Pericles' citizenship law of 451/0). Such a context of upper-class discontent gives added meaning to Pericles' insistence that his lands, too, should be ravaged by Archidamus (Thuc. 2.13) and in case they were not, they should become public property.

Against the suggestion that the public funeral fostered desire for peace, it can be argued that the 'heroic' equation of the dead might *raise* the morale of the bereaved and the community, while modern analogies suggest that it is harder to argue against the wisdom of a particular war once casualties have been incurred because to do so seems to devalue the sacrifice made by the dead. Mourning could also be exploited for political ends, as was done by Theramenes and his supporters after Arginusae (Xenophon, *Hellenica* 1.7.8).

Therefore, the circumstantial evidence suggests that the effect of the women at the public funeral on anyone's desire for peace or war was problematic, but that depending on the context it could have intensified existing strains or revived arguments about strategy. In any case, an empathetic approach suggests that bringing together female mourners on a public occasion might have had considerable effects on the crowd, and Thucydides specifically says that 'Everyone who wishes can join in the procession and the women who are related to the dead are to make their laments at the tomb' (2.34). This indicates they were not just restricted to private lamentation at the equivalent of the *prothesis*. Here we are dealing with public demonstration of an aspect of women's behaviour which was expected and institutionalized in the conventions of funeral ritual.

4. What was the women's role at the funeral? Was it a focus of debate?

It has been well shown that, where not derived from the kinship of males, a woman's status was defined in terms of ritual functions.[21] In the case of funeral rites, the two sources of female status were combined. In addition, the occasion of a Public Funeral for the war dead adds an extra dimension to what I. Morris has called 'the Communal use made of the dead, in rituals evoking and creating the structure of society'.[22] Therefore, it is relevant to consider the extent to which the ritual at the public funeral, and especially the women's role in it, was in accordance with traditional practices.

In recent years, extensive work has been done on Greek attitudes to death and mourning.[23] Particularly important has been the characterization of what was meant by dying a 'good death' – what Loraux calls 'la belle mort'. Loraux takes up in a historical context the anthropological concept of Tame Death, which is defined as involving a glorious affirmation of the lasting fame of the dead man who dies young and courageously, avoiding the gradual loss of powers and unlovely death associated with old age.[24] Thus, death in battle becomes the paradigm uniting the Homeric hero with the military values of the classical *polis*. Although the *kleos* associated with the hero might extend outside his native land, this concept of death also involved being mourned at *home*.

There was essential continuity in attitudes towards death through the archaic to the classical period and beyond.[25] What did change, however, was the ritual use

---

[21] Gould, op. cit.

[22] I. Morris (1989), 'Attitudes Towards Death in Archaic Greece', *CA* 8, 296–320.

[23] D. Kurtz and J. Boardman (1971), *Greek Burial Customs* (London); S. Humphreys (1983), 'Family Tombs and Tomb Cult in Ancient Athens: Tradition or Traditionalism', in *The Family, Women and Death* (London); R. Garland (1985), *The Greek Way of Death* (London).

[24] Loraux (1978), op. cit., builds on the distinction between Tame Death and Death of the Self drawn by P. Ariès (1981), *The Hour of Our Death* (New York) and (1974), *Western Attitudes to Death from the Middle Ages to the Present* (London and Baltimore).

[25] I. Morris, op. cit., argues that there was no large-scale change in the individual psychology of death in response to the rise of the polis, *contra* C. Sourvinou-Inwood (1983), 'A Trauma in Flux: Death in the Eighth Century and After' in (ed) R. Hägg, *The Greek Renaissance of the Eighth Century BC* (Stockholm).

made of the dead to 'create' the *polis* community, the 'ideologies of death'. It is possible to show how the parameters of thought and practice were defined and put into practice and to draw some conclusions about the underlying assumptions. When considered in context the public funeral in the first year of the war suggests significant tensions in the response to earlier traditions.

On the one hand there is a move away from the aristocratic ideology which claimed comparison with heroic forebears through family and individual tombs and poems.[26] There is not, however, a complete break. The confluence of the aristocratic ethos and the heroic tradition provided Greeks with a collective past through which they defined themselves and this paradigm shapes the civic identity of the fifth century, in which the citizen 'hero' is admitted to a share of the collective *kleos* of the *polis*. Inevitably, this tended to dim the privileged aura of the aristocrat.

There is evidence of a long continuous tradition in important aspects of the women's role in funeral ritual. Women participated in the three phases of a funeral – the washing and preparing of the body and the house; the *prothesis* or vigil over the prepared body; the *ekphora* or procession to the cemetery. The tradition included sung lament, ritual gestures, dancing, and waving of branches.[27] Vase painting is a key source of evidence for the participation of women in funeral rituals. Funerary amphorae from the mid-eighth century emphasize the social context of death and include a visual equivalent of the ceremony. The large crowd scenes in geometric art are confined to funerary vases. Such scenes continue to be represented on Black Figure vases and plaques and on a small number of Red Figure ritual *loutrophoroi*. Fifth-century *lekythoi* do not feature crowd scenes and have a special significance. They will be discussed below.[28]

The social aspect of most of the funeral scenes has been emphasized by E. Vermeule. 'A good funeral has always been a lot of fun, a reunion stirring open emotions and bringing news to exchange, the periodic intersection of the family, the clan and the city.'[29] This last phrase – the intersection of the family, kinship group, and city – points us towards possible constraints in the women's role. As the relationship between social institutions and the *polis* changed, so the funeral, as a sign of interaction, was bound to be affected and the ideologies expressed in death ritual challenged and redefined. This can be seen in the early sixth-century Solonic legislation against excessive display in mourning (Plutarch, *Solon* 21). The laws were not anti-female and probably not even directed at class rivalry but were an attempt to prevent *horizontal* rivalry, that is aristocratic families competing to display conspicuous wealth and following.[30]

---

[26] For the evidence on archaic attitudes to hero-cult see A.M. Snodgrass (1989), *An Archaeology of Greece* (Berkeley and LA), p.162. E. Stein-Hölkeskamp (1989), *Adelskultur und Polisgesellschaft: Studien zum Griechischen Adel in Archaischer und Klassischer Zeit* (Stuttgart). J.-P. Vernant (1982), 'La Belle Mort et Le Cadavre Outragé' in (eds) G. Gnoli and J.-P. Vernant, *La mort, les morts dans les sociétés anciennes* (Cambridge).

[27] M. Alexiou (1974), *The Ritual Lament in Greek Tradition* (Cambridge), esp. cc. 1 and 6. G. Holst-Warhaft (1992), *Dangerous Voices – women's laments in Greek literature* (London), discusses the *epitaphios logos* (ch. 4) but misses the political significance of the point that Pericles is trying to get *male* silence.

[28] A selection of vases is illustrated and discussed in C.M. Havelock (1982), 'Mourners on Greek Vases: Remarks on the Social History of Women' in (eds) N. Broude and M.D. Garrard, *Feminism and Art History: Questioning the Litany* (New York). See also R.G. Osborne (1988), 'Death Revisited: Death Revised. The death of the artist in archaic and classical Greece', *Art History* 2.1, 1–16 and A.M. Snodgrass, op. cit., ch. 5 (Osborne rightly draws attention to the element of personal feeling expressed in the commemoration of individuals).

[29] E. Vermeule (1979), *Aspects of Death in Early Greek Art and Literature* (Berkeley and LA), ch. 1.

[30] J.R. Ellis and G.R. Stanton (1968), 'Factional Conflict and Solon's Reforms', *Phoenix* 22, 95–110.

Significantly, Diogenes Laertius suggests that funerals of battle casualties were exempt from restrictions (1.7.55).

The ceremonial aspects of burial in archaic Athens were protracted, expensive, and *enjoyable to aristocrats*.[31] 'Enjoyable' needs a further gloss – a source of display, rivalry and envy. The statements on archaic tombstones are not sentimental and domestic or concerned with the after-life. They display pride and a sense of loss, not unlike fifth-century public inscriptions. But the differences of course are that the fifth-century epitaphs are collective and do not name individuals and that the lists of names do not display patronymics. In the fifth century, competition was not necessarily confined to rivalry between aristocrats; it could also take place between aristocrats and the *polis*.

Once war funerals came under public control they had two functions – to distribute honour from the *polis* and to channel competition and envy into safe rituals (and thus discourage *stasis*). Therefore, the relationship between the kinship group and the *polis* was redefined. If the public ceremony differed from private traditions it is necessary to consider who were affected by the differences.

Thucydides tells us that three days before the ceremony 'the bones of the fallen are laid out in a tent which has been erected and their friends bring to their relatives such offerings as they please' (2.34). The transport home of the dead implies (state) wealth. Because they were dealing with bones and not bodies, the stage involving washing of the dead was missed out. Because the occasion was communal the preparation of the house was also omitted but other aspects of the traditional role of women were preserved or adapted. The vigil was presumably collective and gave the opportunity for semi-public display and even competition. It lasted longer than the customary one day. In Greek tradition the female relatives were seen to be the prime guardians of kinship and religion (compare reactions in *Antigone, Seven against Thebes* and *The Suppliant Women* when these rights were threatened by the *polis*). At the public funeral any female relative of the dead appears to have been able to attend (in contrast to Solon's restriction of entitlement to the over-sixties and those within the degree of second cousin, at least for non-military funerals). However, the public procession seems to have been arranged so as to minimize competition, the bones of the deceased being carried in coffins, one for each tribe (with a symbolic bier for the missing). The procession was open to all (including *xenoi*) and Thucydides explicitly states that female relatives attended at the burial which was in the public cemetery. While the private and personal aspects of the kinship ritual were displaced by a more public civic display those aspects which remain were strongly linked with past tradition. Other aspects of the individuality of the fallen were submerged into tribe and civic identity. The inference is that a high-profile role for the women was the most significant opportunity which remained for celebration of kinship and of the individual prominence of the dead.

There is also evidence that fifth-century aristocrats continued earlier traditions in private commemoration of their dead. Analysis of family tombs and funerary vases shows that social distinctions were still desired. S. Humphreys has suggested that the themes and images depicted on the white-ground *lekythoi* dating

---

[31] Vermeule, op. cit., p.3.

from the Peloponnesian wars were a prelude to more conspicuous material expression, the monumental enclosures of the late fifth century and early fourth. Some vases not only stress the emotional aspects of mourning but also show elaborate tomb markers.[32] These may well be the precursors for later monuments such as the *stele* of Dexileos. He was actually buried with his fellow horsemen at Corinth and his name is recorded on the public casualty list but he was also privately commemorated by an elaborate carved *stele*.[33]

State funerals could not meet a continued desire for individual commemoration nor fit into a context of kinship ritual in which the family tomb was a mark of social distinction. The fact that aristocrats still desired these shows that they did not find the state provision satisfactory. We can infer that they would nevertheless have tried to maximize their impact on public ceremonial. An extreme reaction is dramatized by Euripides in *The Suppliant Women*, when Evadne prefers to throw herself on her husband's pyre rather than to participate in the ceremony organized by the *polis* (948ff.). However, less drastic public measures were possible. Although fifth-century funerary vase painting records private family tombs, a different emphasis is evident on public sculpture. This has been interpreted to suggest that the élite *did* manage to obtain a public differential in the mid-fifth century. R.G. Osborne has asked whether the Parthenon Frieze actually contains a concession to the élite. He suggests that while the Frieze appears to parallel the Funeral Oration in its heroizing of the Athenian citizen, the difference is that it shows young cavalrymen. Osborne further argues that on public monuments to war dead, the cavalry is over-represented in sculpture in comparison with the infantry.[34]

Thus it is clear that in spite of (or because of) the communal nature of the civic funeral, greater public prominence of the élite could still have been desired. Archaeological and literary evidence shows the persistence of notions of women as the guardians of religious and kinship obligations and the desire of the élite for a public commemoration of their status, which in the context of the civic funeral for the war dead only the women could give.

Examination of the context of Pericles' comment to the women suggests that its real purpose was to suppress argument about contentious issues and to prevent outbursts of rivalry, whether among the élite or between them and the ordinary citizens. This conclusion can be supported from the rest of his speech, which also attempts to promote civic unity by appealing to reluctant democrats as well as to the ordinary Athenian. Loraux's stress on the significance of the speech as a landmark for the admission of ordinary citizens to heroic status has tended to divert attention from the extent to which the picture of democracy presented in the speech is, in fact, élitist. Quite apart from the stress on Greek military values, the praise of political activity in the speech is actually designed to appeal to those who thought that 'the best' should hold public positions (e.g. the stress on 'merit' and 'reputations for capacity' rather than sortition in 2.37). S. Hornblower suggests that the speech may even be

[32] Humphreys, op. cit., for a range of examples with iconographical notes, see D.C. Kurtz (1975), *Athenian White Lekythoi* (Oxford), especially Plates pages 19–23, 26, 29–33, 35–41. Garland, op. cit., ch. 7 discusses the *Nomizomena*, annual rites performed by a family on behalf of its members. For the relation between funerary iconography on Athenian *lekythoi* and gravestone reliefs, see J. Boardman (1989), *Athenian Red Figure Vases: The Classical Period* (London), pp.129ff. Boardman (1985), *Greek Sculpture: The Classical Period* (London), pp.183ff., discusses the interruption in the production of decorated gravestones in early fifth-century Athens and the small number of individual warrior stones even after the tradition resumed *c*.430. I. Morris (1992), *Death-ritual and social structure in Classical Antiquity* (Cambridge), evaluates the evidence relating to strategies of display and restraint in Athens (cc. 4 and 5).

[33] M.N. Tod (1949), *A Selection of Greek Historical Inscriptions*, Vol. II (from 403 to 328 BC), Nos. 104 & 105.

[34] R.G. Osborne (1987), 'The Viewing and Obscuring of the Parthenon Frieze', *JHS* 107, 98–105.

'subversive of democratic ideology in some ways', citing the rather casual attitude to military training which is praised by Pericles (2.39) as indicative of an
appeal to the cavalry ethos (reliant on 'natural courage' and based on a life of
leisure not labour, a contrast with the rigid training given to Spartan infantry).[35]
In addition, there were quasi-aristocratic accompaniments to the public funeral
ceremony. Thucydides is silent about these but Plato in the *Menexenus* (233f.)
mentions musical competitions, athletes, and horse events, emphasizing the
aristocratic *ethos,* while Lysias (2.80) refers to contests of strength, wisdom, and
wealth.

However, Pericles only goes so far in his attempt to placate the upper classes
and crypto-oligarchs. The reference to the *apragmones* in 2.40 as having no business in the Athenian *polis* is not just a spur to the apathetic but a criticism of
those who took a conscious decision to distance themselves from Pericles'
policies.[36] The subtext is that Pericles wanted to keep civic unity as far as possible and was willing to go some way to pacify the potentially disaffected by pri-
vileging their role and values in his coded use of language and allusions, but
the reference to the *apragmones* shows that some could not be induced to keep
up even the pretence of participating. The character of the Funeral Speech as a
unity speech is further supported by the stress on good social relations and lack
of envy within the Athenian *polis*, as compared with the aggression and competition which is projected *outwards* in the sections dealing with the *arche* (2.39–
43).

The difficulty faced by Pericles in preserving unity is clear from Thucydides'
emphasis on the setbacks which occurred in the first year of the war, especially
the invasions by Sparta and the disagreement about policy. Those who had had
their land devastated by the Spartans were influential. Thucydides records in
2.59 the drop in morale after the *chora* of the Athenians was devastated for the
second time. There was even an embassy to Sparta.

The Last Speech (2.60ff.) is an important control on our interpretation of the
Funeral Speech and further strengthens the argument that Pericles' position
was not particularly secure in the late 430s. Thucydides 2.63 shows how
Pericles had to use the rhetoric of aggressive *arche* in order to ensure the support of the Assembly. Here, too, there are repeated attacks on the *apragmones*
(which becomes almost a code word for the negative attitudes of oligarchy,
whereas *sophrosyne* signals the positive or approved aspects). Thucydides 2.65
sets out the *general* ill-feeling towards Pericles from both rich and poor: 'The
common people having been deprived of the little that they possessed, while
the higher orders had lost costly establishments and buildings in the country,
and, worst of all, had war instead of peace', and of course Pericles was im-
peached.

Thus, the occasion of the public funeral emphasized at one and the same time
various stresses with which Pericles had to deal. His defensive strategy had denied the traditional forms of war (devastation, looting, and skirmishing) which
had been practised in the countryside by the farmers and hoplites on whom the
city depended. Because of the Long Walls, the navy, and the wealth gained from
the *arche*, Pericles had an alternative strategy through which he could avoid
major land battles with Sparta. But pressure from the land interest and the keen
young citizens meant that he had to make some tactical use of his forces in
Attica, including cavalry. The funeral thus highlighted *both* the discontents over
his policy *and* the bereavement caused by the action he had taken. The ordinary
citizens might be placated by the public honours, but the upper classes missed
their conspicuous social distinctions and kinship rituals now largely replaced
by the communal use made of the dead. Also they had yet to be convinced that
the democracy did not operate against their interests. Thus the speech had as
far as possible to placate those whose loss of exclusivity and élite status was

---

[35] I am grateful to Dr Simon Hornblower for discussion of this point.

[36] For a study of the various groups identified by the term *apragmones*, see L. Carter
(1986), *The Quiet Athenian* (Oxford).

exposed by the nature of the ritual, yet at the same time civic unity and balance had to be preserved.

Through analysis of the comment about the women in the Funeral Speech we can uncover something of the religious and social impact of the bereavements suffered in the first year of the war (especially among the better off), and can at least speculate about the ensuing rivalry, gossip, and debate which kept their policy disagreements with Pericles in the public eye. Writing perhaps with hindsight, Thucydides uses the Funeral Speech and the Last Speech to show the complexity of Pericles' balancing act, which he singles out for special comment in 2.65.

It may be the case that Pericles, although leader of the *demos*, was tolerated and approved by the upper classes from which he came. However, in the first year of the war it was hard to keep both sections on his side. The public funeral was an intense and emotional occasion. This gave added force to the traditional role of the women and explains why their presence and participation was particularly 'high profile'. In the political context of the time Pericles did not want any of the issues which were highlighted by their role to be the subject of intense debate. Pericles was neither the first nor the last politician in history to wrap political convenience in the cloak of an appeal to honour. His words to the women encode the silencing of men – his critics.

An earlier version of this paper was given at the Annual Conference of the Classical Association in 1991. I warmly acknowledge the helpful comments offered by participants. I also thank my colleagues in the Women in the Humanities Research Group at the Open University, especially Dr Catherine King for encouraging me to look at artistic representations of women's history.

LAW, CUSTOM AND MYTH: ASPECTS OF THE SOCIAL POSITION OF WOMEN IN CLASSICAL ATHENS

Source: *Journal of Hellenic Studies*, vol. C, 1980, pp.38–59.

By J.P. Gould

In memoriam E.R. Dodds

1   Introduction

It is some years now since the Oxford anthropologist Edwin Ardener in his article 'Belief and the problem of women' drew attention to the striking lack of progress that had been made in understanding traditional societies as they are seen from the point of view of women: 'the models of a society made by most ethnographers tend to be models derived from the male portion of that society'. The result, as he pointed out, is that, in considering social structure, 'we are, for practical purposes, in a male world. The study of women is on a level little higher than the study of the ducks and fowl they commonly own.' He went on to put forward an explanation of the fact, by suggesting that, since the dominant structure of society is articulated and communicated in terms of a male world-position, women constitute a 'muted group', made inarticulate by the lack of a language in which to communicate their particular sense of society and its relationship to the totality of experience.

With the society of Athens in the fifth and fourth centuries BC we are in much the same situation. In some respects, we might think, better off, but in one crucial point, actually worse. Better off, as we might suppose, since in the imaginative literature of classical Athens we have what seems to be a highly articulate and prominent, not marginal, presentation of women, and their role in society: in this world, it seems, women 'speak' and share the centre of attention with men. But this is a mirage: we can have no direct access to the model of Athenian society to which women subscribed, even as it might have been expressed in the dominant language of men. For the evidence available to us is almost without exception the product of men and addressed to men in a male-dominated world. It takes the assumptions of the masculine order of things for granted, in a sense that goes beyond even the experience of the anthropologist in the field. We have to be quite clear about this: it is all too easy to imagine, thoughtlessly, that we are somehow in a position to look at ancient Greek society, and particularly that of fifth- and fourth-century Athens, from some sort of central 'ethnographic' point of vantage, from where we can see the social scene spread out before us without distortion of perspective and starting from which, warned by Ardener's observations, we can proceed to look at the world as it was seen by women. Of course I have only to say that for it to become immediately obvious that it is not so; but it does require a constant effort of thought and imagination to remember that the words of a Lysistrata or a Medea, for example, are the product of a man's imagination and addressed to men, and it is absolutely essential that we make that effort, and continuously. Here then there is ground for vigilance. Of course, in a male-dominated world such as the one we shall be examining, or indeed our own, it is possible that some women (perhaps even a majority) will have come to accept the assumptions that prevail among men and will have come to think of themselves as men have taught them to think (that point is indeed implicit in Ardener's description of women as 'inarticulate'): it is possible that if we could interrogate the women of classical Athens, that is what we should find – but we are not, in fact, in a position to interrogate them and it is mere arrogance simply to assume it. It follows, then, that it is with the dominant, male model of society that we shall perforce be largely concerned here, and that is a fact of which we must remain conscious throughout this discussion.

The subject of this paper will appear positively trendy, in view of the spate of work recently produced, including two whole numbers of *Arethusa* (vi I [1973]; xi 1–2 [1978]) devoted to the subject of women in antiquity. But I make no apology for it on that account: if one reads a sample of the better things written on this subject, from Gomme's classic essay of more than fifty years ago down to the most recent, I think it is fair to say that almost no progress has been made and that much further study is needed. But if this is so it certainly calls for some explanation. The explanation, I am quite sure, is largely a matter of methodology: the question has been put in terms that are naive and misleadingly, even grossly, over-simple. It has been put always from a male perspective, not through any explicit awareness of the determining nature of the evidence, but as though there were no other perspective, and as though to ask 'were women regarded [by men] with "contempt" or "respect"?' were a question capable of a simple 'yes' or 'no' answer, as though there were some single and univocal scale of values on which it should be possible to place 'women' as evaluated by 'men'. In these terms the question is simply unanswerable: however long we go on discussing it we shall not reach agreement. But why has the question been put in these terms?

Before we can answer that question there are two further points we should notice. The first of these is the fact recently stressed by Sarah Pomeroy, that different investigators have drawn on quite different, indeed mutually exclusive, categories of evidence to support their case: one group drawing largely on myth and imaginative literature, particularly Homer and the theatre, as Gomme does; and the other on the orators of the fourth century and on the evidence of inscriptions. This curious selectivity, which is usually justified, if at all, by *a priori* generalizations about the 'representativeness' of the various available sets of data, is itself sufficiently striking, especially when coupled with an equally arbitrary and generally casual approach to the whole question of the juridical position of women and its implications. But when these facts are combined with a marked tendency to demonstrably false assertion we must begin to feel that we are faced with a question of quite peculiar methodological status. And so we are. But I had first perhaps best try to substantiate my claim that demonstrably false assertions are characteristic of this particular field of enquiry.

Two examples will have to do. The first is from Gomme's essay. Discussing the controversial (and slippery) question of 'seclusion', Gomme turns to fifth-century tragedy and refers to 'the freedom with which they [women] come and go on the stage'. 'Ismene, most timid of women ... does not censure Antigone (and herself) for appearing outside the *gynaikonitis* [women's quarters] and still more for proposing to walk through the streets of Thebes. Neither does Medea hurry indoors when the stranger Aigeus appears, and the latter – a perfectly respectable Athenian – does not seem to expect her to.' Quite apart from the stylization of social life to which it could be argued that the conventions of the fifth-century theatre inevitably led (I shall return to this point later), Gomme's assertion rather breathtakingly ignores a fair number of counter examples from tragedy itself. Consider, for example, the *Teichoskopia* [view from the walls] scene of *Phoenissae*: the *paidagogos* [tutor] emerges first from the palace of the Labdacidae and only after he has assured himself that there are no strange males in sight does Antigone appear, with her mother's specific permission to leave the *parthenones* (the girls' quarters). At the end of the sung section of the scene she returns inside, to remain 'in the girls' quarters', the *paidagogos* commenting this time on the approach of strange women, prone (as women) to gossip. In Euripides' *Electra* Electra's peasant husband criticizes her for being seen loitering and talking to strange young males outside the house. Nor are these moments indicative of some special Euripidean concern with social 'realism' or of any change in social norms during the fifth century (on this last point I would agree with Gomme's effective demolition): in Sophocles' *Electra* Clytemnestra accounts to her own satisfaction for Electra's 'wandering untethered' in public view and 'bringing shame on her *philoi*' by the absence of

Aegisthus' male control. Aeschylus' Eteocles orders the women of the chorus in *Seven* to return home with the words:

μέλει γὰρ ἀνδρί, μὴ γυνὴ βουλευέτω,
τἄξωθεν· ἔνδον δ' οὖσα μὴ βλάβην τίθει.

> It is the concern of men – no place for women's schemes –
> what lies outside: you stay within and cause no hurt.

And even in the case of one of Gomme's own examples, Medea, is it not reasonable to see in her opening words to the women of the chorus (Κορίνθιαι γυναῖκες, ἐξῆλθον δόμων – 'Women of Corinth, I have come out of the house ') some implication of conscious abnormality in what she is doing? It is not just true that 'in Attic tragedy women come and go from their houses at will'.

My second example is more open to debate: it comes from a more recent article by Prof. Le Gall. In the course of an interesting discussion of the relationship between social and political status as it concerns women, Le Gall asserts in passing that though women were not technically citizens and were thus not entered on the *lexiarchikon grammateion* [i.e. the official records] of the *deme*, the birth of female children was declared to the phratry-members of their father. I find that assertion surprising. It is supported by reference to evidence assembled by Glotz-Cohen, but the passages referred to there not only do not prove the point that Le Gall is asserting, they amount to something very like proof of its converse. In none of them is there any reference to the presentation of daughters to the phratry and in several the evident differences between the ways in which the speaker attempts to prove the legitimacy of his two parents tells strongly in favour of the conclusion that they were not presented. For example, in [Dem.] lvii 67 Euxitheos lists as witnesses of his father's legitimacy first five of his father's male agnatic kinsmen and a number of male affines (his father's female cousins' husbands); then his father's *phrateres*, the *Gennetai* with whom he shares his Apollo Patroos and Zeus Herkeios and the same ἡρία (family tombs), and his father's fellow demesmen. For his mother's legitimacy, on the other hand, he cites, as well as a similar range of male agnatic kinsmen and affines, only the *phrateres* and fellow demesmen of her [male] kinsmen: the conspicuous absence of reference to *phrateres* of his mother makes Le Gall's assertion at the least highly improbable. Again the roundabout way in which the speaker of Isaeus viii sets about establishing his mother's legitimacy in contrast to the direct citation of *phrateres* among those who attest his own status supports the same conclusion. He calls the witnesses at his mother's wedding, the *phrateres* of his grandfather who were present at the marriage feast, and invokes the fact that the wives of his fellow demesmen chose his mother to hold office at the Thesmophoria, as well as the fact that he was himself accepted into his father's phratry. In fact such indirect and informal evidence for the status of women is absolutely normal, and in the instances relied upon by Le Gall there is no evidence for the formal presentation of female children even to the phratry.

There is one instance which might seem to support Le Gall's assertion, but it seems to have attracted little recent attention and is not referred to by Le Gall. It is, I would suggest, the exception that proves the rule for which I have been arguing. The speaker of Isaeus iii has been asserting throughout that the woman whose *kyrios* is his opponent is not the legitimate daughter of the γυνὴ ἐγγυητή (betrothed wife) of Pyrrhos whose estate is the object of dispute in this case, but is νόθη (not legitimate) since her mother was the *pallake* (woman with whom he was living) and not the wife of Pyrrhos. In ch. 73 he suddenly and belatedly produces the argument that if things had been as Xenokles, the *kyrios*, asserts, Pyrrhos would have been able to present and introduce (ἀποφανθεῖσαν ... εἰσαγαγόντι) his daughter by this alleged wife to his *phrateres*, thus leaving her as *epidikos* [assignable] with the whole of his estate, and could have requested his *phrateres* to admit (εἰσαγαγεῖν) one of the sons produced by his daughter as his (adoptive) son. The language used is that which Isaeus regularly uses elsewhere of the presentation and admission of male children to the phratry, but the essential point here is clearly that the daughter would be, if Xenokles is telling the truth, an *epikleros*, that is a female descendant of quite special significance in the transmission of family property, since it is only through her that the male line can continue and the *oikos* not become technically 'empty'. Thus introduction to the phratry is being presented as the only step that Pyrrhos can take, since the daughter has as yet no male offspring, in legitimating his male descendants. The uniqueness of the instance may be due as much to unusual circumstances (as Wyse points out, we are never told by Isaeus how old the daughter in question was at her father's death) as to Isaeus' well-known penchant for throwing sand in the eyes of juries. Nevertheless, the instance is unique: to set beside it there are only a puzzling passage in Harpocration about something which Phanodemus did not say, two schematic and muddled passages in the Lexicographers and a scholium on Aristophanes which looks as if it derives from the same source. The silence of all our other sources constitutes very much more impressive evidence and I infer that girls were not introduced to, still less registered as members of, the phratry.

To summarize then. Discussion of the social position of women in antiquity has been characterized by over-simplification of the issues, by concentration on the part of different investigators on mutually exclusive sets of data, and by a tendency (I think it is fair to say more marked here than elsewhere) to false statement which the actual evidence is enough to rebut. If we ask why, as we must, the answer is surely clear. It is that we are dealing with a question which involves powerful and deep-seated emotional drives and in which, therefore, rationalization plays a correspondingly large role. Part of the pleasure in reading Gomme's essay (and part of the danger in believing him) comes from our sense of the extent to which he is engaged emotionally in the quest for a satisfactory answer to the question as he puts it. But we have to be aware that the answer is going to have to satisfy emotional as well as rational requirements; and here is a second, and by far the most important ground for vigilance, for the tendency to rationalize can lead to strange conclusions. When Gomme sums up his position by saying that to the unprejudiced reader of Homer, Sappho, Alcman, Simonides and the three tragedians there is nothing 'remarkable about the position of women in Athens, except perhaps the special honour paid to them' I can only gasp: that seems to me a simplistic fantasy.

What I want to do is look briefly at the real complexities of the question from three points of view, in the belief that the ways in which any society defines its own structure to itself and communicates that structure to its members are likely to constitute a composite of formal and informal, of conscious and unconscious, of explicit rules and implicit norms and patterns, and that to grasp the thing with any faithfulness we need to look at more than one of these ways: the formal rules of law will tell us one thing, the half-conscious paradigms of myth perhaps another. I hope to show that my three aspects stand in a complementary relationship to each other.

II Law

Before I come to the first I think I should draw attention to one crucial ambiguity in my title (and in the titles of most other essays which deal with this question). When we speak of the social position of women, and mean by that more than just the social milieu in which they move, we are being dangerously vague in the terms we use, for it will make a very great difference whether we are speaking of women as daughters, as sisters, or as wives, and whether as wives or mothers; and it may make an equal difference whether we are speaking of the women of the rich or of the poor. We shall have to bear this vagueness in mind as we proceed: for the moment I only draw attention to it.

I have already mentioned the striking lack of interest in discussions of the social position of women in their juridical status. Gomme, as we would expect, defends this omission, but by arguing, it seems, that there is no connection between legal and social status. I do not imagine that most women today, let alone

J.P. Gould

supporters of women's lib or the suffragettes of two generations ago, would
agree. We cannot simply say that status before the law is no part of what we
must attend to if we are to define the place of women within the structure of a
given society, even though from a male point of view (since laws in antiquity, as
largely today, were made by men) this might be a comfortable way out. The law
is surely beyond dispute one of those sets of social institutions by which society
seeks to define its inner structure. We cannot simply ignore it. In the case of
Athens during the fifth and fourth centuries the factual position is well enough
known and can be treated fairly briefly: I shall be more concerned with the significance of the facts and their relation to other facts which help to define the
position of women.

The juridical status of women in Athens is beautifully indicated by the single
entry under 'women' in the index to Harrison's *Law of Athens* i: it reads simply
'women, disabilities'. A woman, whatever her status as daughter, sister, wife or
mother, and whatever her age or social class, is in law a perpetual minor: that
is, like a male minor, but throughout her life she was in the legal control of a
male *kyrios* who represented her in law. If unmarried she was in the *kyrieia* of
her father, her brother(s) by the same father, or her paternal grandfather. Upon
marriage a kind of divided *kyrieia* arose: the evidence seems to suggest that a
father could dissolve his daughter's marriage, even against her wishes, whereas
in other respects the husband acts as *kyrios*. On her husband's death she either
passes to the *kyrieia* of her son(s) (if any) or reverts to that of her father if still
alive: if her sons are minors she falls under the *kyrieia* of their *kyrios*. If she is
pregnant on her husband's death she may (and perhaps must) remain in the
kyrieia of whatever male affine will become her future child's guardian, that is
to say, in the *oikos* of her deceased husband. In relation to marriage the most
instructive case of female disability at law is, of course, the situation of the *epikleros*. If a man dies leaving only a daughter or daughters, none of whom is married to one whom the father had already adopted as his son, such daughters
become ἐπίδικοι, 'assignable', and are 'assigned' by the archon eponymos to
the nearest male kinsman in a fixed order of precedence. Even if already married her existing marriage could be (and sometimes was) dissolved in order to
allow her to be assigned in this way. The order of precedence proceeds through
the agnatic line, starting with the dead father's brothers, and failing any in this
line, through the cognatic: the set of those to whom an *epikleros* could be assigned is the *anchisteia* and this set exhausts the class, not only of those who may
marry an *epikleros,* but also of those who may inherit and those who may
avenge in law the death of a murdered man: this coincidence of rules of marriage, rules of succession and rules of vengeance is certainly significant.

The position of the *epikleros* is an extreme instance of the general rule that a
woman has in law no standing in any question relating to her marriage, just
as she has no legal right to own or dispose of property (I am using 'just as' here
in its strongest sense: the two disabilities are parallel and connected): in other
cases it is her *kyrios* who, in law, determines whom a woman shall marry, and
included in this right of the *kyrios* is a husband's right to dispose of his widow-
to-be in prospect of his death. The connection with property is maintained in
the rules governing dowries: any dowry that went with the woman in marriage
is controlled by her husband *qua kyrios* but cannot be disposed of by him; on the
husband's prior death or on dissolution of the marriage the dowry passes with
her to her new *kyrios*; on the death of the wife without children born to her, the
dowry reverts to her original *kyrios*. The maintenance of these rules, like those
which govern the care and protection of wives, *epikleroi* and wards, are the concern of society in its formal, legal aspect and were probably the responsibility of
the archon – again just as the oversight of 'empty *oikoi*'. In all this, what is most
striking is the strict parallelism between the formal rules controlling the treatment of women and those that govern the transmission and inheritance of
property and of the right or obligation to avenge. Two further points will serve
to bring this parallelism into sharper focus. The first act of the archon on
entering office was to proclaim ὅσα τις εἶχεν πρὶν αὐτὸν εἰσελθεῖν εἰς τὴν ἀρχήν,
ταῦτ' ἔχειν καὶ κρατεῖν μέχρι ἀρχῆς τέλους:) 'all that any man possessed before

he entered upon his office, that he should possess and control until the end of that office'. It is hard not to see the archon's responsibility for preventing the ill treatment of women who are potential transmitters of property as stemming from this primary duty of protecting the rights of property. And the association of women and property is beautifully realized in the dual use of the word ἐγ- γύη: Harrison rightly draws attention to H.J. Wolff's observation that 'in origin the word ἐγγύη (marriage), like ἐγγύη (surety), implied transference with a re- served right to the transferor'. The common element of a retained right in what is transferred derives, in the case of marriage, as Wolff points out, from the fact that the role of the woman in the transmission of property is a dual one: she may be required to produce the son necessary to ensure continuity of the *oikos* in the descent line of her father as well as (or instead of) in that of her husband: hence, of course, the institution of the *epikleros.*

It is thus in their role as transmitters of property that the community displays concern for and extends protection to its women, and expresses such concern and protection within its formal, legal rules and institutions. The way in which it does so defines the woman as incapable of a self-determined act, as almost in law an un-person, outside the limits of those who constitute society's respon- sible and representative agents; and yet, at the same time, as precious and es- sential to the maintenance of a continuing social order and in particular to the continuity of property.

This contradictoriness of status becomes even more marked in the anomalous situation which we find when we try to define formally the sense in which a woman is a member of the community. In one sense, as we have already noti- ced, she clearly stands outside: she is not registered on the *deme* register and she is not a member of a phratry. It is significant that the pattern of naming and re- ferring to women in public contexts reflects this: here we have a clear instance of 'muting' in Ardener's sense. On Attic tombstones of women, even of the Hellenistic period, when a demotic (indicating membership of the community) occurs it agrees invariably with the name of the dead woman's father or hus- band, not with her own name: this contrasts with the case of non-Athenians, where the ethnic normally agrees with the name of the woman. The situation in legal contexts is even more striking. In the private speeches of Demosthenes twenty-seven women are actually named, in eight speeches fourteen of these occur in one speech, Apollodorus' speech *Against Neaira*, and significantly ten of these are alleged to be *hetairai*: the remaining four are slaves. There are for comparison five hundred and nine male names spread over thirty-three speeches. Demosthenes' own mother and sister, though he refers to them repeatedly in the five speeches devoted to the tangled issues of his inheritance, are never named. Neither is the unfaithful wife at the centre of Lysias' first speech, though the story of the marriage is told in considerable detail. This is not accidental: David Schaps has recently shown how systematic is the avoid- ance of women's names throughout the speeches of the Attic orators. The only exceptions are women of low status or none (prostitutes, slaves); women connected with one's opponent (a clear extension of the first category); and the dead. Thus the names of women who have a respected place in the community are suppressed and they are referred to by complex periphrases which stress their status-dependence upon male kinsmen. Respect requires that they be treated, almost, as part of the property of father or husband. We may compare these facts both with our own system of surname changing by women upon marriage and with modern Greek usage, whereby a woman's surname is that of her father, then of her husband, in the possessive: 'so and so's Miss or Mrs'. Maniote [Mani is the name of a Greek village which was used in anthropologi- cal study] custom is even more extreme: to address a married woman by the possessive use of her husband's Christian name, and never utter the woman's first name at all. Recently Caroline Humphrey has described and analysed a complementary system of naming behaviour among the nomads of Mongolia, where a woman is not allowed to utter the name (or any homophone of the name) of any of her senior male affines (her husband's older brothers, his father, his father's brothers, or grandfather): she explains this taboo persuasively as being grounded in the social necessity not to command the attention of any senior affine to 'someone whom [their own] agnatic ideology insists on suppressing'.

Thus in these contexts it is as though the woman has no personality and exists only as an extension of her male *kyrios*. On the other hand, after Pericles' citizenship law of 451/50 and its re-enactment in 403/2 the citizenship of a male Athenian and hence his legal personality depend upon his being the son of a mother who was, in Plutarch's formulation, 'Athenian'; the word regularly used is ἀστή [literally, town-dweller]. But status as an ἀστή is not easy to define. It is noticeable that Aristotle offers no definition in the *Politics*. As we have seen, it is characteristically through her relationship to males or by her participation in *deme* or other rituals and by evidence of her marriage that a woman's status is upheld in courts of law: in other words, where it is not derived from kinship with males, a woman's status tends to be defined in terms of ritual functions.

In terms of law we are left then with a situation which appears internally contradictory and with definitions that seem inherently circular: women stand 'outside' society, yet are essential to it (and in particular to its continued, ordered existence); their status derives from males but theirs, in turn, from the women who are their mothers.

III   Custom

In talking of law we have been talking about formal structures, the formal rules by which society attempts to regulate its own inner relationships and in so doing inevitably gives these relationships definition. When we speak of 'custom' we are speaking of something much less easy to define but which embraces roughly the informal patterns of behaviour and the norms and attitudes which are implicit in such behaviour. We shall be interested both in the actual patterns of behaviour that we can discern and also in the expected patterns, the set of roles in terms of which men and women express their sense both of themselves and of the other, and of the relationship between them which the ordered existence of society requires. That Athenians in particular had a highly articulated sense of such a set of roles is clear from such well-known instances as Meno's attempt to define *arete* [excellence] in Plato's dialogue.

Now in approaching the question of custom as it concerns the social position of women at Athens it is important, once again, to make ourselves aware of and be on our guard against the dangers of rationalization and *a priori* argument. Those who, like Gomme, have sought to deny that anything that might be termed 'seclusion' was characteristic of the customary treatment of women have evidently been largely motivated by their sense that if Athenian women were 'secluded' it must follow that they were regarded and treated by men with 'contempt'; that in some way, occupying the same space as men or moving in space with the same freedom is a necessary condition of equality of regard, or even of any degree of 'respect' felt and shown by men to women. Gomme and his followers seemed to feel that if it is accepted that there were physical boundaries separating men from women in Athenian society, then in the eyes of men women are disregarded and despised and no account taken of their feelings in decisions that we should see as involving both. But of course it does not follow and the evidence is enough, I think, to show that it was not so.

On the one hand evidence for the existence of separate spheres of activity and within the house for separate areas of customary life is so strong and widespread that only a very powerful rationalizing need could account for its being denied or ignored. I have already mentioned cases where this customary separation impinges on the social order of Greek tragedy; the orators provide us with more than enough to satisfy the most sceptical that such separation of male and female areas of life was normal. The evidence of the orators on this point has been well used by Lacey, and I have space only for two examples. One of the climaxes of the sad and tangled story of the ship's gear that is the subject of

[Dem.] xlvii brings the speaker to the house of the devious Theophemos: his need is now becoming desperate; the fleet is about to sail and the Council has passed a resolution requiring all trierarchs to regain possession of missing gear from their predecessors in office 'by any means they could'. Theophemos is out but the slave girl who answers the door is sent to fetch him. The trierarch waits at the door and Theophemos returns, but he prevaricates and is insulting. The trierarch sends his slave to gather witnesses as to what happens next; he tries further argument with Theophemos and declares that if the gear is not forthcoming he will seize ἐνέχυρα (securities). This he does by grabbing the slave girl (they are still standing by the door). Theophemos resists and now the trierarch goes into the house to seek an alternative object to seize as security for the gear. At this point he pauses for a moment in his narrative to the jury and explains (a) that the door was open (he was not breaking in) and (b) that he had [to act] immediately with Theophemos punching him in the mouth and his [need to make a] dramatic return to the meeting of the Council. It is the brief aside that we should notice: even in this crisis a self-respecting Athenian is not going to run the risk of coming face to face with another man's wife in his own home. The trierarch's admirable restraint is clearly intended to contrast with the outrageous behaviour of Theophemos' brother and brother-in-law who later in the story, in a balancing episode, break into the speaker's country farmhouse and confront his wife and children and an old nurse eating in the courtyard: the remaining slave women of the household were in the 'tower', 'where they lived' and barred themselves in. Violence breaks out (the trierarch describes his house as 'in the process of being sacked') and the shouting attracts the attention, first of neighbours' slaves and then of a passing neighbour, Hagnophilos. None of these enters the house: the slaves stand on the roofs of their own farm buildings or go into a nearby lane, trying to attract the attention of passers-by, and Hagnophilos stands on another neighbour's land and witnesses the scene. Hagnophilos did not go in, the trierarch explains to the jury, because 'he did not think he was justified in the absence of the head of the family (*kyrios*) from the house'. Few passages, perhaps, bring out so clearly the sense of an inviolable boundary separating the free women of a household from unrelated males and of the outrage implicit in male entry upon the women of another kinship group. But several others, less dramatically, point to the same conclusion.

The speaker of Lysias i, Euphiletos, is charged with murder: it is therefore vital for him to show that there was no premeditation, and he provides a highly circumstantial account of all that led up to the killing of his wife's lover. He lays stress on the (apparent) normality of relations between himself and his wife: whether he is telling the truth or not is irrelevant to us. All we need bear in mind is that Euphiletos' domestic life is intended to sound normal. He describes the lay-out of his house, with its separate quarters for men and women, and how his wife, who was feeding their baby, frequently slept in the women's quarters so that she could feed and wash it in the night. The picture that emerges is, as it is intended to be, simple and convincing: a wife who leads a private, sheltered life, who goes out little (the affair with Eratosthenes begins, as so often in Menander, with a first sight of her at a public religious ritual, in this case a funeral); whose shopping is done by a slave woman; who, once her child is born, is no longer under her husband's surveillance, but who is not expected to be present when Euphiletos brings home a male friend for an evening meal. This last is of course a well-known feature of relationships within marriage in classical Athens: evidence of eating and drinking together with males who are not kinsmen is frequently presented in Athenian law courts as by itself establishing that a woman is a *pallake* [concubine/mistress] or *hetaira* [or courtesan] but not a wife.

This overall picture is not one that we have any *a priori* right, or evidence on which, to challenge. It can be reinforced in two ways. The first is from the evidence of house plans and vase paintings, as well as the comparative evidence of other cultures. Greek houses seem almost always to have one external door only: there is no 'back door' at or through which women may come into contact with other outsiders than those who enter the house through the 'front door'.

The men's quarters are commonly near to this street door or across the court-yard from the sole entrance. In two-storey houses it is a fair inference from the evidence of Lysias i that the women's quarters were normally on the upper floor: hence, it seems likely, the association between the women's quarters and the μυχός, 'recesses', of the house. On Attic vases women are characteristically seen indoors and in the company of other women. Outside the house they are shown fetching water and taking part in religious rituals, or in the doorway saying farewell to men leaving the house. In ancient Greece, as in modern, the woman's orientation is domestic: 'of the house' as against 'of the road'. Moreover, the spatial distinction has its analogue in the temporal definition of a woman's role. It is of the essence of women's tasks that they be time-consuming; the provision of food, combing and spinning wool, weaving. The significance of this has recently been brought out by Hirschon in her study of female sexuality in a Peiraeus neighbourhood: just as spatial seclusion protects the woman from contact with males not of her own kin, so time-consuming tasks keep her out of mischief (the symbolism of Penelope's weaving is certainly relevant here, as is the night-milling slave woman of *Od.* xx).

The description I have been offering is sometimes qualified by the *caveat* that it can only be true of those Athenians wealthy enough to own slaves and thus keep their women from the necessity of leaving the house to buy food or even to work. I am not happy about this if it is taken to mean that the sense of an inviolable boundary marking the separateness of male and female 'territories' and areas of activity was a preoccupation only of the rich. Of course the women of the poor worked outside the house, but I would suggest that such activity may not have been seen as a normal part of the female role and that its exceptional nature may have been marked by some residual sense of a boundary still separating them and marking them off from the strange males with whom they must have come face to face. I have in mind two parallels from modern Greece. The first is from Ernestine Friedl's account of life in a Boeotian village:

> for the most part ... the world of the *aghora* [which in the case of Vasilika is merely a stretch of the one village street defined by social custom], and, indeed, the public world of the village, is a male world penetrated sporadically by children of both sexes ... men do the marketing from the pedlars of fresh foods and buy whatever items are needed from the village stores. Little girls up to the age of twelve or fourteen, alone or with their brothers, may be sent to the *aghora* on errands, but older girls and women will venture into the area only to pass through it on their way to church or to the fields. I have seen a young mother from the eastern end of the village, when she heard the calls of a tomato vendor, walk to the edge of the *aghora* area. She stood some two hundred feet from the tomato wagon, shouted to the pedlar to ask what his prices were and then waited in the same spot until she could send a passing child to buy her tomatoes for her.

The other is from an experience of my own. Driving through Crete I passed a remote threshing floor on which a man and two women were winnowing wheat. I got out of the car to take a photograph and as I came nearer the two women retreated rapidly and, while I remained, stayed crouching more than half out of sight in the heavy shade of a tree: the man continued with his work while I took my photographs. Physically, the women were in the public world, but in a privileged and bounded position within it: the approach of a male stranger activated the sense of separateness implicit in their role and forced physical expression of it. I think we have to bear in mind the possibility of such submerged lines of demarcation in Classical Athens also.

However, as I have suggested, it does not follow from this state of things that 'contempt' is the appropriate term to describe male attitudes to, or behaviour towards, women. The evidence indeed contradicts any such assumption. But in examining it we have to make three preliminary distinctions: the first between private and public worlds, between 'inside' and 'outside' and the behaviour appropriate to each; the second between relationships which associate women with male kinsmen and the absence of any such relationships with unrelated males; and the third between relationships with men in general and those with other women, in particular the network of gossip relationships with neighbouring women. There is a nice example of the last in the water-rights case against Kallikles, Dem. 1v. The speaker is arguing that any flood damage caused on Kallikles' estate by his father's having built a wall along the road separating the two estates, was minimal, and he produces the hearsay evidence of a conversation between his mother and Kallikles' mother which took place during a visit made by the former (by implication a normal occurrence). The impression left by this speech is of two parallel networks of relationship between unrelated neighbours, one involving the men, the other the women. What we do not find is any sort of relationship pattern between neighbours of opposite sex, and that is what we should expect from the evidence already produced.

On the other hand, relationships between women and their male kinsmen can be very close, can display a very high degree of warmth, tenderness and concern; of mutual understanding and tolerance; and of male acceptance, not only of the right of women to be consulted, but also of the initiative of women in the affairs of the family. On the other hand, of course, we can find in the evidence examples of an equally striking absence of these qualities. These facts will surprise only those who have accepted Gomme's tacit assumption and infer from the evidence for 'seclusion' that such human feelings cannot have existed between men and women or, conversely (like Gomme himself) feel certain of the latter, and find themselves therefore impelled to deny the former.

Let me look at some examples. Lacey has made good use of the scene described in Lysias xxxii in which Diodotos' widow makes a long and impassioned speech to her male kinsmen on the subject of her husband's will and her father's infamous behaviour over what was left in trust for her and for her children. It is a striking instance of free and equal interchange between men and women on the domestic interests of the family. A narrative in Isaeus is less dramatic but equally revealing. In Isae. ii the speaker describes how he and his brother are approached by their brother-in-law, Menekles, whose marriage with their sister has been childless. The reason, in Menekles' view, is his own age: it would be wrong, he suggests for him to take advantage of his wife's 'goodness' and for her to grow old with him in childlessness. He asks the speaker and his brother to give their sister in marriage to another, with his consent. The speaker then describes how he and his brother urged Menekles to persuade his wife, their sister, to accept this: 'I would do, I said, whatever she agreed to'. The sister at first resists, then with reluctance agrees. Here, apart from the legal framework within which the conversation takes place, we do find certainly a familiar sense of human warmth in relations between men and women. Equally familiar, however different the circumstances, is the tone of voice in which Euphiletos and his wife talk to one another on that night when Euphiletos came home unexpectedly from his farm in the country. His wife's lover is in the house and the old slave makes the baby cry to give its mother an excuse to go downstairs. At first she acts reluctance and puts on a performance of pleasure at her husband's return after being away some time: Euphiletos begins to lose his temper and tells her to go down. 'Oh yes', she says, 'I know why: you want a chance to get your hands on the little slave girl. You have done it before when you were drunk'. Euphiletos laughs and his wife goes out, shuts the door behind her and pushes the bar across – it was meant to look like a joke and it worked. Here are relations between a 'secluded' woman and her husband, warm, intimate, familiar relations, and if there are others which display neglect and bitterness and misery that, too, is something we can find familiar. Not all husbands, certainly, could have replied as Kritoboulos to Socrates, that there were few, if any, to whom he talked less than to his wife. Indeed, even on the subject of the public life of a husband or brother or father, Apollodorus presents the women of the family as taking a lively, and at times an embarrassing interest: when you go home, he tells the jury in the Neaira case, you will have to explain and defend what you have done here in court, and he then describes a vigorous cross-examination followed by forthright comment. Again, not all men would have brushed aside such questions with the effortless superiority of Lysistrata's husband.

But these examples, to repeat, are examples of relations between men and women who are kindred, οἰκεῖοι καὶ φίλοι, and they occur 'inside' in the private, enclosed and often secret world of the Greek household. The world 'outside', the public world, is the world of men. In that world it is true that silence is the only ornament a woman has – with one striking exception. In the sacred and ritual activities of the community the active presence of women in the public world is not merely tolerated but required. As priestesses in many of the major cults of the *polis* (priestesses of gods as well as of goddesses), as *kanephoroi* [basket-bearers] and *hydrophoroi* [water-carriers] in the great religious processions, as the *arrhephoroi* of Athena Polias [the carriers of the robe and other holy things of Athena Polias], the 'bears' of Artemis Brauronia, as raisers of the ritual scream, the ὀλολυγή at the blood sacrifice, in mourning and at funerals, in the rituals of marriage, the participation of women is indispensable to the sacral continuity, the ordering of society. The magnificent Panathenaic procession of the Parthenon frieze displays the ritual splendour and solemnity of the woman's role. And alongside the great civic rituals in which women stand with men as equal participants are those other rituals, just as much part of the sacred action of the community, which are either the exclusive domain of women or in which women play the leading role – rituals such as the Arrhephoria, the Skira, the Thesmophoria, the Lenaia, the Adonia. In these too the community expresses its sense of the necessary participation of women in its continuing life. Walter Burkert has recently shown that the eight-month-long ritual tasks of the two young girls called *arrhephoroi*, chosen by the archon basileus from the great families of Athens, constitute a rite of initiation and incorporation into the community; and how the sacred objects round which the ritual revolves – the peplos of Athena Polias and the snake or phallos, the ἄρρητα ('secret [unspoken] things') contained in the covered basket that the girls carried in their night descent to the cave and well under the north cliff of the Akropolis – celebrate and symbolize the dual function of women in the community: spinning and weaving, the making of clothes, the ἔργα γυναικῶν ('tasks of women'); and sex and marriage, the conception of the child, the continued existence of the community itself.

The participation of women in the cults of the community raises problems of interpretation. It cannot be wholly explained by adopting I.M. Lewis' recent suggestion, that these are 'peripheral' cults and that the role of women in them is to be understood as part of a strategy which can be widely illustrated from traditional societies, whereby women and others of low status, excluded from participation in the social and political life of the community, have found a mechanism to establish indirect claims to status and attention through possession and ecstasy, in a way which 'ventilates aggression and frustration largely within an uneasy acceptance of the established order of things'. Such an explanation seems helpful with rituals such as the Adonia, or with the cult of Dionysus at the Lenaia. It seems less helpful when applied to the ritual of the sacred marriage at the Anthesteria, between Dionysus and the wife of the archon basileus, or the cult of Demeter at the Thesmophoria. And it is surely quite untenable as an explanation of the participation of women in the cult of Athena Polias, from her priestess downwards. The cult of Athena, as expressed in rituals such as the Panathenaia, is not 'peripheral', but 'central', in Lewis' terminology: that is, its function is to reinforce official, 'male' morality and the dominant structures of society, and the role of women in it must seem anomalous.

Moreover, in the ritual participation of women in community religion there are once again counter-indications to be noted, signs of that ambivalence and contradiction we have already seen in the judicial status of women. In the rituals of the Skira and Thesmophoria is enacted not the ordered continuity of society, but precisely its opposite, inversion and disruption: the women gather outside the house and apart, sexual relations are ritually in suspense, the norms of society disrupted. And at the Adonia the other pole of the ambivalence surrounding the role of women in ritual appears: sexual promiscuity and sterility.

But with the intricate, half-hidden significations of ritual we have come close to my third aspect, myth.

IV Myth

With myth, we face major and intractable problems, both of definition and of method: no one who is familiar with Prof. Kirk's book and its reception can be in any doubt of that. I propose to be cavalier about both. For definition I shall offer nothing more than what might charitably be called ostensive, and I think that no great harm will be done. Whether we define myth in terms of 'charter', 'archetype', 'fantasy' or whatever else, we are dealing with something recognizably different from what we have so far considered and which, however dreamlike, can serve as a vehicle for the mapping and understanding of experience in terms which are not available to a society in its more explicit rules and customary norms: myth can, and does, supplement these things, and may draw our attention to what is not otherwise visible to us, nor even, in all probability, consciously grasped by the tellers and hearers of it. As to method, I agree with many of the misgivings recently expressed by Brian Vickers, and faced with some of the more schematic binary interpretations of the structuralist school feel drawn irresistibly towards Mary Douglas' splendid remark: 'On this subject the stolid English suspicion of cleverness begins to crystallize'. I shall be eclectic, perhaps impressionistic, and hope that the results may justify me.

Let me begin with what will at first appear a random set of data. We have already noticed an example of the symbolic force of spinning and weaving in defining the social role of women in ritual. So too in myth. Louis Gernet has drawn attention to the interesting fact that in the mythical theme of the 'don fatal', it is commonly a garment of death that is the woman's gift: we have only to remember Eriphyle, Deianeira, Medea. The contribution to society has become the source of its destruction. Encounters between men and women in Greek myth regularly associate women with the wild and the sacred, with what is outside the limits of ordered civilization, and with the forces of life, with mountains and forests, with rivers, springs and fountains. The correlation with fountains has its counterpart in modern Greek culture and has been well documented by Nicholas Richardson in his commentary on the Homeric hymn to Demeter. To his primary examples we can add, as well as Odysseus and Nausikaa, Odysseus' men and the Laistrygonian princess at the fountain Artakie (*Od.* x 103ff.), Teiresias and Athena; and for the wilds, Aktaion and Artemis, Anchises and Aphrodite, Paris and the three goddesses, Paris and Oinone, Daphnis and the nymph, Hesiod and the Muses. In most of these, the encounter ends in the destruction of the man. On the other hand, there is an alternative pattern which stresses the secluded privacy of the woman (a young girl) and in which the encounter leads to her destruction: Kore and Hades, Kreousa and Apollo, Europa and Zeus, Helen and Hermes (Eur. *Hel.* 241ff.), Stratonike and Apollo (Hes. *fr.* 26.18ff.), Oreithyia and Boreas (Choer. *fr.* 5 Kinkel). The motifs of this second pattern of encounter revolve around the gathering of flowers, or the washing of clothes, and the peace and domesticity of the world of women, invaded by men. The ambiguities of the encounter are richly presented in the Kirke episode of the *Odyssey* (x 135ff.). In this, the association of normal and abnormal in sexual relations, of sex, witchcraft and the fear of castration, is reinforced by a parallel ambiguity in the physical and social setting of the scene: the wild, forested island inhabited by stags but with the civilized, domestic column of smoke rising from it; the stone-built palace in the forest clearing; the domesticated guard animals who are lions and wolves; the singing of the witch as she weaves at the loom. Nothing, we know, is as it should be, and yet everything is familiar. Even the civilized norms of the proper reception of the stranger-guest are (on the surface) minutely observed, but what results is the horror of dream-work, and Odysseus stands, sword in hand, as Kirke invites him to go to bed with her.

For the moment without comment, I will add some observations on the language of metaphor (male metaphor, we should remind ourselves) as it relates to women, sex and marriage. The formula required by custom if not by law, for giving in marriage is several times attested in Menander: 'I give (ἐγγυῶ, δίδωμι ἔχειν) you this woman (my daughter) γνησίων παίδων ἐπ' ἀρότῳ 'for the ploughing of legitimate children'. This traditional formula is part of a network of imagery and metaphor which associates women and their role in sex and marriage with animals, especially the taming, yoking and breaking in of animals, and with agriculture. Marriage is a yoke; virgins are wild, unbroken or untamed (ἀδμής, ἄδμητος, ἀδάματος); unyoked (ἄζυγος); the three goddesses proceeding to the judgement of Paris are τρίπωλον ἅρμα δαιμόνων ... τὸ καλλιζυγές, 'a three-horse team of gods ... beauty harnessed'. Girls are young, unbroken horses (πῶλοι); women are bitches (and here the overtones are of sexuality, not maliciousness). In the horrified *kommos* which crowns *Oedipus Tyrannus*, in Oedipus' words cited in the messenger speech, and already in the final stasimon, the imagery of plough-land and seed and furrow comes to dominate the coda of the play. Nor are these just the images of the extremity of horror: Deianeira speaks of Heracles' marriage with her in the prologue of *Trachiniae* as of a peasant visiting a distant field to sow and reap.

Let me complete this job-lot of examples by two stories from Herodotus (with a little help from Plato): Herodotus will have thought them history, but I see no reason not to call them myth. The story of Gyges tells how an inferior member of the king's *oikos* (in Plato a shepherd wage-labourer who becomes a royal messenger, in Herodotus a favoured member of the palace guard) kills the king and succeeds to his power: the common factor to both versions is Kandaules' wife (another anonymous woman). Her seduction (if that is the right word) is a mere unobtrusive step in the story in Plato: the weird happenings – the earth quaking and opening, the bronze horse with little doors in its side, the huge corpse, the gold ring of invisibility – are already passed, the rest is matter of fact; and yet of course it is not – those other things had to happen to make it possible. In Herodotus the seduction is central: it follows instantly and it seems automatically upon an outrageous breach of the taboos of seclusion. The symmetry of outrage and revenge is brought out in the queen's orders to Gyges, to carry out his murderous attack on Kandaules 'from the same spot from which he displayed me, naked'. The story of Gyges clearly deals with the theme of the abnormal succession of male power through violation of the boundaries that separate women from unrelated males (in the one version, through abnormal visibility; in the other, through abnormal invisibility).

My second story from Herodotus is in reality a pair of episodes whose interconnections are made explicit by Herodotus himself. The earlier of the two is narrated second and is set first in Attica, then Lemnos: it concerns the feud between the Athenians and the Pelasgian settlers on Lemnos. The story begins with the building of the Pelasgian wall around the Akropolis, the *polis* of Athenian tradition. The Pelasgians are rewarded with land, marginal land under the slopes of Mt Hymettos. The quarrel starts, in Hecataeus' version, over this land: under cultivation it becomes an object of jealousy and desire (φθόνος καὶ ἵμερος) to the Athenians. In the Athenian account, the quarrel is over women: Pelasgian men and Athenian women encounter one another at the fountain Enneakrounos, and the result is rape, followed by a murderous plan against the men of Athens. The Athenians, in a striking deviation from the norms of such a tale, take no blood revenge but merely exile the Pelasgians, who remove to Lemnos. Exile, however, itself calls for revenge, and the Pelasgians descend on Brauron at a time designed to coincide with the festival of Artemis. They seize large numbers of the Athenian women who are gathered there to carry out the rituals of the goddess and take them back to Lemnos, where they become *pallakai* [concubines]. The sons of these Athenian women speak Attic, and behave as Athenians: they will not mix with the sons of the Pelasgian women, they display complete solidarity in responding to insult or violence, and they establish superiority over the Pelasgian boys. If this is how they behave as children, the Pelasgians naturally ask themselves, how will they behave as grown men? The answer to this question issues in another act of violence: the Pelasgians kill all the Athenian-born boys, and their mothers. But the sons of Athenian women are also the sons of Pelasgian men and their murder brings about sterility in the earth, in women and in flocks. Delphi orders recompense to be made to Athens. The Athenians demand Lemnos, and they are promised it, upon fulfilment of an *adynaton* [a condition impossible to satisfy]. When ('many years later', says Herodotus) Miltiades sails to Lemnos from the Chersonese in high summer, he claims that the *adynaton* is fulfilled, and against some scepticism makes good his claim by force. The astonishing richness of theme in this last story makes comment difficult, but perhaps unnecessary. It deals, evidently, with ambiguous questions of legitimacy and inheritance, with the mysterious and dangerous 'otherness' of women; it suggests interchangeability of women and land, of exile, rape and death, even of women and slaves; it touches on the establishment of cities (the Akropolis wall), and communities (the settlement of Lemnos), on life-giving fountains and rough land made good by agriculture, on kinship solidarity and feud, on sterility as the outcome of some misreading of the boundaries separating strangers from kin. In it women are seen as linked with the sacred, as necessary to the continuity of society and disruptive of it, the victims and the cause of violence and bloodshed.

The second episode takes place at Sparta and involves the 'grandsons' (παίδων παῖδες) of the crew of the Argo, expelled from Lemnos by the same Pelasgians who raped the Athenian women from Brauron. It responds reciprocally to the first episode. In it the Minyan descendants of the Argo arrive above Sparta on Mt Taygetos and kindle fire. On enquiry by the Spartans, they explain their presence by declaring that they have 'returned to their fathers', and request a share of land and status. Moved by the presence of Castor and Pollux on the Argo, the Spartans agree; Minyans and Spartans exchange women, and the Minyans are distributed among the Spartan tribes. Soon after, the Minyans demand a share in the Spartan kingship and behave insultingly to the Spartans: they are arrested and are due to be executed. But in the night fixed for their execution they are visited by their Spartan wives, who exchange clothes with them and allow them to escape in women's dress; whereupon they return to Taygetos until some are eventually persuaded to join the expedition to Thera and others seize land in Elis. This time we have to do with incoming males, agnatic kinsmen of the inhabitants, who detach the women, daughters of leading members of the community, from their loyalties through marriage, who dress as women and threaten the community from the mountains. Women are seen as points of weakness in the solidarity of the community, and as forming strong and fast-wrought ties with incomers who are also subverters of order.

My random set of data was, then, not quite random: it displays certain recurrent themes and anxieties, and through it we can begin to see, I think, that myth may significantly add depth to that sense of the woman's role in society that we have so far been able to reach. This is because it brings into view ambiguities, tensions and fears, deep-seated fears, which the norms of law and custom are intended to control and even suppress: myth in some sense contradicts the comfortable surface normality of the social structure defined by law and custom, and points to conflict at a deeper level within the dominant structure. But the significations of myth are implicit, half-hidden and disguised, and need to be disengaged and made articulate. Before I turn to some recent attempts to do this, I will add, by way of recapitulation, a stasimon from the *Choephoroe*, which is itself an attempt to articulate the role of women in myth.

The first stasimon of *Choephoroe* immediately precedes the first encounter of Orestes and Clytemnestra, of son and mother, male and female. Generically it belongs with the πολλὰ τὰ δεινά stasimon of *Antigone* but it takes a different course. The opening strophe alludes to the sources of terror and destruction, the δεινὰ δειμάτων ἄχη, that breed and swarm on earth, in the sea, and in the sky between. The antistrophe continues: but who could recount the aggressive pride of men, the passions and desires (ἔρωτες) of women that recognize no bounds, 'that make society with man's destruction'? 'The desire, out of all desire (ἀπέρωτος ἔρως) that overpowers women' (or 'that gives women power' [θηλυκρατής]: the ambiguity is revealing) 'defeats and perverts the common yoke and yard of beast and man' (συζύγους ... ὁμαυλίας ... παρανικᾷ κνωδάλων τε καὶ βροτῶν). The remaining strophic pairs recall the paradigms of myth: Althaia (ἁ παιδολυμὰς, τάλαινα Θεστίας, 'Thestios' iron-hearted daughter, who maimed her child'); the murderous Skylla (ἁ κυνόφρων, 'minded like a bitch'), who destroyed a *philos* (her father) for the good of enemies; the women of Lemnos, and Clytemnestra herself. Meleager and Nisos were magically safe from death, until a mother and a daughter destroyed that magic; on Lemnos a whole society was destroyed – γοᾶται δὲ δημόθεν κατάπτυστον, 'bewailed by a whole community, detestable' – that is the ultimate paradigm of woman's evil. Men have their own unlimited and competitive aggression to fear, but they have to fear too the devious and consciously destructive sex of women, and what that brings is death.

So Aeschylus. The most interesting of recent attempts to disengage from myth its signification of the role of women in human society are those, on the one hand, of the French structuralist school of Vernant, Vidal-Naquet and Detienne, and on the other, of the American analytical psychologist Philip Slater. Methodologically they are poles apart, and it is therefore surprising and significant that they should have produced accounts which are recognizably similar in their general drift. What they point to, in the mythical imagination of Greece (and let us remind ourselves, for one last time, that we are speaking of the imagination of men), is a profound and ambivalent disquiet, an oscillation between obsessive fear and revulsion, on the one hand, and, on the other, an implication of total dependence. Women figure, with a quite extraordinary prominence, in Greek myth, but the roles that they play are shot through with implications of antagonism and ambivalence. Let me just list some obvious examples. The catalogue of women who figure as the destroyers of men, usually with marked sexual overtones, forms a long procession: Althaia, Skylla, Clytemnestra and the women of Lemnos we have already met in Aeschylus. Without going far afield we can add Helen, Medea, Phaidra, Agaue, Stheneboia, Tyro, Eriphyle, Ino, Astydameia, Eidothea, the daughters of Danaos, of Proitos and of Minyas, even Deianeira; some, like Semele or Io or Europa, are destroyed by male divinities, some figure in both roles (Hekabe, even Helen); sometimes a pair of women act together as destroyer and destroyed, as Prokne and Philomela or as Hermione and Andromache in Euripides' play. Women act as 'rescuers' (Ariadne, Medea) or as 'rescued' (Andromeda); they are guarded and protected (as precious and vulnerable) but they are also imprisoned (as dangerous) – Danae, Antiope, Kleopatra; they are confined but they have longings for the wild (as Phaidra in Euripides' *Hippolytus*). Recurrently women act as the shacklers and inhibitors of men: Omphale perhaps springs first to mind, but Kakridis has recently pointed out how it is the role of the women of the Homeric poems to restrain and inhibit men from the assertion of their *arete*, and the inhibitory feeling of *aidos* is characteristically descriptive of encounters between men and women. The terrifying nightmare figures of Greek mythology – the Moirai, the Erinyes, Harpies, Graiai, Sirens, Skylla and Charybdis, Medusa and the Sphinx – and bogies of folklore, such as the μειξοπάρθενος (half woman, half snake) of Hdt. iv 9.1 or she of Dio of Prusa v 12, are, again, characteristically women. The monstrous Minotaur is offspring of Pasiphae and an uncanny bull from the sea.

But it is the ambivalence of sex, and the uncertainties of femininity and of sexual roles which is perhaps most striking and interesting. Detienne has shown how an ambivalent attitude to sex is implicit not only in the rituals of the Thesmophoria and Adonia but also in such myths as those of Myrrha, Ixion and Phaon, as well as of Adonis himself. The ambiguity of a figure such as Helen is obvious, and we have already seen the polarization of incompatible aspects of the female role in pairs of women such as Hermione and Andromache: this is a recurrent motif in Sophocles (the obvious examples are

Antigone and Ismene, Electra and Chrysothemis; more ambiguously Deianeira
and Iole) and it leads us, I think, to an instructive perception of how ambiguous, in Greek male imagination, is the masculine/feminine polarity. In one
sense, it is the function of women in Greek society to define the male role by
opposition: Pierre Vidal-Naquet and Simon Pembroke have made fascinating
use of this opposition and its recurrence in Greek myth and tradition.
Oedipus' words to Ismene in *Oedipus at Colonus* are a classic instance of the
way in which the opposition male/female is seen as defining social structure.
To call a man 'woman', as the chorus do to Aigisthos in *Agamemnon*, is the gros-
sest insult and humiliation. But what of the converse? Clytemnestra has an
ἀνδρόβουλον κέαρ, 'a man-scheming heart': do we admire her or fear her?
When Orestes exclaims to Electra

ὦ τὰς φρένας μὲν ἄρσενας κεκτημένη ...
ὡς ἀξία ζῆν μᾶλλον ἢ θανεῖν ἔφυς

Oh, the mind you have, it is a man's ...
your gifts deserve to live, not die!

on a superficial reading the valuation is positive, but by now the whole action
of *Orestes* has become ambiguous, not least the role of Orestes himself.
Xenophon's Socrates is more straightforward; or is he? But the issue is wider
than the mere explicit attribution of male characteristics to women. A friend recently described the impression made on her by the female figures of Euripides
as one of 'men in drag'. In terms of literal theatre history that is, of course, true
– and the fact itself is significant. But beyond that there is a discernible
'masculinization' of women in Greek tragedy. Let me take just two indications
of it. A defining trait of masculine competitive aggression is the horror of being
humiliated by laughter and mockery and a determination to retaliate against
even an imagined instance: Sophocles' Ajax and Philoctetes provide classic
instances. But we should notice that the trait reappears in several of the women
in tragedy: in the Erinyes of the *Oresteia*, in Medea, even in Antigone. Though
she is a 'destroyer', Deianeira is, many would say, Sophocles' most 'feminine'
character, but she dies by the sword: that is a horrifyingly masculine way to
die, and the shock of it reverberates through the play. I have argued elsewhere
that, in part, this 'masculinization' of women is the consequence of theatre conditions and conventions: the inner life of the *oikos* is projected on to the public
world of 'outside' and there are inevitable distortions of social role as a result.
But that is not all. We have only to look at the motif of exchange of sexual roles
and the recurrence of transvestism as a mythological (and ritual) theme, to see
that it is not: Heracles and Omphale, Achilles on Skyros, Dionysus among the
nymphs of Nysa, Pentheus himself. Indeed, the ambiguities of the myth and ritual of Dionysus are as much sexual as they are moral: Dionysus repeatedly
taken for a woman, the Maenads descending on Hysiae and Erythrae like an
army of men, the voyeurism of Pentheus. We can add the sex-change myths of
Teiresias and Kaineus.

It emerges then from an examination of Greek myth that male attitudes to
women, and to themselves in relation to women, are marked by tension,
anxiety and fear. Women are not part of, do not belong easily in, the male
ordered world of the 'civilized' community; they have to be accounted for in
other terms, and they threaten continually to overturn its stability or subvert
its continuity, to break out of the place assigned to them by their partial incorporation within it. Yet they are essential to it: they are producers and bestowers
of wealth and children, the guarantors of due succession, the guardians of the
oikos and its hearth. Men are their sons, and are brought up, as children, by
them and among them. Like the earth and once-wild animals, they must be
tamed and cultivated by men, but their 'wildness' will out.

The ambiguous correlation between women and the wild is not, of course,
peculiar to Athenian or to ancient Greek culture at large. The tendency to categorize experience in terms of an opposition between 'culture' (what is accessible to and under the ordering control of human intelligence and human
skills) and nature (what is 'outside', alien to human order and not subject to

its control) has been widely documented by anthropologists. And in the terms of such an opposition, women, or certain facets of the social personality of women, are often seen (by men) as aligned with 'nature' rather than 'culture', or as 'liminal', existing in the dangerous no-man's land between these mutually exclusive categories. Much of the symbolic transactions of social life, in many cultures, can be best understood as expressive of the 'liminality', or even the alienness, of women's existence. Ardener himself, for example, in the article from which I began this essay, went on to discuss myths and rituals of the Bakweri in the Cameroon which associate women with possession by the 'mermaids' of the rain-soaked forest, and to analyse the relationship between women and 'nature' implicit in these; and Bourdieu has analysed the complex symbolism of Kabyle social life in such a way as to underline similar associations. More recently Sherry Ortner has pointed to behavioural and psychological factors which tend, cross-culturally, to align women with 'nature' as against 'culture'. Moreover in the Greek context, the sharpness of the physical boundary between the enclosed world of house, high walls and narrow streets and the stark openness of the mountain beyond is a source of powerful imagery. We have seen how, in terms of the categorization of Athenian society, of the boundaries between inclusion and exclusion, women are 'boundary-crossers', anomalous beings who belong and do not belong, are 'within' and 'without'. And we have learnt from Mary Douglas how potent are the fears released by such anomalies to the dominant system of categorization in any culture: 'all margins are dangerous ... Any structure of ideas is vulnerable at its margins.'

The marginality of women may explain some aspects of their role in Athenian ritual. In so far as the gods are unambiguously seen as an extension of the dominant structure of society, that is, as analogous to (male) humans in motivation, behaviour, even appearance, then relationships with divinity may themselves be construed as an extension of human interaction, and be regulated according to the norms and categories of the (male) social order. But much in the imagery of Greek religion shows that this is not altogether so; that gods may be seen not as super-humans but as bestial; as 'natural', not 'cultural' powers; wild, not tamed. Divinity too is, potentially at least, anomalous: the divine powers are and are not part of the structure of 'social' relationships. Thus the contradictions that co-exist in the imagery of divinity are parallel to those that mark the social and ritual roles, and the mythical personality, of women, and the parallelism should have some explanatory value.

One of the most sustained attempts in Greek myth to order these contradictions is Hesiod's story of Prometheus and the creation of Pandora, brilliantly analysed in a recent paper by Vernant. Vernant has shown how the themes of the loss of bliss and ease, the creation by the gods of a new order, the present 'civilized' order of agriculture, animal sacrifice and fire, are articulated with the birth of woman and the onset of κακά and πήματα, 'evils and pains'. Pandora is beautiful; clothed and disguised by the skill of craft, she is a *dolos* [deceiver] that men will not be able to handle, a consumer of men, their sex, their strength and the food and wealth that their strength produces. But without her, society, the world as it is, cannot continue; and the world as it once was, without women, has been stolen and hidden by Zeus and cannot be stolen back: ὡς οὐκ ἔστι Διὸς κλέψαι νόον οὐδὲ παρελθεῖν – 'so there is no way to avoid what Zeus has intended'.

V Conclusion

I have tried in this paper to show something of the true complexity of what we men summarize, brashly and arrogantly, as the social position of women, and to display the 'complementarity' of law, custom and myth as they can contribute to a fuller grasp of that complexity. I am conscious that I have only produced a preliminary sketch. The reason is as much my ignorance as the pressure of time and space. This is an enormous subject and there is still a vast amount of work to be done. I have not discussed such important things as philosophical and physiological traditions and theories about women; I have not pursued Mr de Ste Croix's important and far-reaching suggestion (which I would accept) that we should consider women in classical Athens as an exploited class, in the Marxist sense; I have not touched on a number of major Greek myths about women (for example, the Amazon myth); I have not even discussed the Funeral Speech and Ischomachus' wife. Above all, I have not been able to make adequate use of the great repository of relevant ethnographic material, or of the full range of theoretical discussion among anthropologists. For all these short-comings I apologize. I would like to end by going back to Gomme. It was the stimulation of qualified disagreement with him that first set me thinking about this subject: I hope it will be clear how much I owe to him. He was right, of course, to make such full use of the evidence of myth and imaginative litera-ture; but surely wrong to insist that everything there is perfectly familiar to us and unsurprising. He refers, among other things, to the significance of 'love' in the literature of Athens. When it is a matter of the 'happy ever after' endings of Menander's comic universe, we are on familiar ground, indeed, but Gomme also quotes *Antigone* Ἔρως ἀνίκαιε μάχαν, Ἔρως ... ('*Eros*, undefeated in battle, *eros*...)' and there I want to say that *Eros* is not 'love', and that Gomme might have gone on to quote the rest of the chorus. The *Eros* of that chorus is an im-placable antagonist in an all-out war, Eros 'falls on property' (as a destroyer); he who 'has *eros*' is out of his mind; *eros* warps the minds of the just (δίκαιοι) to injustice (ἀδικία) and destruction: above all, *eros* produces 'quarrels between men who are tied by blood' (νεῖκος ἀνδρῶν ξύναιμον). It seems to me that any contemporary of Sophocles would have understood very well the bafflement of the Fingo elders when confronted with the impact of 'love' on things as they understood them. They were trying, in 1883, to explain to the Cape Government Commissioners the sudden increase in illegitimate births and run-away marriages in their community, and they said: 'the trouble arises through a thing called love. We do not comprehend this at all ... This thing called love has been introduced.'

ATHENIAN DEMAGOGUES[1]

Source: *Studies in Ancient Society*, Routledge and Kegan Paul, 1974, Chapter 1, pp.1–25.

By M.I. Finley

When the news of their defeat in Sicily in 413 BC reached the Athenians, they received it with disbelief. Then came the realization of the full scale of the disaster, and the people, writes Thucydides, 'were indignant with the orators who had joined in promoting the expedition, as if they [the people] had not themselves decreed it [in assembly]'.[2] To this George Grote made the following rejoinder:[3]

> From these latter words, it would seem that Thucydides considered the Athenians, after having adopted the expedition by their votes, to have debarred themselves from the right of complaining of those speakers who had stood forward prominently to advise the step. I do not at all concur in his opinion. The adviser of any important measure always makes himself morally responsible for its justice, usefulness, and practicability; and he very properly incurs disgrace, more or less according to the case, if it turns out to present results totally contrary to those which he had predicted.

These two opposing quotations raise all the fundamental problems inherent in the Athenian democracy, the problems of policy-making and leadership, of decisions and the responsibility for them. Unfortunately Thucydides tells us very little about the orators who successfully urged on the Assembly the decision to mount the great invasion of Sicily. In fact, he tells us nothing concrete about the meeting, other than that the people were given misinformation by a delegation from the Sicilian city of Segesta and by their own envoys just returned from Sicily, and that most of those who voted were so ignorant of the relevant facts that they did not even know the size of the island or of its population. Five days later a second Assembly was held to authorize the necessary armament. The general Nicias took the opportunity to seek a reversal of the whole programme. He was opposed by a number of speakers, Athenian and Sicilian, neither named by the historian nor described in any way, and by Alcibiades, who is given a speech which throws much light on Thucydides himself and on his judgment of Alcibiades, but scarcely any on the issues, whether the immediate ones being debated or the broader ones of democratic procedure and leadership. The result was a complete defeat for Nicias. Everyone, Thucydides admits, was now more eager than before to go ahead with the plan – the old and the young, the hoplite soldiers (who were drawn from the wealthier half of the citizenry) and the common people alike. The few who remained opposed, he concludes, refrained from voting lest they appeared unpatriotic.[4]

The wisdom of the Sicilian expedition is a very difficult matter. Thucydides himself had more than one view at different times in his life. However, he seems not to have changed his mind about the orators: they promoted the expedition for the wrong reasons and they gained the day by playing on the ignorance and emotions of the Assembly. Alcibiades, he says, pressed hardest of all, because he wished to thwart Nicias, because he was personally ambitious and hoped to gain fame and wealth from his generalship in the campaign, and

---

[1] This is a revised text of a paper to the Hellenic Society in London on 25 March 1961, of which a shortened version was broadcast on the Third Programme of the BBC and published in the *Listener* of 5 and 12 October 1961. I am grateful to Professors A. Andrewes and A.H.M. Jones, Messrs P.A. Brunt and M.J. Cowling for advice and criticism.

[2] Thuc., 8.1.1.

[3] *A History of Greece*, new edn (London, 1862), v, p.317 n.3.

[4] Thuc., 6.1–25.

because his extravagant and licentious tastes were more expensive than he could really afford. Elsewhere, writing in more general terms, Thucydides says this:[5]

> [Under Pericles] the government was a democracy in name but in reality rule by the first citizen. His successors were more equal to each other, and each seeking to become the first man they even offered the conduct of affairs to the whims of the people. This, as was to be expected in a great state ruling an empire, produced many blunders.

In short, after the death of Pericles Athens fell into the hands of demagogues and was ruined. Thucydides does not use the word 'demagogue' in any of the passages I have been discussing. It is an uncommon word with him,[6] as it is in Greek literature generally, and that fact may come as a surprise, for there is no more familiar theme in the Athenian picture (despite the rarity of the word) than the demagogue and his adjutant, the sycophant. The demagogue is a bad thing: to 'lead the people' is to mislead – above all, to mislead by failing to lead. The demagogue is driven by self-interest, by the desire to advance himself in power, and through power, in wealth. To achieve this, he surrenders all principles, all genuine leadership, and he panders to the people in every way – in Thucydides' words, 'even offering the conduct of affairs to the whims of the people'. This picture is drawn not only directly, but also in reverse. Here, for example, is Thucydides' image of the right kind of leader:[7]

> Because of his prestige, intelligence, and known incorruptibility with respect to money, Pericles was able to lead the people as a free man should. He led them instead of being led by them. He did not have to humour them in the pursuit of power; on the contrary, his repute was such that he could contradict them and provoke their anger.

This was not everyone's judgment. Aristotle puts the breakdown earlier: it was after Ephialtes took away the power of the Council of the Areopagus that the passion for demagogy set in. Pericles, he continues, first acquired political influence by prosecuting Cimon for malfeasance in office; he energetically pursued a policy of naval power, 'which gave the lower classes the audacity to take over the leadership in politics more and more'; and he introduced pay for jury service, thus bribing the people with their own money. These were demagogic practices and they brought Pericles to power, which, Aristotle agrees, he then used well and properly.[8]

But my interest is neither in evaluating Pericles as an individual nor in examining the lexicography of demagogy. The Greek political vocabulary was normally vague and imprecise, apart from formal titles for individual offices or bodies (and often enough not even then). The word *demos* was itself ambiguous; among its meanings, however, was one which came to dominate literary usage, namely 'the common people', 'the lower classes', and that sense provided the overtones in 'demagogues' – they became leaders of the state thanks to the backing of the common people. All writers accepted the need for political leadership as axiomatic; their problem was to distinguish between good and bad types. With respect to Athens and its democracy, the word 'demagogue' under-

---

[5] Thuc., 2.65.9–11.

[6] Used only in 4.21.3, and 'demagogy' in 8.65.2.

[7] Thuc., 2.65.8.

[8] *Const. of Athens*, 27–28; cf. *Pol.*, 2.9.3 (1274a3–10). A.W. Gomme, *A Historical Commentary on Thucydides* (Oxford, 1956), ii p.193, points out that 'Plutarch divided Perikles' political career sharply into two halves, the first when he did use base demagogic arts to gain power, the second when he had gained it and used it nobly'.

standably became the simplest way of identifying the bad type, and it does not matter in the least whether the word appears in any given text or not. I suppose it was Aristophanes who established the model in his portrayal of Cleon, yet he never directly applied the noun 'demagogue' to him or anyone else;[9] similarly with Thucydides, who surely thought that Cleophon, Hyperbolus, and some, if not all, of the orators responsible for the Sicilian disaster were demagogues, but who never attached the word to any of these men.

It is important to stress the word 'type', for the issue raised by Greek writers is one of the essential *qualities* of the leader, not (except very secondarily) his techniques or technical competence, not even (except in a very generalized way) his programme and policies. The crucial distinction is between the man who gives leadership with nothing else in mind but the good of the state, and the man whose self-interest makes his own position paramount and urges him to pander to the people. The former may make a mistake and adopt the wrong policy in any given situation; the latter may at times make sound proposals, as when Alcibiades dissuaded the fleet at Samos from jeopardizing the naval position by rushing back to Athens in 411 BC to overthrow the oligarchs who had seized power there, an action to which Thucydides gave explicit approval.[10] But these are not fundamental distinctions. Nor are other traits attributed to individual demagogues: Cleon's habit of shouting when addressing the Assembly, personal dishonesty in money matters, and so on. Such things merely sharpen the picture. From Aristophanes to Aristotle, the attack on the demagogues always falls back on the one central question: in whose interest does the leader lead?

Behind this formulation of the question lay three propositions. The first is that men are unequal – both in their moral worth and capability and in their social and economic status. The second is that any community tends to divide into factions, the most fundamental of which are the rich and well-born on one side, the poor on the other, each with its own qualities, potentialities, and interests. The third proposition is that the well-ordered and well-run state is one which overrides faction and serves as an instrumentality for the good life.

Faction is the greatest evil and the most common danger. 'Faction' is a conventional English translation of the Greek *stasis*, one of the most remarkable words to be found in any language. Its root-sense is 'placing', 'setting' or 'stature', 'station'. Its range of political meanings can best be illustrated by merely stringing out the definitions to be found in the lexicon: 'party', 'party formed for seditious purposes', 'faction', 'sedition', 'discord', 'division', 'dissent', and, finally, a well-attested meaning which the lexicon incomprehensibly omits, namely, 'civil war' or 'revolution'. Unlike 'demagogue', *stasis* is a very common word in the literature, and its connotation is regularly pejorative. Oddly enough, it is also the most neglected concept in modern study of Greek history. It has not been observed often enough or sharply enough, I believe, that there must be deep significance in the fact that a word which has the original sense of 'station' or 'position', and which, in abstract logic, could have an equally neutral sense when used in a political context, in practice does nothing of the kind, but immediately takes on the nastiest overtones. A political position, a partisan position – that is the inescapable implication – is a bad thing, leading to sedition, civil war, and the disruption of the social fabric.[11] And this same tendency is repeated throughout the language. There is no eternal law, after all, why 'demagogue', a 'leader of the people', must become 'mis-leader of the people'. Or why *hetairia*, an old Greek word which meant, among other things, 'club' or 'society', should in fifth-century Athens have come simultaneously to mean

---

[9] Aristophanes uses 'demagogy' and 'demagogic' once each in the *Knights*, lines 191 and 217, respectively. Otherwise in his surviving plays there is only the verb 'to be a demagogue', also used once (*Frogs*, 419).

[10] Thuc., 8.86.

[11] The only systematic analysis known to me, and that a brief one, is the inaugural lecture of D. Loenen, *Stasis* (Amsterdam, 1953). He saw, contrary to the view most common among modern writers, that 'illegality is precisely not the *constant* element in *stasis*' (p.5).

'conspiracy', 'seditious organization'. Whatever the explanation, it lies not in philology but in Greek society itself.

No one who has read the Greek political writers can have failed to notice the unanimity of approach in this respect. Whatever the disagreements among them, they all insist that the state must stand outside class or other factional interests. Its aims and objectives are moral ones, timeless and universal, and they can be achieved – more correctly, approached or approximated – only by education, moral conduct (especially on the part of those in authority), morally correct legislation, and the choice of the right governors. The existence of classes and interests as an empirical fact is, of course, not denied. What is denied is that the choice of political goals can legitimately be linked with these classes and interests, or that the good of the state can be advanced except by ignoring (if not suppressing) private interests.

It was Plato, of course, who pursued this line of its reasoning to its most radical solutions. In the *Gorgias* he had argued that not even the great Athenian political figures of the past – Miltiades, Themistocles, Cimon and Pericles –were true statesmen. They had merely been more accomplished than their successors in gratifying the desires of the *demos* with ships and walls and dockyards. They had failed to make the citizens better men, and to call them 'statesmen' was therefore to confuse the pastrycook with the doctor.[12] Then, in the *Republic*, Plato proposed to concentrate all power in the hands of a small, select, appropriately educated class, who were to be freed from all special interests by the most radical measures, by the abolition insofar as they were concerned of both private property and the family. Only under those conditions would they behave as perfect moral agents, leading the state to its proper goals without the possibility that any self-interest might intrude. Plato, to be sure, was the most untypical of men. One does not safely generalize from Plato; not only not to all Greeks, but not even to any other single Greek. Who else shared his passionate conviction that qualified experts – philosophers – could make (and should therefore be empowered to enforce) universally correct and authoritative decisions about the good life, the life of virtue, which was the sole end of the state?[13] Yet on the one point with which I am immediately concerned – private interests and the state – Plato stood on common ground with many Greek writers (much as they disagreed with him on the answers). In the great final scene of Aeschylus' *Eumenides* the chorus expresses the doctrine explicitly: the welfare of the state can rest only on harmony and freedom from faction. Thucydides implies this more than once.[14]

The most empirical of Greek philosophers, Aristotle collected vast quantities of data about the actual workings of Greek states, including facts about *stasis*. The *Politics* includes an elaborate taxonomy of *stasis*, and even advice on how *stasis* can be avoided under a variety of conditions. But Aristotle's canons and goals were ethical, his work a branch of moral philosophy. He viewed political behaviour teleologically, according to the moral ends which are man's by his nature; and those ends are subverted if the governors make their decisions out of personal or class interest. That is the test by which he distinguished between the three 'right' forms of government ('according to absolute justice') and their degenerate forms: monarchy becomes tyranny when an individual rules in his own interest rather than in the interest of the whole state, aristocracy similarly becomes oligarchy, and polity becomes democracy (or, in the language of Polybius, democracy becomes mob-rule).[15] Among democracies, furthermore, those in rural communities will be superior because farmers are too occupied

---

[12] *Gorgias*, 502E–519D.

[13] See R. Bambrough, 'Plato's political analogies', in *Philosophy, Politics and Society*, ed. Peter Laslett (Oxford, 1956), pp.98–115.

[14] It is developed most fully in his long account (3.69–85) of the *stasis* in Corcyra in 427 BC. And it underlies the theory of the mixed constitution as we find it in Aristotle's Politis.

[15] Arist., *Pol.*, 3.4–5 (1278b–79b), 4.6–7 (1293b–94b); Polyb., 6.3–9.

to bother with meetings, whereas urban craftsmen and shopkeepers find it easy to attend, and such people 'are generally a bad lot'.[16]

On this matter of special interest and general interest, of faction and concord, the available exceptions to the line of thinking I have summarized are strikingly few and unrewarding. One deserves particular mention, and that, ironically enough, is the pamphlet on the Athenian state by an anonymous writer of the later half of the fifth century BC who now generally goes under the too amiable label of the Old Oligarch. This work is a diatribe against the democracy, hammering at the theme that the system is a bad one because all its actions are determined by the interests of the poorer (inferior) sections of the citizenry. The argument is familiar enough; what gives the pamphlet its unusual interest is this conclusion:[17]

> As for the Athenian system of government, I do not like it. However, since they decided to become a democracy, it seems to me that they are preserving the democracy well by the methods I have described.

In other words, the strength of the Athenian government comes precisely from that which many merely criticize, namely, the fact that it is government by a faction acting unashamedly to its own advantage.

The great difference between political analysis and moral judgment could not be better exemplified. Do not be misled, says the Old Oligarch in effect: I and some of you dislike democracy, but a reasoned consideration of the facts shows that what we condemn on moral grounds is very strong as a practical force, and its strength lies in its immorality. This is a very promising line of investigation, but it was not pursued in antiquity. Instead, those thinkers whose orientation was anti-democratic persisted in their concentration on political philosophy. And those who sided with the democracy? A.H.M. Jones has recently tried to formulate the democratic theory from the fragmentary evidence available in the surviving literature, most of it from the fourth century.[18] Still more recently, Eric Havelock made a massive attempt to discover what he calls the 'liberal temper' in fifth-century Athenian politics, chiefly from the fragments of the pre-Socratic philosophers. In reviewing his book, Momigliano suggested that the effort was foredoomed because 'it is not absolutely certain that a well-articulated democratic idea existed in the fifth century'.[19] I go further: I do not believe that an articulated democratic theory ever existed in Athens. There were notions, maxims, generalities – which Jones has assembled – but they do not add up to a systematic theory. And why indeed should they? It is a curious fallacy to suppose that every social or governmental system in history must necessarily have been accompanied by an elaborate theoretical system. Where that does occur it is often the work of lawyers, and Athens had no jurists in the proper sense. Or it may be the work of philosophers, but the systematic philosophers of this period had a set of concepts and values incompatible with democracy. The committed democrats met the attack by ignoring it, by going about the business of conducting their political affairs according to their own notions, but without writing treatises on what they were about. None of this, however, is a reason why we should not attempt to make the analysis the Athenians failed to make for themselves.

No account of the Athenian democracy can have any validity if it overlooks four points, each obvious in itself, yet all four taken together, I venture to say, are rarely given sufficient weight in modern accounts. The first is that this was a direct democracy, and however much such a system may have in common

---

[16] Arist., *Pol.*, 6.2.7–8 (1319a); cf. Xen., *Hell.*, 5.2.5–7.

[17] Pseudo-Xenophon, *Const. of Athens*, 3.1; see A. Fuks, 'The "Old Oligarch"', *Scripta Hierosolymitana*, i (1954), pp.21–35.

[18] *Athenian Democracy* (Oxford, 1957), ch. iii.

[19] E.A. Havelock, *The Liberal Temper in Greek Politics* (London, 1957), reviewed by A. Momigliano in *RSI*, lxxii (1960), pp.534–41.

with representative democracy, the two differ in certain fundamental respects, and particularly on the very issues with which I am here concerned. The second point is what Ehrenberg calls the 'narrowness of space' of the Greek city-state, an appreciation of which, he has rightly stressed, is crucial to an understanding of its political life.[20] The implications were summed up by Aristotle in a famous passage:[21]

> A state composed of too many ... will not be a true state, for the simple reason that it can hardly have a true constitution. Who can be the general of a mass so excessively large? And who can be herald, except Stentor?

The third point is that the Assembly was the crown of the system, possessing the right and the power to make all the policy decisions, in actual practice with few limitations, whether of precedent or scope. (Strictly speaking there was appeal from the Assembly to the popular courts with their large lay membership. Nevertheless, I ignore the courts in much, though not all, of what follows, because I believe, as the Athenians did themselves, that, though they complicated the practical mechanism of politics, the courts were an expression, not a reduction, of the absolute power of the people functioning directly: and because I believe that the operational analysis I am trying to make would not be significantly altered and would perhaps be obscured if in this brief compass I did not concentrate on the Assembly.) The Assembly, finally, was nothing other than an open-air mass meeting on the hill called the Pnyx, and the fourth point therefore is that we are dealing with problems of crowd behaviour; its psychology, its laws of behaviour, could not have been identical with those of the small group, or even of the larger kind of body of which a modern parliament is an example (though, it must be admitted, we can do little more today than acknowledge their existence).

Who were the Assembly? That is a question we cannot answer satisfactorily. Every male citizen automatically became eligible to attend when he reached his eighteenth birthday, and he retained that privilege to his death (except for the very small number who lost their civic rights for one reason or another). In Pericles' time the number eligible was of the order of 45,000. Women were excluded; so were the fairly numerous non-citizens who were free men, nearly all of them Greeks, but outsiders in the political sphere; and so were the far more numerous slaves. All figures are a guess, but it would not be wildly inaccurate to suggest that the adult male citizens comprised about one-sixth of the total population (taking town and countryside together). But the critical question to be determined is which four or five or six thousand of the 45,000 actually went to meetings. It is reasonable to imagine that under normal conditions the attendance came chiefly from the urban residents. Fewer peasants would often have taken the journey in order to attend a meeting of the Assembly.[22] Therefore one large section of the eligible population was, with respect to direct participation, excluded. That is something to know, but it does not get us far enough. We can guess, for example, with the aid of a few hints in the sources, that the composition was normally weighted on the side of the more aged and the more well-to-do men – but that is only a guess, and the degree of weighting is beyond even guessing.

Still, one important fact can be fixed, namely, that each meeting of the Assembly was unique in its composition. There was no membership in the Assembly as such, only membership in a given Assembly on a given day. Perhaps the shifts were not significant from meeting to meeting in quiet, peaceful times when no vital issues were being debated. Yet even then an important element of predictability was lacking. When he entered the Assembly, no policy-maker could be

[20] *Aspects of the Ancient World* (Oxford, 1946), pp.40–5.

[21] *Pol.*, 7.4.7 (1326b3–7).

[22] That Aristotle drew very important conclusions from this state of affairs has already been indicated, at note 16.

quite sure that a change in the composition of the audience had not occurred, whether through accident or through more or less organized mobilization of some particular sector of the population, which could tip the balance of the votes against a decision made at a previous meeting. And times were often neither peaceful nor normal. In the final decade of the Peloponnesian War, to take an extreme example, the whole rural population was compelled to abandon the countryside and live within the city walls. It is beyond reasonable belief that during this period there was not a larger proportion of countrymen at meetings than was normal. A similar situation prevailed for briefer periods at other times, when an enemy army was operating in Attica. We need not interpret Aristophanes literally when he opens the *Acharnians* with a soliloquy by a farmer who is sitting in the Pnyx waiting for the Assembly to begin and saying to himself how he hates the city and everyone in it and how he intends to shout down any speaker who proposes anything except peace. But Cleon could not have afforded the luxury of ignoring this strange element seated on the hillside before him. They might upset a policy line which he had been able to carry while the Assembly was filled only with city-dwellers.

The one clearcut instance came in the year 411. Then the Assembly was terrorized into voting the democracy out of existence, and it was surely no accident that this occurred at a time when the fleet was fully mobilized and stationed on the island of Samos. The citizens who served in the navy were drawn from the poor and they were known to be the staunchest supporters of the democratic system in its late fifth-century form. Being in Samos, they could not be in Athens, thus enabling the oligarchs to win the day through a majority in the Assembly which was not only a minority of the eligible members but an untypical minority. Our sources do not permit us to study the history of Athenian policy systematically with such knowledge at our disposal, but surely the men who led Athens were acutely aware of the possibility of a change in the composition of the Assembly, and included it in their tactical calculations.

Each meeting, furthermore, was complete in itself. Granted that much preparatory work was done by the Council (*boule*), that informal canvassing took place, and that there were certain devices to control and check frivolous or irresponsible motions, it is nevertheless true that the normal procedure was for a proposal to be introduced, debated, and either passed (with or without amendment) or rejected in a single continuous sitting. We must reckon, therefore, not only with narrowness of space but also with narrowness of time, and with the pressures that generated, especially on leaders (and would-be leaders). I have already mentioned the case of the Sicilian expedition, which was decided in principle on one day and then planned, so to speak, five days later when the scale and cost were discussed and voted. Another kind of case is that of the well-known Mytilene debate. Early in the Peloponnesian War the city of Mytilene revolted from the Athenian Empire. The rebellion was crushed and the Athenian Assembly decided to make an example of the Mytileneans by putting the entire male population to death. Revulsion of feeling set in at once, the issue was reopened at another meeting the very next day, and the decision was reversed.[23] Cleon, at that time the most important political figure in Athens, advocated the policy of frightfulness. The second Assembly was a personal defeat for him – he had participated in the debates on both days – though he seems not to have lost his status even temporarily as a result (as he well might have). But how does one measure the psychological effect on him of such a twenty-four hour reversal? How does estimate not only its impact, but also his awareness all through his career as a leader that such a possibility was a constant factor in Athenian politics? I cannot answer such questions concretely, but I submit that the weight could have been no light one. Cleon surely appreciated, as we cannot, what it promised for men like himself that in the second year of the Peloponnesian War, when morale was temporarily shattered by the plague, the people turned on Pericles, fined him heavily, and deposed him for a

[23] Thuc. 3.27–50.

brief period from the office of general.[24] If this could happen to Pericles, who was immune?

In the Mytilene case Thucydides' account suggests that Cleon's was a lost cause the second day, that he tried to persuade the Assembly to abandon a course of action which they intended to pursue from the moment the session opened, and that he failed. But the story of the meeting in 411, as Thucydides tells it, is a different one. Peisander began the day with the feeling against his proposal that the introduction of an oligarchical form of government should be considered, and he ended it with a victory. The actual debate had swung enough votes to give him a majority.[25]

Debate designed to win votes among an outdoor audience numbering several thousands means oratory, in the strict sense of the word. It was therefore perfectly precise language to call political leaders 'orators', as a synonym and not merely, as we might do, as a mark of the particular skill of a particular political figure. Under Athenian conditions, however, much more is implied. The picture of the Assembly I have been trying to draw suggests not only oratory, but also a 'spontaneity' of debate and decision which parliamentary democracy lacks, at least in our day.[26] Everyone, speakers and audience alike, knew that before night fell the issue must be decided, that each man present would vote 'freely' (without fear of whips or other party controls) and purposefully, and therefore that every speech, every argument must seek to persuade the audience on the spot, that it was all a serious performance, as a whole and in each of its parts.

I place the word 'freely' in inverted commas, for the last thing I wish to imply is the activity of a free, disembodied rational faculty, that favourite illusion of so much political theory since the Enlightenment. Members of the Assembly were free from the controls which bind the members of a parliament: they held no office, they were not elected, and therefore they could neither be punished nor rewarded for their voting records. But they were not free from the human condition, from habit and tradition, from the influences of family and friends, of class and status, of personal experiences, resentments, prejudices, values, aspirations, and fears, much of it in the subconscious. These they took with them when they went up on the Pnyx, and with these they listened to the debates and made up their minds, under conditions very different from the voting practices of our day. There is a vast difference between voting on infrequent occasions for a man or a party on the one hand, and on the other hand voting every few days directly on the issues themselves. In Aristotle's time the Assembly met at least four times in each thirty-six-day period. Whether this was also the rule in the fifth century is not known, but there were occasions, as during the Peloponnesian War, when meetings took place even more frequently. Then there were the two other factors I have already mentioned, the smallness of the Athenian world, in which every member of the Assembly knew personally many others sitting on the Pnyx, and the mass-meeting background of the voting – a situation virtually unrelated to the impersonal act of marking a voting paper in physical isolation from every other voter; an act we perform, furthermore, with the knowledge that millions of other men and women are simultaneously doing the same thing in many places, some of them hundreds of miles distant. When, for example, Alcibiades and Nicias rose in the Assembly in 415, the one to propose the expedition against Sicily, the other to argue against it, each knew that, should the motion be carried, one or both would be asked to command in the field. And in the audience there were many who were being asked to vote on whether they, personally, were to march out in a few days, as officers, soldiers, or members of the fleet. Such examples can be duplicated in a number of other, scarcely less vital areas: taxation, food supply, pay for jury duty, extension of the franchise, laws of citizenship, and so on.

[24] Thuc., 2.65.1–4.

[25] Thuc., 8.53–54.

[26] See the valuable article by O. Reverdin, 'Remarques sur la vie politique d'Athènes au Ve siècle', *Museum Helveticum*, ii (1945), pp.201–12.

To be sure, much of the activity of the Assembly was in a lower key, largely occupied with technical measures (such as cult regulations) or ceremonial acts (such as honorary decrees for a great variety of individuals). It would be a mistake to imagine Athens as a city in which week in and week out great issues dividing the population were being debated and decided. But on the other hand, there were very few single years (and certainly no ten-year periods) in which some great issue did not arise: the two Persian invasions, the long series of measures which completed the process of democratization, the Empire, the Peloponnesian War (which occupied twenty-seven years) and its two oligarchic interludes, the endless diplomatic manoeuvres and wars of the fourth century, with their attendant fiscal crises, all culminating in the decades of Philip and Alexander. It did not often happen, as it did to Cleon in the dispute over Mytilene, that a politician was faced with a repeat performance the following day; but the Assembly did meet constantly, without long periods of holiday or recess. The week-by-week conduct of a war, for example, had to go before the Assembly week by week; as if Winston Churchill were to have been compelled to take a referendum before each move in World War II, and then to face another vote after the move was made, in the Assembly or the law-courts, to determine not merely what the next step should be but also whether he was to be dismissed and his plans abandoned, or even whether he was to be held criminally culpable, subject to a fine or exile or, conceivably, the death penalty either for the proposal itself or for the way the previous move had been carried out. It was part of the Athenian governmental system that, in addition to the endless challenge in the Assembly, a politician was faced, equally without respite, with the threat of politically inspired lawsuits.[27]

If I insist on the psychological aspect, it is not to ignore the considerable political experience of many men who voted in the Assembly – gained in the Council, the law-courts, the *demes*, and the Assembly itself – nor is it merely to counter what I have called the disembodied-rationalism conception. I want to stress something very positive, namely, the intense degree of involvement which attendance at the Athenian Assembly entailed. And this intensity was equally (or even more strongly) the case among the orators, for each vote judged them as well as the issue to be decided on. If I had to choose one word which best characterized the condition of being a political leader in Athens, that word would be 'tension'. In some measure that is true of all politicians who are subject to a vote. 'The desperateness of politics and government' is R.B. McCallum's telling phrase, which he then developed in this way:[28]

> Certainly a note of cynicism and weariness with the manoeuvres and posturings of party politicians is natural and to an extent proper to discerning dons and civil servants, who can reflect independently and at leisure on the doings of their harried masters in government. But this seems to arise from a deliberate rejection ... of the aims and ideals of party statesmen and their followers and the continual responsibility for the security and well-being in the state. For one thing party leaders are in some sense apostles, although all may not be Gladstones; there are policies to which they dedicate themselves and policies which alarm and terrify them.

I believe this to be a fair description of Athenian leaders, too, despite the absence of political parties, equally applicable to Themistocles as to Aristides, to Pericles as to Cimon, to Cleon as to Nicias; for, it should be obvious, this kind of judgment is independent of any judgment about the merits or weaknesses of a particular programme or policy. More accurately, I should have said that this understates the case for the Athenians. Their leaders had no respite. Because

---

[27] P. Cloché, 'Les hommes politiques et la justice populaire dans l'Athènes du IVe siècle', *Historia*, ix (1960), pp.80–95, has recently argued that this threat is exaggerated by modern historians, at least for the fourth century. Useful as his assembling of the evidence is, he lays too much stress on the argument from silence, whereas the sources are far from full enough to bear such statistical weight.

[28] A review in the *Listener* (2 February 1961), p.233.

their influence had to be earned and exerted directly and immediately – this was a necessary consequence of a direct, as distinct from a representative, democracy – they had to lead in person, and they had also to bear, in person, the brunt of the opposition's attacks. More than that, they walked alone. They had their lieutenants, of course, and politicians made alliances with each other. But these were fundamentally personal links, shifting frequently, useful in helping to carry through a particular measure or even a group of measures, but lacking that quality of support, that buttressing or cushioning effect, which is provided by a bureaucracy and political party, in another way by an institutionalized Establishment like the Roman Senate, or in still another way by large-scale patronage as in the Roman clientage system. The critical point is that there was no 'government' in the modern sense. There were posts and offices, but none had any standing in the Assembly. A man was a leader solely as a function of his personal, and in the literal sense, unofficial status within the Assembly itself. The test of whether or not he held that status was simply whether the Assembly did or did not vote as he wished, and therefore the test was repeated with each proposal.

These were the conditions which faced all leaders in Athens, not merely those whom Thucydides and Plato dismissed as 'demagogues', not merely those whom some modern historians miscall 'radical democrats', but everyone, aristocrat or commoner, altruist or self-seeker, able or incompetent, who, in George Grote's phrase, 'stood forward prominently to advise' the Athenians. No doubt the motives which moved men to stand forward varied greatly. But that does not matter in this context, for each one of them without exception, *chose* to aspire to, and actively to work and contest for, leadership, knowing just what that entailed, including the risks. Within narrow limits, they all had to use the same techniques, too. Cleon's platform manner may have been inelegant and boisterous, but how serious is Aristotle's remark that he was the first man to 'shout and rail'?[29] Are we to imagine that Thucydides the son of Melesias (and kinsman of the historian) and Nicias whispered when they addressed the Assembly in opposition to Pericles and Cleon, respectively? Thucydides, who brought his upper-class backers into the Assembly and seated them to form a claque?[30]

This is obviously a frivolous approach, nothing more than the expression of class prejudice and snobbishness. As Aristotle noted, the death of Pericles marked a turning-point in the social history of Athenian leadership. Until then they seem to have been drawn from the old aristocratic landed families, including the men who were responsible for carrying out the reforms which completed the democracy. After Pericles a new class of leaders emerged.[31] Despite the familiar prejudicial references to Cleon the tanner or Cleophon the lyre-maker, these were in fact not poor men, not craftsmen and labourers turned politician, but men of means who differed from their predecessors in their ancestry and their outlook, and who provoked resentment and hostility for their presumption in breaking the old monopoly of leadership. When such attitudes are under discussion, one can always turn to Xenophon to find the lowest level of explanation (which is not therefore necessarily the wrong one). One of the most important of the new leaders was a man called Anytus, who, like Cleon before him, drew his wealth from a slave tannery. Anytus had a long and distinguished career, but he was also the chief actor in the prosecution of Socrates. What is Xenophon's explanation? Simply that Socrates had publicly berated Anytus for bringing up his son to follow in his trade instead of educating him

[29] Arist., *Const.*, 28.3.

[30] Plut., *Pericles*, 11.2. It was against such tactics that the restored democracy in 410 required members of the Council to swear to take their seats by lot: Philochorus 328 F 140 (in *FHG*, ed. F. Jacoby).

[31] Arist., *Const.*, 28.1.

as a proper gentleman, and that Anytus, in revenge for this personal insult, had Socrates tried and executed.[32]

None of this is to deny that there were very fundamental issues behind the thick façade of prejudice and abuse. Throughout the fifth century there were the twin issues of democracy (or oligarchy) and empire, brought to a climax in the Peloponnesian War. Defeat in the war ended the empire and it soon also ended the debate about the kind of government Athens was to have. Oligarchy ceased to be a serious issue in practical politics. It is only the persistence of the philosophers which creates an illusion about it; they continued to argue fifth-century issues in the fourth century, but politically in a vacuum. Down to the middle of the fourth century, the actual policy questions were perhaps less dramatic than before, though not necessarily less vital to the participants – such matters as navy finance, foreign relations both with Persia and with other Greek states, and the ever-present problem of corn supply. Then came the final great conflict, over the rising power of Macedon. That debate went on for some three decades, and it ended only in the year following the death of Alexander the Great when the Macedonian army put an end to democracy itself in Athens.

All these were questions about which men could legitimately disagree, and disagree with passion. On the issues, the arguments of (say) Plato require earnest consideration – but only insofar as he addressed himself to the issues. The injection of the charge of demagogy into the polemic amounts to a resort to the very same unacceptable debating tricks for which the so-called demagogues are condemned. Suppose, for example, that Thucydides was right in attributing Alcibiades' advocacy of the Sicilian expedition to his personal extravagance and to various discreditable private motives. What relevance has that to the merits of the proposal itself? Would the Sicilian expedition, as a war measure, have been a better idea if Alcibiades had been an angelic youth? To ask the question is to dismiss it, and all other such arguments with it. One must dismiss as summarily the objections to oratory: by definition, to wish to lead Athens implies the burden of trying to persuade Athens, and an essential part of that effort consisted in public oratory.

One can draw distinctions, of course. I should concede the label 'demagogue' in its most pejorative sense, for example, if a campaign were built around promises which a clique of orators neither intended to honour nor were capable of honouring. But, significantly enough, this accusation is rarely levelled against the so-called demagogues, and the one definite instance we know comes from the other camp. The oligarchy of 411 was sold to the Athenians on the appeal that this was now the only way to obtain Persian support and thus to win the otherwise lost war. Even on the most favourable view, as Thucydides makes quite clear, Peisander and some of his associates may have meant this originally, but they quickly abandoned all pretence of trying to win the war while they concentrated on preserving the newly won oligarchy on as narrow a base as possible.[33] That is what I should call 'demagogy', if the word is to merit its pejorative flavour. That is 'misleading the people' in the literal sense.

But what then of the interest question, of the supposed clash between the interests of the whole state and the interests of a section or faction within the state? Is that not a valid distinction? It is a pity that we have no direct evidence (and no indirect evidence of any value) about the way the long debate was conducted between 508 BC, when Cleisthenes established the democracy in its primitive form, and the later years of Pericles' dominance. Those were the years when class interests would most likely have been expounded openly and bluntly. Actual speeches survive only from the end of the fifth century on, and they reveal what anyone could have guessed who had not been blinded by Plato and others, namely, that the appeal was customarily a national one, not a

[32] Xen., *Apology,* 30–2. See generally Georges Méautis, *L'aristocratie athénienne* (Paris, 1927).

[33] Thuc., 8.68–91.

factional one. There is little open pandering to the poor against the rich, to the farmers against the town or to the town against the farmers. Why indeed should there have been? Politicians regularly say that what they are advocating is in the best interests of the nation, and, what is much more important, they believe it. Often, too, they charge their opponents with sacrificing the national interest for special interests, and they believe that. I know of no evidence which warrants the view that Athenian politicians were somehow peculiar in this respect; nor do I know any reason to hold that the argument is an essentially different (or better) one because it is put forth not by a politician but by Aristophanes or Thucydides or Plato.

At the same time a politician cannot ignore class or sectional interests or the conflicts among them, whether in a constituency today or in the Assembly in ancient Athens. The evidence for Athens suggests that on many issues – the Empire and the Peloponnesian War, for example, or relations with Philip of Macedon – the divisions over policy did not closely follow class or sectional lines. But other questions, such as the opening of the archonship and other offices to men of the lower property censuses or of pay for jury service or, in the fourth century, the financing of the fleet, or the theoric fund, were by their nature class issues. Advocates on both sides knew this and knew how and when (and when not) to make their appeals accordingly, at the same time that they each argued, and believed, that only their respective points of view would advance Athens as a whole. To plead against Ephialtes and Pericles that *eunomia*, the well-ordered state ruled by law, had the higher moral claim, was merely a plea for the status quo dressed up in fancy language.[34]

In his little book on the Athenian constitution, Aristotle wrote the following:[35]

> Pericles was the first to give pay for jury service, as a demagogic measure to counter the wealth of Cimon. The latter, who possessed the fortune of a tyrant ... supported many of his fellow-demesmen, every one of whom was free to come daily and receive from him enough for his sustenance. Besides, none of his estates was enclosed, so that anyone who wished could take from its fruits. Pericles' property did not permit such largesse, and on the advice of Damonides ... he distributed among the people from what was their own ... and so he introduced pay for the jurors.

Aristotle himself, as I indicated earlier, praised Pericles' regime and he refused responsibility for this silly explanation, but others who repeated it, both before and after him, thought it was a telling instance of demagogy pandering to the common people. The obvious retort is to ask whether what Cimon did was not pandering in equal measure, or whether opposition to pay for jury service was not pandering, too, but in that case to the men of property. No useful analysis is possible in such terms, for they serve only to conceal the real grounds for disagreement. If one is opposed to full democracy as a form of government, then it is wrong to encourage popular participation in the juries by offering pay; but it is wrong because the objective is wrong, not because Pericles obtained leadership status by proposing and carrying the measure. And vice versa, if one favours a democratic system.

What emerges from all this is a very simple proposition, namely, that demagogues – I use the word in a neutral sense – were a structural element in the Athenian political system. By this I mean, first, that the system could not function at all without them; second, that the term is equally applicable to all leaders, regardless of class or point of view; and third, that within rather broad limits they are to be judged individually not by their manners or their methods, but by their performance. (And that, I need hardly add, is precisely how they *were* judged in life, if not in books.) Up to a point one can easily parallel the

[34] 'Eunomia ... the ideal of the past and even of Solon ... now meant the best constitution, based on inequality. It was now the ideal of oligarchy': Ehrenberg, *Aspects*, p.92.

[35] Arist., *Const.*, 27.3–4.

Athenian demagogue with the modern politician, but there soon comes a point when distinctions must be drawn, not merely because the work of government has become so much more complex, but more basically because of differences between a direct and a representative democracy. I need not repeat what I have already said about the mass-meeting (with its uncertain composition), about the lack of a bureaucracy and a party system, and, as a result, the continuous state of tension in which an Athenian demagogue lived and worked. But there is one consequence which needs a little examination, for these conditions make up an important part (if not the whole) of the explanation of an apparently negative feature of Athenian politics, and of Greek politics generally. David Hume put it this way:[36]

> To exclude faction from a free government, is very difficult, if not altogether impracticable; but such inveterate rage between the factions, and such bloody maxims are found, in modern times, amongst religious parties alone. In ancient history we may always observe, where one party prevailed, whether the nobles or people (for I can observe no difference in this respect), that they immediately butchered ... and banished ... No form of process, no law, no trial, no pardon ... These people were extremely fond of liberty, but seem not to have understood it very well.

The remarkable thing about Athens is how near she came to being the complete exception to this correct observation of Hume's, to being free, in other words, from *stasis* in its ultimate meaning. The democracy was established in 508 BC following a brief civil war. Thereafter, in its history of nearly two centuries, armed terror, butchery without process or law, was employed on only two occasions, in 411 and 404, both times by oligarchic factions which seized control of the state for brief periods. And the second time, in particular, the democratic faction, when it regained power, was generous and law-abiding in its treatment of the oligarchs, so much so that they wrung praise even from Plato. Writing about the restoration of 403, he said that 'no one should be surprised that some men took savage personal revenge against their enemies in this revolution, but in general the returning party behaved equitably'.[37] This is not to suggest that the two centuries were totally free from individual acts of injustice and brutality. Hume – speaking of Greece generally and not of Athens in particular – observed 'no difference in this respect' between the factions. We seem to have a less clear vision of Athens, at least, blocked by the distorting mirror of men like Thucydides, Xenophon and Plato, which magnifies the exceptional incidents of extreme democratic intolerance – such as the trial and execution of the generals who won the battle of Arginusae and the trial and execution of Socrates; while it minimizes and often obliterates altogether the even worse behaviour on the other side, for example, the political assassination of Ephialtes in 462 or 461 and of Androcles in 411, each in his time the most influential of the popular leaders.

If Athens largely escaped the extreme forms of *stasis* so common elsewhere, she could not escape its lesser manifestations. Athenian politics had an all-or-nothing quality. The objective on each side was not merely to defeat the opposition but to crush it, to behead it by destroying its leaders. And often enough this game was played within the sides, as a number of men manoeuvred for leadership. The chief technique was the political trial, and the chief instrumentalities were the dining-clubs and the sycophants. These, too, I would argue, were structurally a part of the system, not an accidental or avoidable excrescence. Ostracism, the so-called *graphe paranomon*, and the formal popular scrutiny of archons, generals and other officials, were all deliberately introduced as safety devices, either against excessive individual power (and potential tyranny) or against corruption and malfeasance or against unthinking haste

[36]'Of the populousness of ancient nations', in *Essays*, World's Classics edn (London, 1903), pp.405–6. Cf. Jacob Burckhardt, *Griechische Kulturgeschichte* (reprint Darmstadt, 1956), i, pp.80–1.

[37] *Epist.*, VII 325B; cf. Xen., *Hell.*, 2.4.43; Arist., *Const.*, 40.

and passion in the Assembly itself.[38] Abstractly it may be easy enough to demonstrate that, however praiseworthy in intention, these devices inevitably invited abuse. The trouble is that they were the only kind of device available, again because the democracy was a direct one, lacking a party machinery and so forth. Leaders and would-be leaders had no alternative but to make use of them, and to seek out still other ways of harassing and breaking competitors and opponents.

Hard as this all-out warfare no doubt was on the participants, unfair and vicious on occasion, it does not follow that it was altogether an evil for the community as a whole. Substantial inequalities, serious conflicts of interest, and legitimate divergences of opinion were real and intense. Under such conditions, conflict is not only inevitable, it is a virtue in democratic politics, for it is conflict combined with consent, and not consent alone, which preserves democracy from eroding into oligarchy. On the constitutional issue which dominated so much of the fifth century it was the advocates of popular democracy who triumphed, and they did so precisely because they fought for it and fought hard. They fought a partisan fight, and the Old Oligarch made the correct diagnosis in attributing Athenian strength to just that. Of course, his insight, or perhaps his honesty, did not extend so far as to note the fact that in his day the democracy's leaders were still men of substance, and often of aristocratic background: not only Pericles, but Cleon and Cleophon, and then Thrasybulus and Anytus. The two latter led the democratic faction in overthrowing the Thirty Tyrants in 403, and in following their victory with the amnesty which even Plato praised. The partisan right was not a straight class fight; it also drew support from among the rich and the well-born. Nor was it a fight without rules or legitimacy. The democratic counter-slogan to *eunomia* was *isonomia*, and, as Vlastos has said, the Athenians pursued 'the goal of political equality ... not in defiance, but in support of the rule of law'. The Athenian poor, he noted, did not once raise the standard Greek revolutionary demand – redistribution of the land – throughout the fifth and fourth centuries.[39]

In those two centuries Athens was, by all pragmatic tests, much the greatest Greek state, with a powerful feeling of community, with a toughness and resilience tempered, even granted its imperial ambitions, by a humanity and sense of equity and responsibility quite extraordinary for its day (and for many another day as well). Lord Acton, paradoxically enough, was one of the few historians to have grasped the historic significance of the amnesty of 403. 'The hostile parties', he wrote, 'were reconciled, and proclaimed an amnesty, the first in history'.[40] *The first in history*, despite all the familiar weaknesses, despite the crowd psychology, the slaves, the personal ambition of many leaders, the impatience of the majority with opposition. Nor was this the only Athenian innovation: the structure and mechanism of the democracy were all their own invention, as they groped for something without precedent, having nothing to

---

[38] The fourth-century legislative procedure by means of *nomothetai* could properly be added to this list; see A.R.W. Harrison, 'Law-making at Athens at the end of the fifth century BC', *JHS*, lxxv (1955), pp.26–35.

[39] G. Vlastos, 'Isonomia', *AJP*, lxxiv (1953), pp.337–66. Cf. Jones, *Democracy*, p.52: 'In general ... democrats tended like Aristotle to regard the laws as a code laid down once for all by a wise legislator ... which, immutable in principle, might occasionally require to be clarified or supplemented'. The 'rule of law' is a complicated subject on its own, but it is not the subject of this paper. Nor is the evaluation of individual demagogues, e.g. Cleon, on whom see most recently A.G. Woodhead, 'Thucydides' portrait of Cleon', *Mnemosyne*, 4th ser., xiii (1960), pp. 289–317; A. Andrewes, 'The Mytilene debate', *Phoenix*, xvi (1962), pp.64–85.

[40] 'The history of freedom in antiquity', in *Essays on Freedom and Power*, ed. G. Himmelfarb (London, 1956), p.64. The paradox can be extended: in reviewing Grote, John Stuart Mill wrote about the years leading up to the oligarchic coups of 411 and 404: 'The Athenian Many, of whose democratic irritability and suspicion we hear so much, are rather to be accused of too easy and good-natured a confidence, when we reflect that they had living in the midst of them the very men who, on the first show of an opportunity, were ready to compass the subversion of the democracy...': *Dissertations and Discussions*, ii (London, 1859), p.540.

M.I. Finley

go on but their own notion of freedom, their community solidarity, their willingness to inquire (or at least to accept the consequences of inquiry), and their widely shared political experience.

Much of the credit for the Athenian achievement must go to the political leadership of the state. That, it seems to me, is beyond dispute. It certainly would not have been disputed by the average Athenian. Despite all the tensions and uncertainties, the occasional snap judgment and unreasonable shift in opinion, the people supported Pericles for more than two decades, as they supported a very different kind of man, Demosthenes, under very different conditions a century later. These men, and others like them (less well known now), were able to carry through a more or less consistent and successful programme over long stretches of time. It is altogether perverse to ignore this fact, or to ignore the structure of political life by which Athens became what she was, while one follows the lead of Aristophanes or Plato and looks only at the personalities of the politicians, or at the crooks and failures among them, or at some ethical norms of an ideal existence.

In the end Athens lost her freedom and independence, brought down by a superior external power. She went down fighting, with an understanding of what was at stake clearer than that possessed by many critics in later ages. That final struggle was led by Demosthenes, a demagogue. We cannot have it both ways: we cannot praise and admire the achievement of two centuries, and at the same time dismiss the demagogues who were the architects of the political framework and the makers of policy, or the Assembly in and through which they did their work.[41]

---

[41] See most recently W.R. Connor, *The New Politicians of Fifth-Century Athens* (Princeton, 1971), and my *Democracy Ancient and Modern* (London, 1973).

RELIGION AND THE NEW EDUCATION: THE CHALLENGE OF THE SOPHISTS

Source: Easterling, P. and Muir, J.V. (eds) (1985) *Greek Religion and Society*, Cambridge University Press, pp.191–218 and 228–30.

By J.V. Muir

> We are reaping what was sown in the Sixties. The fashionable theories and permissive claptrap set the scene for a society in which the old virtues of discipline and self-restraint were denigrated. Parents, teachers and other adults need to set clear, consistent limits to the behaviour of children and young people. Children need, respond to and too often lack clear rules.

> (Mrs Margaret Thatcher, reported in the *Sunday Times*, 28 March 1982)

> How sweet it is to be a part of novel and intelligent developments, and to despise the established rules!

> (Pheidippides in Aristophanes, *Clouds* 1399–400)

The feeling that some of the most important things which bind society together are being mocked or abandoned by the young is a symptom of an older generation which has begun to lose its self-confidence. There is the fear that young people are being seduced from the enclosure into forbidden and highly dangerous territory and must be brought back within the limits – a panic nostalgia for a more controllable, safe and stable world. Such sentiments would have been intelligible to many Athenians in the last quarter of the fifth century BC; their city had emerged proudly victorious from the Persian Wars and had seen the rapid expansion of artistic, intellectual, political and economic horizons. Great works of art and literature, increased prosperity, an empire, a participatory democracy, the records of an heroic past, all contributed to the feeling that Athens was at the centre of the world, there to teach others – the school of Hellas. Pericles' Funeral Speech in Thucydides' history recreates this idealized vision of an open society in which toughness and sensibility, adventure and steady calculation, the acknowledgement of excellence and a regard for every individual are held in even balance, and for a few years it was even possible to glimpse the idea of continuous human progress.[1] The war with Sparta which dragged on from 431 to 404 BC with intervals of unsatisfactory peace changed this mood for good and spoilt the vision. There were of course ups and downs, but a series of disasters like the two plagues at the start of the war which reduced the population by as much as a third, the systematic destruction of the farms of Attica year by year, and eventually the failure and annihilation of the great task-force sent to Sicily in 415 BC introduced strident notes of war-weariness and recrimination. Something had gone badly wrong – the standards which had fortified the troops at Marathon and made Athens glorious were no longer upheld. Technical mistakes made by politicians or soldiers were a question of competence, but, when it came to other matters which could be taken as root causes of the trouble, something else was felt to be involved.

At such times it is not uncommon for a decline in religious belief amongst young people together with lapses in moral standards to be taken as both symptoms and prime causes of a more general failure. Two results often follow: first, an accentuation of the 'generation-gap', and, second, a determined and sometimes vindictive hunt for the culprit or culprits. Such a mood was clearly detectable in the latter part of the fifth century in Athens and it is the purpose of this chapter to follow its progress. Well-to-do young men appeared to be embracing dangerous ideas which set them apart from their parents and led them to disregard the beliefs and practices of traditional religion – in extreme cases they even toyed with outright atheism. Traditional moral and social standards

---

[1] Thucydides 2.35–46; E.R. Dodds, *The Ancient Concept of Progress* (Oxford, 1973) 1–13.

were likewise at risk when the new, ambitious generation seemed willing to accept and practise outrageous extremes of ruthless selfishness. Who was responsible? The answer seemed ready to hand, for this phenomenon had an obvious connection with a new and influential development in education (teachers are favourite scapegoats at such moments) – the appearance of the Sophists, those itinerant educators and lecturers who came from various parts of the Greek world to excite, to teach and (in the view of many) to corrupt young men on the verge of manhood. They taught a variety of subjects, the stock-in-trade of most of them being rhetoric, the art of speaking, but it was in the area of morals and religion that their teaching was felt to have the most serious results, and it was for this that some of them were persecuted and condemned.[2] Socrates, who was a part of this same intellectual and educational movement, though at variance with the Sophists in several important ways, died precisely because he had been prosecuted on the twin charges of corrupting the young and maintaining an unacceptable attitude towards religion.

It is first necessary to ask why religion especially was felt to be such a fundamental part of Greek life that the questioning and undermining of it could be seen as posing serious dangers to the whole fabric of society.[3] The reason lies in a curious paradox. Many of the great religions of the modern world have a system of organization which (allowing for wide national variations) is centralized and remarkably uniform. They have a professional priesthood, a central core of sacred writings, common forms of worship and a common stock of dogma and belief. Religion in the Greek world had little or none of this centralism. Priesthood was usually not a full-time occupation – many priesthoods were tenable for only one year and could be variously obtained through birth, election, lot or even purchase; no special qualifications were needed and the priest was not the servant or the representative of some larger corporate body. As might be expected, in earlier times hereditary priesthoods had often been the preserve of aristocratic families like the Eumolpidai at Eleusis or the Asklepiadai on Kos but, by the early fourth century, Isocrates could confidently say 'Any man is thought qualified to be a priest'.[4] Likewise there was very little that could be described as holy scripture or sacred writings. Homer is sometimes cast in this role by modern critics,[5] but though the social functions of the *Iliad* and the *Odyssey* may bear some loose resemblances to the functions of the Bible at some periods of history, they were never read out to the faithful in a temple or commended by priests for private study and meditation. Certain cults like that of the followers of Orpheus did have collections of writings said to derive from their founder, and the pronouncements of Apollo or Zeus through their oracles were sometimes widely remembered, but there was nothing in Greek religion really like the Bible or the Koran. There was a certain similarity in forms and places of worship – the rituals of sacrifice and libation, for instance, were part of everyone's experience and Greek temples shared many similar features – but there were still important differences. The temple itself was not a place built so that a congregation could join in worship but was primarily the house of the god.[6] As for personal belief, there were of course countless stories about the gods in Homer and the poets, but no Greek worshipper was required to subscribe to a body of dogma or to accept a number of common doctrines as a pre-condition of practising religion.

[2] The best modern accounts are W.K.C. Guthrie, *The Sophists* (Cambridge, 1971) = *A History of Greek Philosophy* III part 1 (Cambridge, 1969), and G.B. Kerferd, *The Sophistic Movement* (Cambridge, 1981).

[3] See [...] M.P. Nilsson, *Greek Popular Religion* (New York, 1940), and E.R. Dodds, 'The religion of the ordinary man in classical Greece', *The Ancient Concept of Progress* 140–55.

[4] Isocrates, *Nemean Oration* 7.23.

[5] E.g. P.D. Arnott, *An Introduction to the Greek World* (London, 1967) 96.

[6] See [...] J.E. Sharwood Smith, *Temples, Priests and Worship* (London, 1975).

110

The paradox is that, although Greek religion seems to lack so many of the things which characterize modern religions and which require degrees of personal commitment and faith from their followers, Greeks were involved with religion to a degree which is very hard nowadays to understand. Some form of religion seems to have penetrated all aspects of life. The Greek household had its shrine to Hestia or to Zeus Ktesios, either of whom could give special protection to hearth and home, and the head of the house normally took his duties at the shrine seriously. At a meal the libation or drink-offering to the gods was an automatic custom, and it would have been very odd to eat and drink without offering the gods a small share of what was being consumed. The great landmarks of human life – birth, coming of age, marriage and death – were all marked by rituals with religious significance. Occupations were under the protection of particular gods whose favour had to be maintained, e.g. Castor and Pollux for sailors, Hephaestus for smiths, Prometheus for potters, etc. The literary arts and sport, too, were linked to the gods' favour; the *gymnasium* had its shrine to Hermes, and some god or muse lay behind every sign of poetic inspiration. Both found their highest expression in competition at great religious gatherings like the festival of Zeus at Olympia or the Great Dionysia. Above the level of the individual family, each *deme*, phratry and tribe had its own cult and each city-state its divine guardian: Athens had Athena, Corinth Poseidon and so on. The maintenance of these city-cults was essential for success and no great enterprise was undertaken without proper prayers and offerings. The year was marked by a series of religious festivals and the countryside itself was alive with divine presences; springs, rivers and mountains were all liable to have an in-dwelling god or nymph or hero. Nor was the situation static; the last part of the fifth century and the early part of the fourth saw the introduction of a number of new gods like the Kabeiroi from Samothrace, Ammon from Libya or Bendis from Thrace.

It is against this background of a way of life interpenetrated by an enormous variety of religious ritual, practice and belief – what Gilbert Murray called the Inherited Conglomerate – that the questioning of religion was seen as a dangerous threat. It was not a matter of criticizing a well-defined, separate set of people with clear beliefs and formal institutions – the welfare of every individual, every family and the state itself could be at risk. And who knew whether the disasters and disappointments which Athens suffered in the latter part of the fifth century were not some kind of divine retribution? To understand the threat which some of the Sophists seemed to represent to religion it is necessary to go a little further back in time towards the origins of some of the ideas which they and their pupils discussed.

The essential background is to be found in the work of a small number of remarkable men who lived in Ionia (now Western Turkey) and Magna Graecia (Greek Sicily and South Italy) in the sixth and early fifth centuries BC and who asked and tried to answer fundamental questions about the nature of the physical world and the nature of human knowledge – the Pre-Socratic philosophers.[7] Two aspects of their work are particularly relevant. Three citizens of the Ionian city of Miletus in Asia Minor, Thales, Anaximander and Anaximenes, were credited with the first attempts to give a systematic explanation of the nature of the physical world. However naive these first steps now seem – Thales, for instance, took water to be the origin of all things – these men are rightly remembered with honour in the history of science; all three faced the universe and sought rational answers to the question 'Why are things as they are?' Their enquiries did not lead them in the direction of either agnosticism or atheism – quite the reverse, for the question just posed was, for them, part of a much larger enquiry. Both Anaximander and Anaximenes (and probably Thales too) believed in a single, immortal divinity which was all-powerful and all-embracing – and not human in form; what was the relationship between this supreme power and the way things were? Much of what we know about

---

[7] The best short account is E. Hussey, *The Pre-Socratics* (London, 1972). See also G.S. Kirk, J.E. Raven and M. Schofield, *The Pre-Socratic Philosophers* (2nd edn Cambridge, 1983), and J. Barnes, *Pre-Socratic Philosophers* I and II (London, 1978).

the beliefs of the Milesian thinkers comes through the mediation of Xenophanes, who lived in the second half of the sixth century BC, a poet and travelling rhapsode from Kolophon, a city near Ephesus. He was probably not a very original thinker but he had understood and adopted many of the ideas of his fellow-countrymen and preserves them for us. The idea of a single omnipotent divinity not in human form is explained clearly and unambiguously:

> One god there is in no way like mortal creatures either in bodily form or in the thought of his mind. (fr. 23 trs. Hussey)[8]

> But effortlessly he (= the divinity) agitates all things by the thought of his mind. (fr. 25 trs. Hussey)

This uncompromising monotheism was quite at odds with the varied world of anthropomorphic gods, heroes, nymphs and satyrs with which ordinary Greeks were familiar and it posed a new problem. What could have been the origin of all the accepted and familiar gods and demi-gods? The answer – man made god in his own image – was simple and perceptive:

> But mortal men imagine that gods are begotten, and that they have human dress and speech and shape. (fr. 14 trs. Hussey)

> If oxen or horses or lions had hands to draw with and to make works of art as men do, then horses would draw the forms of gods like horses, oxen like oxen, and they would make their gods' bodies similar to the bodily shape that they themselves each had. (fr. 15 trs. Hussey)

> The Ethiopians say their gods are snub-nosed and black-skinned, the Thracians that they are blue-eyed and red-headed. (fr. 16 trs. Hussey)

If all this was true, what about the poets and especially Homer who regularly depicted the gods as all too human? The answer was that the poets were simply and sometimes maliciously wrong, taken in like everyone else:

> Homer and Hesiod have attributed to the gods everything which brings shame and reproach among men: theft, adultery and fraud. (fr. 11 trs. Hussey)

If divinity could not have a human form, what then could it be like? Xenophanes' contemporary, Heraclitus, the darkly obscure philosopher from Ephesus, had a vision of God as the unifier of opposites, remaining essentially the same though appearing to be different:

> God is day night, winter summer, war peace, surfeit famine; but he is modified just as fire, when incense is added to it, takes its name from the particular scent of each different spice. (fr. 67 trs. Hussey)

He also had challenging things to say about the place of images in worship, a subject which has always been important in Greek popular religion through Byzantine times down to the present day. Praying to a statue seemed to Heraclitus to miss the point; if you wished to communicate with someone, you did not go and talk to his house:

> and men pray to these statues – it is as if someone were addressing remarks to houses – not realizing what gods and heroes really are. (fr. 5 trs. Hussey)

A tendency to scepticism was even more marked in two great thinkers from the Greek West who were born just before and just after the turn of the sixth cen-

---

[8] All quotations of fragments (fr.) are from the standard collected edition by H. Diels and W. Kranz, *Die Fragmente der Vorsokratiker* (Berlin, 1952), usually referred to as DK. In their collection, passages are sorted into two categories: category-B passages are the actual words of the person concerned, category-A passages contain information about the person and his work. In this chapter all references are to category B. A translation – to be used with caution – of category-B passages can be found in K. Freeman, *Ancilla to the Pre-Socratic Philosophers* (Oxford, 1971).

tury: Parmenides (born *c.*515 BC) and Zeno (born *c.*490 BC) both from Elea in South Italy. Their enquiries were not directed towards the investigation of the physical world, but at the nature of knowledge and at the question of how far humans could trust the knowledge they thought they had. They identified for the first time in European history some of the deepest and most troublesome issues in the theory of existence and the theory of knowledge – ontology and epistemology – and Zeno's paradoxes are still, for many contemporary mathematicians who know nothing of Eleatic philosophy, a convenient shorthand way of referring to certain well-known problems. Their arguments are for the most part highly technical, but they put a question-mark over the foundations of human knowledge and at the same time instituted a search for some kind of logical certainty on which true knowledge could be based. They are not reported as being particularly interested in the phenomena of religion, though Parmenides, in the poem in which his philosophy is described, makes the goddess Justice his guide and teacher in a picturesque and rather old-fashioned way. However, thorough-going scepticism is hardly consistent with unquestioned religious attitudes and the doubts these thinkers provoked were certainly transferred to the field of religion by some of those who were influenced by them.

From this background two strands can be followed which are of great importance in the later fifth century. First, there is serious debate about the nature of the gods and some clear dissatisfaction with traditional views. Along with this goes the criticism of Homer and the poets – traditional sources of wisdom and the staples of elementary education – and a clear-sighted, almost anthropological account of how men had arrived at the traditional picture of gods in human form. Second, there is the nagging suspicion that nothing in the world, whether it be observable facts or human values or information about the gods, can be firmly and certainly established – everything may be liable to doubt and possible refutation.

These ideas did not, of course, touch most ordinary Greek citizens; they occupied the minds of a handful of remarkable intellectuals and, however disturbing and revolutionary their theories might be, theories without interpreters and an effective means of diffusion remain relatively harmless. Such a means of diffusion was lacking. Books, in the shape of papyrus rolls, were produced in very small numbers and had a tiny circulation in the sixth and early fifth centuries.[9] Greek society at this time was still largely an oral culture[10] and the only reliable way of spreading information or ideas was by word of mouth – by teaching sympathetic followers who would in their turn go elsewhere and teach others. None of the Pre-Socratics were professional teachers who took regular students and gave courses of instruction in order to earn a living.

The Sophists, however, were teachers first and foremost, making their living by fees received from pupils who made contracts for periods of instruction, and from public lectures and performances for which admission fees were charged. They travelled from city to city, sometimes settling for a time in an area which seemed particularly appreciative, but for the most part on the move, taking with them an ever-changing group of keen students. This was a new phenomenon in Greek education. In the heroic days of the early fifth century when the Greeks were defeating the Persians, professional teachers occupied an essential but lowly place in the scheme of things.[11] There were three types. First was the *paidotribes* or physical trainer who plied his trade in the *palaistra*, an exercise-ground with sanded floor, and who coached boys and

[9] E.G. Turner, *Athenian Books in the Fifth and Fourth Centuries BC* (London, 1952); J.P. Kenyon, *Books and Readers in Ancient Greece and Rome* (Oxford, 1932).

[10] J. Goody and I. Watt in *Literacy in Traditional Societies* (Cambridge, 1968) 27–68; E.A. Havelock, *The Literate Revolution in Greece and its Cultural Consequences* (Princeton, 1982); R. Finnegan in R. Horton and Finnegan (eds) *Modes of Thought* (London, 1973) 112–45.

[11] H.-I. Marrou, *A History of Education in Antiquity* trs. G. Lamb (London, 1956) 36–45. For useful evidence from vase-painting, see F.A.G. Beck, *Album of Greek Education* (Sydney, 1975).

young men in all the regular skills of athletic competition. The *palaistra* and its larger counterpart, the *gymnasium*, together with the Greek custom of exercise in the nude were one of the hallmarks of Greek culture. Second came the *kitharistes* or teacher of the lyre who taught both instrumental technique and that repertory of songs (and especially Homer) which were thought to be a necessary part of every man's equipment for social life. Third was the *grammatistes* who, with the aid of slates and waxed tablets, taught boys to read and form their letters. By the second half of the fifth century the gaps left by this modest provision of education were becoming obvious. Young men who wished to take part in a democracy which was beginning to work in practice as well as in theory could not but be aware that speaking in public and persuading others were skills that some people were better at than others. Could these skills not be acquired or improved? Likewise, Athens, with no professional police force, was notorious for the number of cases which citizens brought against each other in the law-courts. Any citizen might find himself involved, and an appearance in court meant pleading one's case in person before 501 mature male fellow-citizens – public speaking and persuasion again at a premium. Beyond such technical skills, an expanding world and a growth in prosperity and leisure were bringing other doubts and dilemmas about, for instance, morality, the use of power, the rule of law and, of course, religion. Some of these dilemmas were articulated by poets and dramatists – Sophocles' *Antigone* is an obvious example – but poets spoke from a distance under the influence of inspiration. Democracy was bringing things down to earth. It was in this context and to fill such gaps as these that the Sophists came on the scene – both part of a changing world and themselves agents of change. They represented no organized, systematic movement and nearly all of them spent their lives travelling, demonstrating and teaching as rather colourful, much admired, but often slightly suspect figures. Most of them taught the art of public speaking – rhetoric – and with it founded a hugely influential tradition in European education. Gorgias is especially remembered here – what Aeschylus had done for tragedy, Gorgias did for rhetoric. They also taught the skills of argument, both the technique of winning arguments – eristic – and the method of so-called antilogical argument, that is, the art of arguing with equal cogency both for and against a proposition. However, it was not so much their teaching of techniques that provoked fear and opposition, nor even the fact that they offered to teach the art of success to anyone who could pay, but rather the views they proclaimed and taught when debating topics like morals, politics and religion which were of central importance to everyone, and the fact that the diffusion of their teaching put these dangerous novelties into wider circulation.

In the field of religion the first challenge came from one of the first and most remarkable figures of the Sophistic movement, Protagoras. He was born in Thrace at Abdera about 490 BC and probably spent most of his life as a travelling teacher and lecturer, paying several visits to Athens and living for a while in Sicily. He was a friend of Pericles and so highly respected that although he was not an Athenian citizen, he was employed as legal consultant to a new colony sent to found Thourioi near the site of the ancient city of Sybaris in South Italy. Very few indeed of Protagoras' own words survive and much of what we know of him comes through the words of Plato. However, he wrote a famous work *On the Gods* and, according to one source, gave a celebrated reading of it in Euripides' house in Athens.[12] Undoubtedly he will have lectured and taught on the subject as well. We have one statement in Protagoras' own words, probably from the opening of this book, and though short, it sets out a point of view which to many ordinary Greeks must have sounded dangerous in the extreme:

> Concerning the gods I am unable to discover whether they exist or not, or what they are like in form; for there are many hindrances to knowledge, the obscurity of the subject and the brevity of human life. (fr. 2 trs. Guthrie)

---

[12] Diogenes Laertius 9.54.

Religion and the New Education: the Challenge of the Sophists

This was not a statement of atheism but of agnosticism, of suspension of judgement. But even that was a radical departure, for if Protagoras was prepared to suspend judgement on the existence of the gods, it also meant that he was prepared to suspend judgement on them as the guardians or guarantors of much of human life and its standards. If the gods were not responsible, how could life make sense? The answer is partly given in the opening sentence of one of his books which has become almost a slogan of the Sophistic movement:

> Man is the measure of all things, of things that are that they are, and of things that are not that they are not. (fr. 1 trs. Guthrie)

The precise significance of this is still the subject of much debate and Protagoras himself may not have been entirely consistent in its application. The general drift is however abundantly clear – it points to a position of relativism. What seems to me to be the case *is* the case so far as I am concerned. Whatever modifications are made to such a position to avoid the logical conclusion of total anarchy (and Protagoras does seem to have made such modifications), there is little room in it for a stable code of morals depending upon the relations of god to man. Right and wrong, or good and bad, become not a matter of reference to absolute religious standards but a function of the human beings who use them. Shocking inversions are then possible such as Plato puts into the mouth of the sophist Thrasymachus in the *Republic* when he makes him say that Justice consists in the interest of the stronger, or such as Thucydides puts into the mouths of the Athenian negotiators on the island of Melos:

> since you know as well as we do that, when these matters are discussed by practical people, the standard of justice depends on the equality of power to compel and that in fact the strong do what they have the power to do and the weak accept what they have to accept. (Thuc. 5.88 trs. Warner)

Even more thorough-going scepticism was preached by other Sophists. Gorgias, a Sicilian Greek, who was a contemporary of Protagoras, has already been mentioned as one of the first teachers of rhetoric. He was also the author of a treatise 'On that which is not or on Nature' in which the argument proceeded in three stages:

(a) nothing is

(b) even if it is, it cannot be known to human beings

(c) even if it is and can be known, it cannot be indicated and made meaningful to another.

The interpretation of this is again difficult but its effect was plainly to loosen still further a belief in firm, unchangeable certainty.

Doubt about the validity of traditional conceptions of the gods showed in other ways. Some who would not go so far as the open suspension of judgement nevertheless put a distance between gods and men. The notion of a self-sufficient god in need of nothing and the conviction that the gods did not care about men's deeds were both views held by other sophists (Antiphon and Thrasymachus). The quotation is probably not *verbatim* but Thrasymachus is said to have written something like this in one of his speeches:

> The gods do not see what goes on among men. If they did, they would not neglect the greatest of human goods, namely justice (fr. 8 trs. Guthrie)

Even Pericles, who was too experienced a politician to make dangerous statements on great public occasions, is reported as having said that we do not see the gods but are assured of their immortality by the honours paid to them and the good things they provide.[13] This is a cautious step away from a simple anthropomorphic view and it is hardly surprising to find one of the leading

---

[13] Plutarch, *Pericles* 8.

sophists opening up much the same territory as Xenophanes, that is, trying to explain the origin of older conceptions of the gods. Prodicus was a younger man than Protagoras, born on the island of Keos *c.*470–460 BC, and was said to have been Protagoras' pupil. He too spent his life as an itinerant teacher, occasionally employed by his native island as an official representative, but mostly lecturing, discussing and teaching. His views on the subject of religion have to be recovered from many fragmentary sources[14] but the outline is clear enough and of the greatest interest. He said that men considered as gods those elements of the world which were basic to human life, e.g. the sun and moon, rivers, springs, bread, wine, water and fire. In this way bread became called Demeter, wine Dionysus, fire Hephaestus and so on. He also said that men honoured and deified those people who made the first vital discoveries like the basics of food-growing or the earliest practical arts. The association of Greek religion with agriculture was a penetrating and persuasive observation, for the pattern of the farmer's year with its alternations of anxiety and relief was at the heart of the Greek calendar of festivals and embedded in the practice of untold local cults. In Attica, for example, the sowing of the seed in October (Greeks sow in the autumn and harvest in early summer) was associated with the festival of the Thesmophoria whose rituals ensured the fertility of the earth, while the spring saw the festival of the Anthesteria, when amongst other things the new wine was opened and tried for the first time, and there were of course the universal celebrations of the harvest. Likewise the idea of a river or a spring having or actually being a kind of god was entirely familiar. In Homer such gods could be aggressively active as when the river-gods Simois and Scamander attack Achilles with lethal waves after he has dared to defy one of them.[15]

Prodicus' idea of god representing a phenomenon was familiar too. Especially in any form of heightened language, there was an easy association in Greek between the deity and the feeling, quality or substance associated with him or her:

> What is life, what is joy without golden Aphrodite?

> (Mimnermus 1.1: West)

So wrote the lyric poet Mimnermus in the seventh century. In Aeschylus' *Agamemnon* the chorus ask Clytemnestra how the news of the fall of Troy has come so quickly and she begins her great speech:

> Firegod Hephaistos flashed out from Mount Ida
> flame after flame bore the beacon's despatches.

> (*Agamemnon* 281–2 trs. Tony Harrison)

God and what the god represented have become interchangeable. In later antiquity Prodicus was branded as an atheist for his views but there is no evidence for this and there is a vital difference between explaining the origins of man's conception of the gods and denying the existence of divinity altogether.

Although Prodicus was interested in cosmology, the chief figure in this field in the period between the end of the Persian Wars in 480 BC and the start of the Peloponnesian War was Anaxagoras, who was born in Klazomenai, a small city across the Aegean in Ionia. He was not a travelling teacher or lecturer and cannot be called a sophist, but, like Protagoras, he was one of the group of intellectuals and artists known to be friends of Pericles, and his cosmological theories undoubtedly had an influence on current discussions and beliefs about religion. In one respect he was a successor of the Milesian philosophers for he too appeared to redefine deity in terms of one thing – mind:

> All living things, both great and small, are controlled by Mind
> (*Nous*) ... and the kinds of things that were to be and that once were

---

[14] Guthrie, *Sophists* 238–9, gives them in translation.

[15] *Iliad* 21.211ff.

> but now are not, and all that now is and the kinds of things that
> will be – all these are determined by Mind ... (fr. 12 trs. Hussey)

This was a no more daring theory than the Milesians had proposed but it was
put forward at Athens rather than Ionia, and in an atmosphere increasingly sensitive to radical changes in religious views. According to one persuasive interpretation, the sophist Antiphon held a view very similar to this and
doubtless debated it with his pupils.

There were other stirrings, too, in more technical fields.[16] One of the interesting
documents in the early history of Greek medicine is a treatise on epilepsy probably written at the end of the fifth century BC or early in the fourth. It is entitled
On the Sacred Disease, and part of its interest comes from the author's firm re-
solve not to accept divine or magical accounts of epilepsy but to insist that the
disease has a natural cause, divine and magical explanations being attributed to
human ignorance:

> I do not believe that the sacred disease is any more divine or sacred
> than any other disease but, on the contrary, just as other diseases
> have a nature from which they arise, so this one has a nature and a
> definite cause. Nevertheless, because it is completely different from
> other diseases, it has been regarded as a divine visitation by those
> who, being only human, view it with ignorance and astonishment.
> (ch. 1 paras. 2ff. trs. Lloyd)

The author was even more fiercely explicit about how 'sacred' explanations
came about:

> It is my opinion that those who first called this disease 'sacred'
> were the sort of people we now call magi, purifiers, vagabonds and
> charlatans. These are exactly the people who pretend to be very
> pious and to be particularly wise. By invoking a divine element
> they were able to screen their own failures to give suitable
> treatment and so called this a 'sacred' malady to conceal their
> ignorance of its nature. (ch. 1 paras. 10ff. trs. Lloyd)

The determination to search for certain causes only in nature – to establish a
category of events to which only natural explanations are appropriate – is a procedure which throws into serious question the credentials of a religion in which
a god or divine presence may be held responsible for everything that happens;
divine intervention must henceforth be put in a special, *un*natural category. It
might be thought that doctors and their writings would have had little influence on general opinion, and it would be wise not to exaggerate the effect of
such ideas, but it should equally be remembered that the doctor in the fifth century was not a fully-fledged professional with an established round of patients.
Custom and confidence had to be won from the public by persuasion as well as
by results, and demonstrations and defences had to be mounted to maintain a
reputation; the practices of sophists and doctors were closer to each other than
might be thought.[17]

There was of course in Athens at this time someone whose activities are often
sharply distinguished from those of the Sophists but who belonged, as
Aristophanes well knew, to the same movement of thought – Socrates.[18] He
was born in Athens in 470 or 469 BC and spent most of his life there, taking
part in public affairs and, on at least three occasions, serving in the armed forces. He did not, like the Sophists, make a profession of teaching and lecturing
and never offered courses of instruction for money; he never gave public exhi-
bitions of his learning at any of the great festivals and never toured other Greek

[16] See G.E.R. Lloyd, *Magic, Reason and Experience* (Cambridge, 1979) 1–58.

[17] Lloyd, *Magic, Reason and Experience* 96.

[18] Writing a 'neutral' account of Socrates' life and works has always proved to be
impossible. For a full, courteous, sympathetic and balanced account, see W.K.C. Guthrie,
Socrates (Cambridge, 1971) = *A History of Greek Philosophy* III part 2.

cities. Indeed he insisted that his reputation for wisdom rested largely on the honesty with which he recognized his ignorance, and claimed to be an intellectual midwife, helping others to give birth to ideas without necessarily having original thoughts of his own. Above all, he had an unshakeable faith in knowledge as the only firm basis for action. He remained at Athens as a familiar citizen and his 'teaching' consisted of conversations with friends and acquaintances, some of which Plato has recreated in the Dialogues. He left no written works. In all this he was unlike the Sophists, and Plato constantly and vehemently emphasizes the difference. However, Socrates is rightly revered as an outstanding teacher, and in both the subjects and the mode of his teaching he can be seen to have clear affinities with the Sophists and their activities. He shared many of their intellectual interests – morals, politics, education, epistemology, the status of rhetoric – and he too was surrounded by groups of young men who often came to him regularly in the conviction that they would get something of lasting value from their association with him. He died in 399 BC, condemned to death by a jury of 501 fellow-citizens on two counts: first, that he refused to recognize the gods recognized by the state and introduced new divinities, and second, that he corrupted the youth.

Socrates' views on religion remain something of a puzzle. Someone who made such an enormous contribution to our capacity to understand ourselves and our world might be thought to have had something very challenging and penetrating to say on the subject of religion, especially as his views on religion were one of the reasons for his prosecution. In fact he seems to have held to a dignified, sincere and cautious belief in a single divine power in whom there is supreme wisdom and intelligence and who is responsible for the order of the world. In Plato's Dialogues Socrates uses 'the god' or 'gods' indiscriminately but the underlying idea is very like that of Anaxagoras' idea of Mind as the controlling power in the universe. As to notions of immortality, the same word is used in both the *Apology* and the *Phaedo* to describe what happens immediately after this life – a *metoikesis* or 'change of home'.[19] Socrates seems to have believed that the nature of our new home is beyond knowledge and in the *Apology* speculates with gentle humour that it may either be like an eternal dreamless sleep, or a real opportunity to meet our predecessors in a different life (in which case he looks forward with enthusiasm to new opportunities for fresh and stimulating conversation – who would not wish to meet Orpheus, Hesiod or Homer?).[20] One aspect of Socrates' experience was inexplicable and incommunicable, and that was what he called the *daimonion* – 'divine presence' or 'divine sign' – which on several occasions turned him away from a certain course of action (e.g. from taking up a political career) and which he seems to have taken quite seriously. Some of his friends believed that this was behind the phrase in his formal accusation which referred to introducing new divinities. So far as traditional religious belief and practice were concerned, it seems in the highest degree unlikely that Socrates ever made deliberate attempts to denigrate or decry them. His respect for the Delphic oracle was genuine and in none of the Dialogues are there traces of deliberate iconoclasm or of that cheap humour at the expense of religion which is the sure sign of an unhappy agnostic. His belief in a single divine power was certainly a part of the new thinking and was doubtless one of the ideas which rubbed shoulders with more daring and provocative challenges to orthodox belief and practice, but he himself seems to have maintained a scrupulous tact and reticence in such matters.

The one obvious omission in the attitudes examined so far is outright atheism. In fact none of the major sophists about whom there is any information can certainly be said to have been an atheist or to have taught atheistic views. One notorious atheist who was alleged to have written a book describing his personal path to unbelief is mentioned, Diagoras from the island of Melos. He was not a sophist but a poet who lived most of his life at Mantinea and Athens, and became converted to atheism, possibly under the influence of Democritus, but it is

---

[19] *Apology* 40c; *Phaedo* 117c.

[20] *Apology* 40c.

interesting that he is *so* notorious that Aristophanes, when he called Socrates 'the Melian' in the *Clouds*, expected that the audience would immediately take the reference.[21] Diagoras-stories were common. He was said to have been at a friend's house for dinner when his host was called away. He noticed that the lentil soup was not cooking because the fire had burnt too low and there was no wood. Looking round he caught sight of a wooden statue of Heracles, smashed it and threw it on the fire saying that the divine Heracles had just added a thirteenth labour to the other twelve.[22]

Although the major sophists cannot be called atheists, it is clear that views very close to atheism were much in the air in the later fifth century and, even if they were too shocking for any but rebels to embrace publicly, they were put into the mouths of characters on the stage. There are two remarkable examples of mythological characters railing against their fate in language which seems almost self-consciously shocking. Both speeches are fragments – we do not know the context – and one is certainly and the other probably by Euripides, a playwright who was greatly influenced by the Sophists and in whose works clear signs of sophistic terminology and thought have been identified.[23] The first fragment is a speech by Bellerophon:

> Does any man say then that there are gods in heaven? No there are none. If any man says so, let him not be fool enough to believe the old story. Let not my words guide your judgment, look at matters for yourselves. I say that tyranny kills thousands and strips them of their goods, and men who break their oaths cause cities to be sacked. And in doing so they are happier than men who remain pious day after day. I know of small cities that honour the gods, and they are overwhelmed in battle by numbers and are the subjects of greater cities that are more impious than they. (Eur. fr. 286 trs. Kerferd)

The unjust are happier and more successful than the just and this is taken as proof, not of divine injustice, but of the fact that there are no gods. Even more uncompromising is a speech by Sisyphus in a play of that name, which in its form – 'There was a time...' – unmistakably recalls Protagoras' myth of the birth of society in Plato's dialogue:

> There was a time when the life of men was disorderly and beastlike, the slave of brute force, when the good had no reward and the bad no punishment. Then, as I believe, men laid down laws to chastise, that justice might be ruler and make insolence its slave, and whoever sinned was punished. Then when the laws prevented men from open deeds of violence, but they continued to commit them in secret, I believe that a man of shrewd and subtle mind invented for men the fear of the gods, so that there might be something to frighten the wicked even if they acted, spoke or thought in secret. From this motive he introduced the conception of divinity. There is, he said a spirit enjoying endless life, hearing and seeing with his mind, exceedingly wise and all-observing, bearer of a divine nature. He will hear everything spoken among men and can see everything that is done. If you are silently plotting evil, it will not be hidden from the gods, so clever are they. With this story he presented the most seductive of teachings, concealing the truth with lying words. For a dwelling he gave them the place whose mention would most powerfully strike the hearts of men, whence, as he knew, fears come to mortals and help for their wretched lives; that is, the vault above, where he perceived the lightnings and the

[21] *Clouds* 830.

[22] For a collection of all the sources on Diagoras, see F. Jacoby, Diagoras ὁ ἄθεος (Berlin, 1960) 3–8.

[23] Kerferd, *Sophistic Movement* 170–1.

dread roars of thunder, and the starry face and form of heaven fair-wrought by the cunning craftmanship of time; whence too the burning meteor makes its way, and the liquid rain descends on the earth. With such fears did he surround mankind, and so by his story give the godhead a fair home in a fitting place, and extinguished lawlessness by his ordinance ... So, I think, first of all, did someone persuade men to believe that there exists a race of gods. (fr. 25 [Critias] trs. Guthrie)

This explains away the gods as the cunning invention of a brilliant individual, an invention made for social and moral purposes and so disguised by the majesty of nature as to deceive the majority of men. It is a clear statement of atheism – an extreme view – and the kind of thing that made Euripides one of the cult figures of the new movement.

The considered positions of prominent and influential teachers are, however, one thing; the public image of them which unsympathetic critics project is usually rather different – more simplified and more extreme. Plato put into the mouth of Anytus, later one of Socrates' accusers, what many of the older generation must have thought about the Sophists:

I hope no relative of mine or any of my friends, Athenian or foreign, would be so mad as to go and let himself be ruined by those people. That's what they are, the manifest ruin and corruption of anyone who comes into contact with them. (Plato, *Meno* 91c trs. Guthrie)

A reflection of many critical conservative attitudes and some important clues to the results of the Sophists' work in the field of religion can be found in Aristophanes' play, *The Clouds*, first produced in 432 BC and later partly revised. This essentially concerns the encounter of a not-very-bright, conservative father, Strepsiades, and his fast-living, 'modern' son, Pheidippides, with the teaching of the new thinkers typified rather unfairly by Socrates. The father is looking for a way out of his economic problems, caused by a spend-thrift son and an expensive wife (Strepsiades had married 'above his station'). Having heard that the new learning solves all problems and re-arranges values to order, he enrols himself as a pupil in the Thinking-Factory of the Sophists presided over by Socrates. There he encounters in caricature most of the subjects which the Sophists discussed and taught. One of the first is the new view of religion:

Str. ... I'll swear by the gods that I'll deposit whatever fee you ask of me.

Soc. What kind of gods will you swear by? To start with, gods just aren't in circulation with us ...

(*Clouds* 245–8)

Strepsiades finds this hard to grasp. He no longer swears by the gods, but what of Zeus?

Str. Come now, by Earth, don't you believe that Olympian Zeus is a god?

Soc. What Zeus? Don't talk rubbish. Zeus doesn't exist.

(*Clouds* 366–7)

Later in the play, Strepsiades has become thoroughly indoctrinated and talks to his son as if Zeus were a kind of Father Christmas:

Pheid. My god, what's happened to you, father? By Olympian Zeus, you're not in your right mind.

Str. There you are, there you are – Olympian Zeus! How stupid! To believe in that Zeus of yours at your age.

(*Clouds* 816–19)

And later still, when Strepsiades has come to his senses, he has no doubt who was responsible for his flirtation with atheism:

> *Str.* How mad I was when, because of Socrates, I rejected Zeus.

(*Clouds* 1476–7)

There are echoes, too, of rationalist arguments about the actions of the gods. Strepsiades asks Socrates about the thunderbolt, Zeus's weapon against perjurers. Socrates mentions three notable contemporaries who should be prime targets but who have got away with it, and points out by contrast that Zeus strikes his own temple, Sunium, and great oak trees with the thunderbolt. To what purpose? Socrates then goes on to give a meteorological, scientific explanation of the noise of thunder. Explaining the gods away in scientific terms, accounting for the universe by one basic physical principle, and replacing the old pantheon by one new-style deity are cleverly combined in another comic exchange:

> *Str.* But who is it who makes the clouds move? Isn't it Zeus?
>
> *Soc.* Not at all; it's the celestial vortex.
>
> *Str.* Vortex? I'd missed this altogether – that Zeus no longer exists but in his place Vortex now is king.

(*Clouds* 379–81)

All this leaves no doubt that the abandonment of religion was felt to be one of the obvious consequences of sophistic education. Aristophanes makes fun of it, but the fun contains a note of warning; this is not the kind of thing which made Athens great. The new thinkers including Socrates are represented as the prophets of amorality and atheism, lazy, unwholesome, unwashed, ineffective logic-choppers. They are lampooned to the point of not seeming to be worth serious attention, but embedded in the comedy are signs of some revealing trends. One of the most important is the extent to which the new movement had evidently acquired a certain solidarity. The pupils in the Thinking-Factory are represented as an almost religious community and indeed Socrates refers to new pupils as initiates and takes Strepsiades through a little initiation-ceremony before entry; he even makes him subscribe to a mini-creed:

> *Soc.* Will you then believe in no other gods but ours – Chaos, the Clouds and the Tongue, these three?
>
> *Str.* I simply wouldn't talk to the others, not even if I met them; I wouldn't sacrifice or pour libation or make an incense-offering.

(*Clouds* 423–6)

Then the teacher is accorded exaggerated respect and an almost guru-like status. Strepsiades' first encounter with Socrates is intended to inspire awe; shortly after he has entered the Thinking-Factory he catches sight of a figure hanging aloft in a basket and questions one of the students:

> Str. Say, who is this, the man in the basket?
>
> *Stud.* It's himself.
>
> *Str.* Who's himself?
>
> *Stud.* Socrates.

(*Clouds* 218–19)

There is an interesting parallel in the wry humour with which Plato describes Protagoras walking to and fro with his band of pupils in Kallias' house:

> Those who followed behind listening to their conversation seemed to be for the most part foreigners – Protagoras draws them from every city that he passes through, charming them with his voice like Orpheus, and they followed spellbound – but there were some Athenians in the band as well. As I looked at the party I was delighted to notice what special care they took never to get in front

> or to be in Protagoras's way. When he and those with him turned round, the listeners divided this way and that in perfect order, and executing a circular movement took their places each time in the rear. It was beautiful. (Plato, *Protagoras*, 315a–b trs. Guthrie)

It would be an exaggeration and an anachronism to talk of a youth-movement or a youth-cult, but there are clear signs that the Sophists helped to widen the 'generation-gap'. Old customs of everyday social life like songs at the *symposium* are despised, and great, respected authors from the past whom parents had been brought up to revere, like Simonides and Aeschylus, are treated with contempt. Parents belong to the old world and do not understand.

Most intellectual movements have their deliberately shocking extremes which provoke and crystallize opposition and, so far as religion is concerned, the last quarter of the fifth century supplies several examples. There was the notorious club of the *kakodaimonistai* – three aristocratic young men who chose to meet together for dinner on unlucky days to cock a snook at popular superstition.[24] More seriously there were two acts of wanton sacrilege which preceded the departure of the great task-force to Sicily in 415 BC, both rightly or wrongly associated with Alcibiades and his circle. It was said that the holy mysteries of Eleusis had been profaned and mocked in private houses at Athens and – a more obvious and public act of vandalism – the statues of Hermes which stood at the entrance to houses and temples all over the city were discovered one morning to have had their sexual organs removed.[25] This concerted and planned sacrilege on the eve of a great (and finally disastrous) state enterprise made a serious impression; nothing like it occurred again.

The questioning of traditional religious belief and practice, the rise of a new and increasingly self-conscious intellectual movement amongst the young which seemed commonly to lead to scepticism, amorality or even atheism, the diffusion of dangerous ideas by teachers who were not part of the city and who took away some of its promising young men, a growing lack of respect for traditions, customs and the rights of parents – all these might reasonably be expected to have provoked more opposition than the appearance of a satirical play at a dramatic festival. There were doubtless many collisions about which no evidence has survived, but one of the most serious lines of attack by conservatives was a series of prosecutions in the courts for *asebeia* or impiety.[26] *Asebeia* was a conveniently vague term with no set legal definition; injustice – *adikia* – was a matter of wrong-doing in man's relationship with man, *asebeia* involved wrong-doing in his relationship with the gods – a much trickier concept. The prosecutions began in the 430s (the exact date is not known) after a decree was introduced by a soothsayer who was also involved in politics, Diopeithes, the terms of which are very revealing. The decree allowed for the public prosecution of two categories of offender: first, those who did not admit the practice of religion (the Greek word *nomizein* is the same one used by Aristophanes for believing in the gods), and second, those who taught rational theories (*logoi*) about the heavens. The motives behind the prosecutions were not always simple; in some cases political considerations, such as opposition to the policies of Pericles, probably played a part, but the significant fact is that anyone who was even loosely associated with the intellectual revolution and the 'new thinking' on religion was thought to be vulnerable.

Of the Sophists, Protagoras was the most prominent victim. According to the tradition he was condemned on a charge of *asebeia* probably soon after 421 BC and was drowned at sea while escaping from Athens on his way to Sicily. As Diogenes Laertius wryly observed, he escaped the judges but not Pluto. Prodicus is also said to have been condemned to death and, though this is prob-

---

[24] Lysias fr. 53.2 (Thalheim).

[25] Thucydides 6.27–8.

[26] E. Derenne, *Les procès d'impiété intentés aux philosophes à Athènes au Vme et au IVme siècles avant J-C* (Liège, 1930; repr. New York, 1956). Sir Moses Finley has kindly pointed out to me the need for extreme caution in using some of the late sources quoted by Derenne.

ably the result of the sources transferring Socrates' experience to Prodicus, there is evidence that he too ran into opposition and was expelled from a *gymnasium* for 'unsuitable' teaching. Another minor sophist, Damon, was ostracized for ten years. Diagoras was prosecuted and was already in exile by 414 BC. The great playwright Euripides, in whose house Protagoras was said to have read his book 'On the Gods', was attacked in the courts although in his case the prosecution was unsuccessful. Anaxagoras was prosecuted successfully and either had to leave Athens or was imprisoned there. Finally just after the turn of the century Socrates himself was prosecuted and condemned in a trial which has become a legend.[27]

Freedom of thought in education has always been a risky business and it is no wonder that Aristotle in the fourth century said that being a sophist was one of the dangerous occupations, if not quite as dangerous as that of being a general.[28] The Sophists and Socrates can be regarded as the founding fathers of higher education and they have an honourable record. They dared to face some of the most basic questions of personal and social life and to centre some of their discussion and teaching upon them, and this should be set in the balance against the workaday uses to which the skills of the Sophists were also directed. In the field of religion they may not have been the originators of ideas, but they helped to stimulate two lines of speculation which are still eagerly and hotly debated. The first is the study of religion as a social and anthropological phenomenon; this has since taken many forms and modern structuralism is only one of them. The second is the attempt to understand the universe and its apparently miraculous order in terms of one controlling power or principle, and to get behind the absurdities of anthropomorphic deities and too literal an interpretation of 'picture-language'. They also opened the way to a divorce between religion and morals, and to debates about the relativity of moral standards which are still very much with us. These lines of enquiry invited criticism and repression, and, as isolated individuals, the Sophists and Socrates were all too vulnerable. Their successors founded institutions – Plato had his Academy, Aristotle his Lyceum, Isocrates his school – and institutions are notoriously more cautious than committed individuals.[29] The professional teachers of following generations learnt their lesson and not many of them appeared in the courts or dared the displeasure of local rulers. The issues had not changed, but educators had learnt to back off to a safe distance. *Gymnasia* continued to keep their shrines to Hermes and the Muses, success in educational or sporting competition was a regular occasion for thanking the gods, and the 'school calendars' of the Hellenistic world were largely based upon religious celebrations and festivals. Already in the fourth century some of the trials for *asebeia* seem to show an even tighter control over the technicalities and proprieties of religion. Archias, a priest at Eleusis, made a mistake in the ritual by himself sacrificing on a day when a priestess should have offered a basket of fruit. He was a member of a well-known local family but was accused and condemned to death. Another man who got drunk and attacked someone with a whip during a sacred procession suffered the same fate. Even someone who came to blows with another man over a reserved seat at the Great Dionysia found himself accused of impiety. These were, perhaps, unusual and extreme cases but they represented a sharp warning.[30]

[27] M.I. Finley, 'Socrates and Athens' in *Aspects of Antiquity* (London, 1972) 60–73. It is a sad irony that Socrates' execution was delayed by an age-old *religious* observance – the despatch of a ship to the island of Delos as a thanksgiving for Theseus' success in Crete against the Minotaur. The city could not be polluted by executions during the voyage out and back. Plato, *Phaedo* 58a–c; Xenophon, *Memorabilia* 4.8.2.

[28] *Rhetoric* 1397b24.

[29] Both the Academy and the Lyceum had *Mouseia* or shrines to the Muses and a conscious sense of a dedicated community. It is, however, doubtful whether they were legally registered as *thiasoi* or religious communities proper as most modern books say. See J.P. Lynch, *Aristotle's School* (Berkeley, 1972) 112–27.

[30] For the reaction in general, see E.R Dodds, *The Greeks and the Irrational* (Berkeley, 1951) ch. 6.

It is one of the most remarkable features of the age of the Sophists and Socrates that, for a few years and at considerable risk to themselves, a number of gifted teachers dared to bring education face to face with some of the basic problems of religion, morals and politics, in short, with what Plato said philosophy ought to be about – how one ought to live.

CLOUDS

Source: *Aristophanes; Myth, Ritual and Comedy*, Cambridge University Press, 1993, Chapter 5, pp.102–12 and 124–33.

By A.M. Bowie

Clouds is structurally similar to *Wasps*, in that once again an old man is subjected to various trials in an attempt to remedy an unsatisfactory circumstance, and in the process experiences a form of rejuvenation. At the same time, there are a number of important differences: in *Wasps*, the old man is apparently freed by this from all moral and political restraints; whereas in *Clouds* the folly of his attempts is borne in upon him with some force. Both plays use the ephebic mythos, but in *Clouds* there is woven into the text a series of commentaries on Strepsiades' actions which constantly suggest that he is not only reversing the natural pattern of the *ephebeia* but also contravening moral and religious rules that are fundamental to the well-being of the city. The moral disapproval implied by these commentaries can however be prevented from dominating the reading of the play by a consideration of the outcome from two perspectives and by attention to what Aristophanes has to say about himself in the parabasis. This chapter will begin with a discussion of Strepsiades' ephebic odyssey, before looking at the treatments of Socrates and the Cloud-Chorus, which together provide the frameworks through which Strepsiades' errors of choice are to be enjoyed.

Strepsiades' *ephebeia*

The prologue of the play can be analysed in terms similar to those found at the start of *Wasps*. Strepsiades' adult, citizen status is clear from the ill-tempered complaints about his slaves, son and wife with which he opens the play. Where Philocleon was bound to the city by his participation in the lawcourts, Strepsiades is so bound by his debts to other citizens. If Philocleon tells us little of his wife, Strepsiades is eloquent on the subject of his. The account he gives of his marriage has often been read as a nostalgic longing for the countryside, much like Dicaeopolis', and is taken to be typical of Old Comedy's supposed preference for rural over city life.[1] No doubt Greek peasants did feel affection for their lands, especially when comparisons with the city were being made as in Strepsiades' case, but one must none the less beware of imposing on the Greeks views about the countryside that are more characteristic of the Romantic Age: such nostalgic views tend to be found when men have freed themselves from close dependence on the land for their survival. Greek ideology allows us to consider the relationship between city and country in more than one way.

Strepsiades describes his marriage as follows (43–52):

> I had a pleasant rustic life, mouldy, unkempt, lying about as one pleased, full of bees and sheep and pressed olives. Then I married the niece of Megacles, son of Megacles, I a rustic, she from town, classy, luxurious, very much the *grande dame*. When I married her, I lay down with her, smelling of wine-lees, fig-crates, fleeces, and bountiful creation, while she smelled of myrrh, saffron, tongued kisses, expense, gourmandizing, Colias and Genetyllis.[2]

Strepsiades' contrast between himself and his wife is all the more arresting because his wife is portrayed not simply as a city girl, but as a sophisticated woman with high-up connections, both in 'Megacles son of Megacles', who

---

[1] E.g. Segal 1969.

[2] On the last two, see Paus. 1.1.5; Henderson 1987a: 67.

has the name of a man of the Alcmaeonid clan who was Secretary to the Treasurers of Athena in 428/7,[3] and in his mother, Coesura (48), noted for her haughty ways and evident wealth.[4] Strepsiades has therefore moved from a life and smells clearly expressive of 'nature',[5] not just into the life and smells of the *polis* and 'culture', but into the very heart of Athenian political life. Reduced to its simplest terms, it is the move of the ephebe. The emphasis on this contrast is suggestive of more than just nostalgia and seems designed to draw attention to that opposition between city and country which is one code of status-transition rites.

The aged Philocleon occupied a position of ambiguous status, and Strepsiades is a similarly ambiguous figure, though in a somewhat different way. He unites some of the key oppositions of the play and articulates Greek attitudes to country and city by being characterized by aspects of each. He may be viewed in a variety of lights. A countryman might warm to his praise of the country against the sophistication of the city, to his blunt, common-sense approach to intellectual matters and even to his desire to free himself from debt (unless he were a creditor himself), but might find his description of the countryside in 44f. (quoted above) somewhat uncritical, and would not have had much sympathy for a man who had made a match with a rich and sexy woman and was *still* able to complain about debts. A townsman might take a similar view, except that he would see a gap between himself and Strepsiades in the latter's *agroikia*, in the sense both of rusticity and of buffoonery. Only the aristocracy might not feel great affinity with him, though his marriage does presumably come close to making him one of them.

Strepsiades is thus not an easy man to categorize.[6] We cannot take him simply as a peasant, for the reasons just given, and also because the text manages to make problematic exactly where he lives. The Athenian custom whereby wives went to live in their husband's house, and Strepsiades' claim at 138 that 'I live far away in the fields'[7] might suggest his stage-house was in the country. He belongs to the *deme* Cicynna (134), the position of which is uncertain, though Traill places it east of Hymettus.[8] In 1322, he summons the help of his demesmen, which might again support such a country setting for the house.[9] On the other hand, the fact that he can see the Phrontisterion from his house (91f.) would suggest that he lives in the city: it is hardly likely that Socrates would have set up a school for rich young aristocrats in Cicynna. Comedy can tolerate considerable jumps of place and time, but this 'contradiction' seems to have a significance beyond mere dramatic convenience: town and country are juxtaposed not only in the text but also in the theatrical space.[10]

The marginal nature of Strepsiades is complemented by the similar characterization of his son Pheidippides and Strepsiades' attitude to him. Because he is still living at home and a member of the cavalry (120), one might well conceive

[3] On the importance of this office, cf. [Arist.] *Ath. Pol.* 8.1.

[4] Dover 1968a: 99 on 46; Davies 1971: 380f.; Sommerstein 1980a: 187f. on *Ach.* 614.

[5] Strepsiades wishes to return to a life lived lying about εἰκῆ (44, 'at random'), a word used by Prometheus to describe the primitive state of man, before he gave them civilization ([A.] *PV* 450).

[6] On character in Aristophanes, Silk 1990.

[7] On the analogy of the use of *porro* + genitive, though *telou* + genitive elsewhere always means 'far away *from*' (cf. *KG* 1 420f.). The scholia say the phrase is a parody of Euripides' *Telephus* fr. 884 (Page 1962: 130–3) but the two are not so very close.

[8] 1975: map 2.

[9] Although it is equally possible to imagine him calling on other men from the same deme living near by in the city.

[10] For the juxtaposition of two doors that are not to be conceived as 'actually' next to each other, compare vases depicting erotic pursuit between the doors of the houses of the bridegroom and the bride, which doors mark the transfer of the girl, not a case of marrying the boy next door: Sourvinou-Inwood 1991:85–7.

of Pheidippides as being of about ephebic age. That his name is also significant is shown by Strepsiades' account of his dispute with his wife over what the boy should be called: 'she wanted to add 'hippus' to his name – Xanthippus or Chaerippus or Callippides – but I wanted to give him his grandfather's name, Pheidonides' (63–7). They ended up with a compromise that combined elements signifying the thrift of his rural father (*Pheid-*) and the horse-riding, aristocratic background of his mother (*-hipp-*). His name thus situates him ephebe-like on the margins of their two spheres of influence. Furthermore, names with the *hipp-* element are not uncommon in myths of transition.[11] There was a further dispute over the child's career. Strepsiades wanted him to follow in his father's footsteps, as was appropriate for an ephebe about to leave the *oikos*, but curiously desired him to tend goats, not just in the country but on the poorest sort of land,[12] wearing a peasant's cloak: by contrast, his wife wished her son to ride in the Panathenaic procession wearing the saffron-coloured cloak (*xustis*), one of the highest honours which the city could offer an ephebe.[13] Garments and names are again important symbols of status. In his ambition to return himself and his son to a fantasy world of the country, Strepsiades thus goes against the expected movement of men from nature to culture, against, that is, the ideology of the *ephebeia*. Several myths provide a commentary on such reversals or refusals to take the next initiatory step, such as those of Hippolytus, whose rejection of sexuality and attempt to hide from it in his sacred grove in the country[14] led to death in a chariot crash, or Atalanta, who, though she married, refused to leave the countryside for normal married life and was eventually, with her husband, turned into an animal.[15]

Like Philocleon, therefore, the hero is represented as both central and yet in some ways marginal and desirous of becoming more so in his wish for a return to the country. His son is no more willing to undergo the initiations of the Phrontisterion than he was to tend goats on barren land, so that Strepsiades is forced to free himself from his unsatisfactory life in the city by turning to another marginal world, the Phrontisterion, which stands in a similar relationship to the city as does the country, but as it were further up a scale of 'civilization'. If the country is 'insufficiently civilized', the Phrontisterion is 'excessively civilized' as is shown by the extreme forms that things familiar from 'normal' existence take there. It will correspond to the topsy-turvy world of Philocleon's house and domestic lawcourt.[16]

The Phrontisterion is characterized as abnormal or marginal in ways similar to those used in *Wasps*. It is strongly characterized as chthonic: it is the haunt of 'souls', like Hades (94); their pallid complexions are quite unlike those of normal healthy young men such as the Hippeis (103, 119f.),[17] and recall the half-dead Spartan prisoners from Sphacteria (186); their concerns are with the things beneath the earth (188, 192), whence they are said to have sprung, as *gegeneis* (853). The fact that they live permanently inside the school and cannot

---

[11] E.g. Hippolytus. Young unmarried girls are regularly referred to in the imagery of horses: Calame 1977: 1 411 20.

[12] On *phelleus*, cf. Harpocration and LSJ s.v.; Pollux 1.227; Dover 1968a: 103; Osborne 1985a: 20, with reference to X. *Cyn.* 5.18; Arr. *Cyn.* 17.4; *SEG* 24.152.2.

[13] The *xustis* (70) is worn by the riders on the north frieze of the Parthenon; cf. scholia *ad loc.*

[14] E. *Hipp.* 73–87.

[15] Sourvinou-Inwood 1991: 73 and Calame 1977: 1 77–9 on the daughters of Eumelus.

[16] The attempt to change Philocleon was prompted by a 'disease', and Strepsiades is similarly driven to the Phrontisterion by the 'disease' of his son's love for horses (74, 243; for an actual 'horsy' disease, cf. Hp. *MS* 4.23f. (I owe this reference to Mr E.L. Hussey)).

[17] For pale skin as a sign of effeminacy beside the virile sun-tan, *Frogs* 1092, *Thesm.* 191, *Eccl.* 62–4, 699.

stay long in the open air (198) contrasts with the daily journey to school and gymnastic training of normal boys (964f.).[18] One remembers the darkness and hiding of the ephebe. As beasts (184), they differ from normal people: they do not wash, shave (835–7) or wear shoes (103). Their interests and beliefs, and the instruments with which they investigate them, are far from the experience of the ordinary man (200–17). There are admirable emblems of the inverted nature of the school not only in Socrates, a mortal, swinging up in the air in a basket and concerning himself with the heavenly bodies (225–34), but more particularly in the students of 191–4:

> *Str.* What are these doing so bent over like that?
>
> *Student.* They are searching in the nether darkness below Tartarus.
>
> *Str.* Then why are their arses looking at the sky?
>
> *Student.* They are learning astronomy on their own account.

It was a topos of ancient thought that man is distinguished from the animals by the fact that his eyes look up to the heavens, whilst theirs look at the ground.[19]

Philocleon's domestic trial was described as a rite, and Strepsiades' entry into the Phrontisterion is cadenced by 'rituals' marking the stages. The Student, who first broaches the secrets of the school, calls them 'mysteries' (143). When Socrates accepts him as a pupil, he undergoes the enthronement, garlanding and sprinkling that was associated with initiation into mystery cults (255ff.). After this he is introduced to the new gods of the Phrontisterion and prepares for a severely austere life-style: just as the marginal existence prepares the ephebe for becoming part of the centre, so this austerity serves to dramatize his transition, in a reversal of the life of untroubled ease into which he thinks he is being initiated. A second rite is performed when Strepsiades moves into the inner recesses of the Phrontisterion: he asks for a honey-cake as if he were entering the cave of the oracle of Trophonius (508), for which elaborate rituals were prescribed. It is after this that he discovers himself in a new world where everyday things are not as they were outside: *metra*, 'measures', refer not to measures of corn but to poetic metres (639–46); *rhuthmoi*, 'rhythms', not to sex but to prose (647–54); and the names of everyday objects are changed according to new rules of gender (658–91).

It is thus wholly appropriate that the ruler of this topsy-turvy world should be Dinos, the celestial Whirl (380):[20] the key verbs for 'turning', *strephein* and *kamptein*, appear regularly, in connection with rhetoric (317, 884, 901), poetry (331–7, 969–71) and philosophy (700–4).

Like Philocleon, Strepsiades has made a transition from the *nomoi* of normal life to the natural world of *phusis*, which is here signified not so much by reference to animals, but rather in the more appropriate philosophical terms of the *nomos/ phusis* debate, which was central to so many discussions in the fifth century.[21] The more reprobate denizens of the Phrontisterion delight in the overthrow of the *nomoi*. The Worse Argument boasts that 'I was the very first to conceive of speaking against accepted morality and just pleas in court' (1039f.), and Pheidippides exclaims 'How agreeable it is to spend one's time on new and clever things, and to be able to flout the established laws!' (1399f.). He will later

---

[18] Starkie 1911: 53 contrasts Solon's description of Athenian training in Lucian, *Anachar*, 24.

[19] First in X. *Mem.* 1.4.11; cf. Pease 1955 8: 914; Bömer 1969: 46; Lloyd 1983: 30 2, 40f., where note especially Arist. *HA* 502b20f. and *PA* 695a3ff. On man as a standard against which animals are measured, Lloyd 1983: 26 43. Compare the two satyrs on Beazley 1963: 317 n.15 'walking on their hands, with their rear ends in the air, symbolizing their upside-down world' (Lissarrague, 1990: 39f.).

[20] J. Ferguson 1978 9 (1972–3 is remarkably similar) and 1971; on 'turning' in the play, see Marzullo 1953.

[21] Heinimann 1945; Guthrie 1969: 55–134; Nussbaum 1980: 52–67. *Nomizein* is frequent in the play.

show no respect for the laws covering debts (1178ff.). In the *agon*, the Worse Argument offers Pheidippides the chance to do as he pleases: 'if you consort with me, indulge your nature, leap about, laugh, think nothing shameful' (1077f.). Pheidippides learns his lesson well and is soon proving to his father the mere conventionality of the laws: 'Was it not a man, like you or I, who first made this law, who persuaded the ancients by argument? Do I have any less right to make for the future a new law that sons should beat their fathers?' (1421–4). Strepsiades is thus inducted into a world where the *nomoi* that mark Athenian civilization are abrogated in favour of the kind of self-indulgence and lack of restraint seen at the end of *Wasps*: abandonment of *nomoi* leads to a similar kind of chaos to that enjoyed by the rejuvenated Philocleon.

Sadly, the instruction offered by the Phrontisterion is too much for the addled brain of Strepsiades and the attempted initiation fails, so that he turns once again, this time with more success, to his son. Curiously, this pupillage of Pheidippides brings about the change which his elderly father had earlier sought by himself: it enables him to deploy sophistic arguments before his creditors and turns the clock back for him so that he becomes young again. This produces, in realist terms, the comic incongruity whereby Strepsiades is at one moment a stupid old man and the next able, albeit farcically, to use the logic of a Socrates, simply because his son has been to the school. To explain this, one might have recourse to comedy's flexibility in such matters or to the possible incompleteness of the revision of the play, but these are somewhat desperate expedients. There is however a mythical story-type in which a young person, often a relative, is in some way sacrificed so that another may achieve his end.[22] For instance, Elpenor, 'youngest' of Odysseus' Companions, dies as his leader sets off for Hades and has been interpreted as a kind of 'ritual substitute' whose death permits another's return from Hades.[23] Iphigeneia and Creusa, daughter of Erechtheus, are examples of children actually sacrificed so that their fathers may succeed. In Euripides' *Alcestis*, her death keeps her husband Admetus on earth,[24] so that it is appropriate that, when his career as a Knight has been abandoned for the Phrontisterion, Pheidippides should echo a line from that play: compare *Clouds* 1415, 'Children weep, do you think the father should not?', and *Alc.* 691, 'You delight to look on the sun; do you think your father does not?' Can one see Pheidippides, therefore, as a child sacrificed for his father's success?[25] Further support for this idea may be found in the fact that Strepsiades summons him from the school with the words of Euripides' Hecuba summoning her daughter Polyxena to tell her she must be sacrificed at Achilles' tomb, though there the sacrifice of the child is not on behalf of a parent.[26]

Whether or not this be accepted, the scene between the two Logoi continues the theme of transition set out at the start of the play, with Pheidippides now the figure undergoing the transition. As Ernesti was the first to point out, Pheidippides' choice between the Better and Worse Arguments recalls Prodicus' parable of Heracles at the Cross-Roads, where the hero was faced with a choice of two life-styles offered by the allegorical figures of Virtue and Vice.[27] The parallels are close, and, since they have not been spelled out before, I shall do so briefly here. The date of Prodicus' allegory is not known, so we do

[22] See also Vian 1963: 214f.; Bremmer 1983b; J.E.M. Dillon 1989: 32 52.

[23] *Od.* 10.552–60; van Brock 1959; Nagy 1979: 292f. Perithous remained there to allow Theseus to return (Frazer 1921: II 234–7).

[24] Lesky, 1925.

[25] Strepsiades' requests to Pheidippides to suffer on his behalf also parallel Admetus' requests to his parents to die for him (*Alc.* 614ff.).

[26] Cf. 1165f. and E. *Hec.* 173f. (for the possible corruption of the text, Diggle 1984: 347).

[27] X. *Mem.* 2.1.21 34; cf. Schultz 1909 (who notes the ephebic element in the story). For the 'roads of life' cf. M.L. West, 1978 on *Op.* 287 92. If Aristophanes is writing after Prodicus, for those who spot the parallel with Prodicus' tale, there is a mischievous reference to Heracles in 1048 52.

not know whether Aristophanes was imitating it directly, but it and the Judgement of Paris, with its demonstration of what can happen when a young man chooses bodily pleasures instead of political and military power, provide parallel stories of youths making their transition to manhood: when the wrong choice is made, disaster follows.

Heracles faced this choice, which concerned his education (30, 34), 'when he came to maturity from childhood' (21); Pheidippides, as we have seen, is of ephebic age and character. Prodicus depicted the character of his figures by means of their dress (22), and the Better Argument describes the effects of the two kinds of education on Pheidippides' dress and physique (1002–23; cf. 1112, 1171). Virtue is dressed in white, is attractive and adorned with *sophrosune* (22); Pheidippides will be garlanded with white reeds and white poplar (1006f.), his body will be 'shining and blooming' (1002) and his companion will be *sophron* (1006), a virtue shared by the Better Argument (961 etc.). Virtue's eyes are full of *aidos*, whose statue Pheidippides will learn to revere (995). Vice offers indulgence in boys, food and drink (23, 24f., 30), as does the Worse Argument (1071–82). Virtue tells Heracles that training, toil and sweat are needed for bodily strength (28) and that Vice makes the young feeble (31); Better says that Pheidippides will shine in the gymnasia (1002) and complains that, since the young ignore the wrestling schools (1054), they are too feeble to hold their shield properly (987–9). Finally, under Virtue, young and old stand in a proper relationship: the young rejoice in the praise of the old and the old in the respect of the young; Better claims he will teach Pheidippides not to snatch food from his elders (982), to give up his seat to them, and to avoid being mischievous towards them (994), answering them back or calling them names (998f.). Virtue claims Heracles, but the victor in the ephebic *agon* in *Clouds*, as in the Apaturia myth and in *Wasps*, is the 'unexpected' one, the Worse Argument.

When Pheidippides returns, however, Strepsiades is unaware of the moral warning carried in such tales, and sings an encomium to himself (1206–12). The use of songs in these metres before a calamity in tragedy bodes ill for Strepsiades,[28] but he proceeds to deploy his sophistic skills. It is here that he appears to have achieved his desire to be a Sophist and even to have been rejuvenated. Earlier in the play, two things characterized the young, the competing interests of philosophy and horses; Strepsiades now displays his control of both. To 'Pasias' he denies the gods and plays with language just as Socrates taught him (1233–51), and with 'Amynias' he uses a neatly spurious set of analogies from meteorology and geography to argue that, just as the sea does not get any bigger as the rivers flow into it, so debts ought not to increase as time flows on (1278–96). He then calls for a goad and drives him off as a horse and chariot (1298–1302):

> *Str.* Go on! What are you waiting for? Won't you get a move on, you thoroughbred?
>
> *Cred.* What is this but violent assault?
>
> *Str.* On you go! I'll lay into you and poke your thoroughbred arse! On your way, are you? I knew I'd make you move, wheels, chariot, pair and all!

Then, in their subsequent song, the Chorus declare him a *sophistes* (1309), albeit one about to come to grief. Strepsiades thus possesses the two youthful qualities of philosopher and horse-driver, but their sharp opposition earlier suggests that this combination is not to be stable.

Indeed, Pheidippides demonstrates its superficial quality immediately, by taking it quite literally, through the proverb 'old men are in their second childhood' (1417), and uses this as a justification for beating his father. Strepsiades' new 'childhood' is then confirmed, when he contrasts his own past treatment of Pheidippides with what Pheidippides has done to him (1380–90):

---

[28] On the metres, Rau 1967: 148 50; also Macleod 1981 on 'self-*makarismos*'.

I brought you up, and understood everything you meant by your lisping. If you said 'bru', I'd understand and bring you a drink; if you asked for 'mamma', I'd bring bread; you'd scarcely said 'kakka' before I'd carry you outside and hold you out. But now, when you were strangling me, as I cried and shouted that I wanted to go, you didn't think to carry me outside, you villain, but you choked me until I did my 'kakka' where I was.

As at the end of *Wasps*, the roles of father and son are reversed: Strepsiades now behaves like, and is beaten as, a child.[29]

Strepsiades' reversed rite of passage has thus ended, as both comparable myths and the perverse direction and intent of the rite always portended, in disaster: all his twisting has left him with his debts still to pay (1463f.), but without his cloak and shoes (856–9); his son has abandoned the *cursus honorum* of the rich and, where he was earlier willing to obey, in some things at least, his father and mother, will now beat them both (1443). Strepsiades appears as an *agroikos*, 'a rustic', in the fullest sense of the word. By replacing the upbringing of his son (*trephein*) with twisting (*strephein*) in an attempt to escape his 'debts' (*tokoi*), he has only succeeded in losing his son (*tokos*) and maintaining those debts.[30]

Some lines of Pheidippides highlight the futility of Strepsiades' attempts to become a young man and a sophist. Explaining why his father need not fear the 'Old and New' day, on which debt-settlements had to be made,[31] he says (1181–4):

> *Pheidippides*. Those who make their deposits will lose them, because there's no way that one day could become two days.

> *Strepsiades*. It couldn't?

> *Phedippides*. No, how could it, unless a woman could be both aged and young at the same time?

For 'old woman' read 'old man'. The immortal Clouds may be able to change their nature in order to deceive wrongdoers (348–50), but this is denied to the mortal Strepsiades: his desire to mock at the Old and New day by becoming at once old and young is not permitted to succeed [...]

The Cloud-Chorus

That the Clouds, who have earlier acted as the sophistic deities of Socrates, should at the end reveal themselves as agents of divine justice has sometimes been felt to be a problem in the play. In fact, as Segal 1969 has shown, the Clouds give ample indication of their true nature throughout the play from their very first entry. Their delight in the open air (275–90) contrasts strongly with the enclosed nature of the Phrontisterion (198f.). Their father is Ocean (277), who is hardly a sophistic deity, and they hymn Athens for the richness of its celebrations of the Olympians (299–313, quoted above). Socrates thinks they support the idle (331–4), but they praise hard work (414–19); they praise too the Stronger Argument but not the Weaker (1024–30; cf. 959f.). They give warnings of the consequences of Strepsiades' actions on three occasions (810–12, 1114, 1303–20). In the parabasis, they relay the complaints of the Sun and Moon and the other Olympians, whom they hymn as rulers of the universe

[29] For the use of the imagery or memory of childhood at a point of transition, compare the story of Odysseus' scar, related when his nurse Eurycleia realizes who he is (*Od.* 19. 392ff.), and the sad reminiscences of a similarly incontinent if less vocal Orestes by his nurse Cilissa (A. *Cho.* 734ff., esp. 755–60).

[30] For this pun, cf. *Clouds* 1156 9; *Thesm.* 839 45; Pl. *Rep.* 507A, 555E; Arist. *Pol.* 1258b4 5.

[31] Kassel 1981.

(563–74) and as protectors of cities (595–606).[32] In all of this there is little to encourage Socrates in his belief that they are on his side.

Furthermore, their change of character is of a piece with their normal method of operation. We have quoted Socrates' explanation of their shape-changing and how they 'become whatever they want' to mock men's folly (348–50): if they have turned themselves into appropriate animals to deride the infamous they have now become goetic, sophistic deities in order to mock at and punish a goetic Sophist. That the 'wise' Socrates is unable to see what is happening is not only comic in itself, but also in the tradition of seers who can see the future for others but not for themselves.[33] One might even say they have twisted their nature to mock at Strepsiades, 'the son of Twister'.

It has not I think been noticed that alongside these indications of their true role there are in the early part of the play several warnings given to Strepsiades in the form of weather signs which in traditional weather-lore portended a storm. Strepsiades has this very morning conceived his plan (75f.) and immediately there are 'portents' which, as a self-proclaimed *agroikos*, he really ought to recognize as telling him that a stormy encounter with clouds is ahead.[34]

The first sign comes at 56, when the oil runs out in the lamp and Strepsiades threatens to beat the slave for having put in a 'thirsty' wick. This might be a comic demonstration of Strepsiades' meanness, but lamps at all times in antiquity were held to give indications about the weather.[35] According to the pseudo-Theophrastan *De Signis*, 'If a lamp does not wish to light, it is a sign of a storm.'[36] It might be objected that this is not a precise parallel to the *Clouds* passage, because the lamp goes out simply because of the lack of oil, but a passage in the parabasis suggests that the lamp's behaviour is significant. When the Athenians were electing Cleon as general, the Clouds thundered and 'the Moon left its orbit, and the Sun, immediately drawing its wick into itself; said it would not shine for you if you elected Cleon general' (584–6). In each case, the extinguishing of wick gives a warning which the mortals will ignore at their peril:[37] the election of Cleon was a 'mindless expedition (*exodos*)' (579f.), just like the 'path' (*atrapos*) pursued by Strepsiades (76).[38]

The frequent biting of insects was another rain-sign: 'The popular saying about flies is true: when they bite a good deal it is a sign of rain.'[39] Aratus combines the two signs we have looked at: 'If flies bite and desire blood more than before, or snuff gathers around the wicks of lamps on a damp night, [it is a sign of rain].'[40] There are several references to the biting of various sorts of insect in *Clouds*, some of them of a surprising kind. Strepsiades complains from his bed that he is 'being bitten by expense and fodder and debts' (12f.), and later (37f.) that the demarch, responsible for the regulation of debts,[41] is biting him. In the Phrontisterion, the bed-bugs will not let him bring his bed out and he begs

---

[32] Scodel 1987.

[33] X. *Symp.* 4.5. Plato makes much of the ignorance of *manteis* concerning the things they talk of: *Apol.* 22B C, *Meno* 99C D, *Ion* 534B E; Otto 1890: s.v. *sapere*.

[34] For a collection of ancient weather-lore, see McCartney's sequence of articles in *CW* from 1921 onwards (cf. 1929: 2 n.1), and 1929 on clouds.

[35] Ganszyniec, *RE* 13.2115–19, s.v. *luchnomanteia*.

[36] 42. On this work, see Heeger, 1889. Cf. also Aratus 976 81, 1033 6; Virg. *Geo.* 1.390 2; Plin. *NH* 18.357f.

[37] On eclipses as portents, Pritchett, 1979: 108–13. For a link between bad politicians and bad weather in comedy, Philippides fr. 25 (R.C.T. Parker, 1983: 269).

[38] See Harry 1910 on this latter word, and the proverb 'When the road (*hodos*) is there, why do you take the side-track (*atrapos*)?' (Apostol. 12.34); cf. also Ar. fr. 47.

[39] *De Sign.* 23.

[40] 974–7.

[41] Whitehead 1986: 124–7.

Socrates to allow him to sleep on the ground to avoid them (699); at 709–26 he describes their merciless torture. At 146, a flea-bite is the starting point for some research into mosquitoes.

Not unnaturally, clouds played an important role in weather-lore. Their very gathering pointed to rain,[42] and Strepsiades curses himself for not having brought a hat when Socrates announces their arrival (267f.). The shapes assumed by clouds were also significant. To Strepsiades some of the Clouds resemble 'fleeces of wool stretched out' (343), which was a bad sign: 'When the clouds are like fleeces of wool, it signifies rain.'[43] Aristotle warns of the times when clouds are to be seen moving about on the earth:[44] 'Again, clouds have often been seen borne over the earth itself with a great noise, in a way that is terrifying to those who see and hear them, because they seem to portend some great event.' In the same way, when Strepsiades hears the voice of the Clouds, he too is struck with awe (293) and finds it 'holy and august and ominous' (364). Clouds on mountain-tops were an especially bad sign: 'When Athos and Olympus and mountain-tops generally are covered in clouds, it is a sign of a storm';[45] and it is over mountain-tops (279–81) that the Cloud-Chorus arrives. More significantly, De Signis says: 'If the parts of Mount Parnes towards the west and Phyle are covered with clouds, when the north wind is blowing, it is the sign of a storm.'[46] Our Clouds too first appear over Mount Parnes, as Socrates says: 'look towards Parnes; I can already see them coming down in silence' (323f.). The commentators note that Parnes is not visible from the theatre of Dionysus because the Acropolis is in the way, and Dover has suggested that there may be a 'compromise with theatrical conditions',[47] but Aristophanes could easily have chosen another mountain to avoid that problem: did he not choose Parnes because of its popular connection with stormy weather?[48]

There is a final sign to complete this section. At 169–74, the Student tells of the gecko that deprived Socrates of a thought by excreting on him. This animal was generally thought to be ill-omened, although there seems to be no connection between the gecko itself and rain. On the other hand, we find 'When the lizard they call the salamander appears, it signifies rain.'[49] Perhaps one should not be too particular about which lizard is involved.[50]

A knowledge of Greek mythology would also have helped Strepsiades, since clouds regularly feature in myth as the agents of divine retribution, not least in cases where a mortal has received some boon from the gods and has misused it. Parallels between Clouds and cloud mythology have been noted before,[51] but further scrutiny will be profitable. Clouds are often used by gods in their commerce with mortals, as when they save their favourites in battle.[52] In Hesiod,

[42] Aratus 1018–20; De Sign. 45; Plin., NH 18 355; McCartney, 1929: 3.

[43] De Sign. 13; also Aratus 938f.; Lucr. 6.502 4; Virg. Geo. 1.397; Plin. NH 18.356; Lydus, De Ostentis 9D (p.27 Wachsmuth).

[44] Meteor. 348a24–8.

[45] De Sign. 43; McCartney, 1929: 4–7; Frazer on Paus. 1.32.2.

[46] 47; cf. 43.

[47] 1968a: 143.

[48] The point about Parnes is also made by Lalonde, 1982: 80f.; see too Böker, RE Supplbd. 9.1645f. The fact that De Signis has this piece of obviously Attic lore suggests that other pieces may have been current in Attica too.

[49] De Sign. 15.

[50] On the gecko, cf. Gossen-Steier, RE II.1966.60ff.; Keller, 1909–13: 278–81; Douglas, 1928: 132–4; Nock, 1972: 1 271 6; Waegeman, 1984; Davies & Kathirithamby, 1986: 173. For the gecko's connection with divination, cf. Frazer on Paus. 6.2.4. For a similar tale told about Gorgias, cf. Arist. Rhet. 1406b15–19.

[51] By Dover, 1968a: lxviii and Köhnken, 1980 (esp. 163).

[52] Wagner, LGRM 111 179f.; e.g. Il. 3.373 82; see also Od. 13.187ff.

A.M. Bowie

the thirty thousand guardians of justice cloak themselves in mist to watch over mankind's misdoings.[53]

More specifically, there is a group of myths in which a 'cloud' plays a prominent role in the punishment of transgressors. The most revealing example is that of Ixion, which has a structure with striking similarities to that of *Clouds*.[54] Ixion married Dia, daughter of Eioneus, but refused to pay the debt generated by this marriage, the bride price; in revenge, Eioneus stole his mares. Strepsiades has married the niece of Megacles, son of Megacles, who may not have the exalted name of Eioneus' daughter but is still a major catch; he is reluctant to pay the debts, arising from his son's horse-racing, which have been made the result of this marriage into affluent society. Ixion invited Eioneus to collect the debt but murdered him in a fiery pit; Strepsiades' creditors also come for their money and are maltreated. Ixion went mad as a result of the subsequent pollution, and Strepsiades' attempts to escape his debts are referred to as madness (844–6, 1476–80). Zeus alone was willing to purify Ixion and invited him to heaven, but he abused this divine kindness by attempting to seduce Hera. Strepsiades too has the divine help of the Clouds and makes illegitimate use of it. Both men are eventually punished by clouds. Zeus created one to look like Hera to test the truth of her claim that Ixion had made advances to her; when the truth was established, Ixion was punished by being tied to a blazing wheel by Hermes and whirled through the universe as a warning to others not to maltreat their benefactors.[55] *Clouds* ends in a slightly different way, although the 'mythemes' of the Ixion story do appear: Strepsiades punishes Socrates and his confrères by burning the Phrontisterion down to teach them not to believe in the divine 'whirl' but to revere the gods (1472ff.); Hermes prompts him to this (1478–85). The fruit of Ixion's union with the cloud was the violent and uncivilized race of the centaurs; the fruits of Strepsiades' meeting with the Cloud-Chorus are an alienated son who beats father and mother, continued debts and impending lawsuits; in short, a life in tatters.

The two stories convey the same message: the failure to maintain a relationship involving mutual responsibility results in disaster.[56] In *Clouds* this point is underlined by the two complaints in the parabasis by the Clouds and the Sun and Moon that, though they are the city's greatest benefactors, the Athenians do not make offerings to them (575ff., 607ff.). This is also the substance of Aristophanes' complaint, again in the parabasis, that the Athenians maltreated him despite the many benefits conferred on them by his comedies (518ff.). Such relationships form a central topic of play and parabasis.

The second myth, that of Athamas, though it differs rather more from *Clouds*, carries a not dissimilar set of messages. Many and varied are the stories about this man and his wives, but I shall confine myself here to the version given in the scholia to 257 where Athamas is explicitly mentioned, since this appears to be a summary of one of Sophocles' versions.[57] Athamas sired Phrixus and Helle on his divine wife Nephele, but then transferred his affections to the mortal Ino. Nephele retired to heaven in dudgeon and blighted Athamas' land with infer-

[53] *Op.* 252–5. West 1966: 155 (on *Th.* 9) says that it is misleading to translate *aer* as 'mist' in such contexts: 'mist is something visible, and *aer* is the very stuff of invisibility.' However, see *Od.* 8.562 and 11.5 (of the Phaeacian ships and cities of the Cimmerians) and *Il.* 17.649, which suggest the distinction is not so rigorous; see in general Roeger, 1924: esp. 26–49.

[54] For the stories about Ixion, *LGRM* 11 766–72; Pi. *Py.* 2.21ff. (with scholia); Pherecydes, *FGH* 3 F 51; S. *Phil.* 676ff.; Diod. 4.69; schol. E. *Phoen.* 1185; Detienne, 1977: 86 9.

[55] As on the Ixion Vase (*LGRM* 11 769f., 3.183f., but see Simon, 1955: 19f.) Hermes appears regularly in the punishment scenes.

[56] See Simon, 1975 for an interpretation of the Ixion myth depicted in the Parthenon's southern metopes as showing the unfortunate results of the failure of *charis*-relationships.

[57] *LGRM* 1 669 75; schol. Lycophr. 22; Apollod. 1.9.1 (with Frazer 1926 9: 74f); Pearson, 1917: 1 1ff.; Dover, 1968 on 257; *TGF* 4.99 102. The details of the earlier part of the story come principally from Tzetzes' and the Thoman-Triclinian scholia to Aristophanes, but the older ones also seem to presuppose a similar sequence of events.

tility. He sent ambassadors to Delphi, who were bribed by Ino to say that Apollo demanded the sacrifice of Nephele's children. They were saved by the ram with the golden fleece, and Nephele forced Athamas to repay her by being sacrificed himself; Heracles saved him at the last moment. Here we have a man who, like Strepsiades, is dissatisfied by a marriage which he might have been expected to find great satisfaction in, and suffers at the hands of a 'cloud'.

The most famous cloud-myth is that version of the Helen story, first attested in Stesichorus, in which an *eidolon* ('phantom') took her place at Troy.[58] The details of Stesichorus' version are now lost, but the story was revived in Euripides' *Helen*, where the *eidolon* is regularly referred to as a *nephele*.[59] Paris is another man who, as a result of his judgement of the goddesses, is given an exceptional wife by the gods, but is subsequently destroyed by the agency of a cloud. Paris, like Pheidippides, is faced with a choice between the world of pleasure and sensuality offered to him by Aphrodite and that of power and dominion offered by Hera and Athena, and we have already seen that the message of such myths is that young men should not choose the life of luxuriousness but, like Heracles in Prodicus' parable, the more arduous road to fame and virtue. Strepsiades is pleased to see Pheidippides educated by the Worse Argument, another wrong decision, and as a result his *oikos* is also turned upside down.

The other two myths are less well attested but have similarities to these main parallels. Hesiod tells how Endymion was given the gift of dying when he wished. He was taken to heaven by Zeus, but fell in love with Hera, was deceived like Ixion by a cloud, and was cast into hell.[60] Iasion (or, in Hesiod, Eëtion) made a similar attempt on a *phasma* or *agalma* of Demeter, which Kannicht plausibly suggests may also have been a cloud.[61]

That the Clouds should turn out to be agents of divine justice should therefore be no surprise, given what they themselves say, the weather-portents, and the traditional significance and function of clouds in Greek mythology. Strepsiades may be thankful that, though he has broken the oaths of the gods in refusing to pay his debts (1227), his family has suffered less disruption than that of Ixion or Athamas, or indeed of Glaucus, the man of legendary honesty, who asked the Delphic oracle if it was right for him to break his oath. The oracle replied that asking to break an oath was tantamount to breaking it and that 'Oath has a son, nameless, without hands or feet, who moves swiftly until he captures and destroys a whole race and house'. Of Glaucus and his house nothing remains.[62]

Morality and humour

Strepsiades' refusal to pay his debts, the unnaturalness of his reversed *ephebeia*, his involvement with a *goes* and the example of the typical cloud-myth all serve to characterize his activities in a negative fashion, but it would be wrong to conclude that all of this endows *Clouds* with an unrelieved moral seriousness that is absent from, for instance, *Wasps*.[63]

---

[58] Stes. 192; Kannicht, 1969; 1 21 77; S.R. West, 1982.

[59] 705, 707, 750, 1219.

[60] Fr. 260; also in Peisander, *FGH* 16F 7, Acusilaus, *FGH* 2 F 36, and Pherecydes, *FGH* 3 F 121; cf. scholia A.R. 4.57 and Theoc. 3.49b.

[61] 1969: 1 36. For completeness, cf. the sad tale of Cephalus and Procris (Pherecydes, *FGH* 3 F 34).

[62] Hdt. 6.86a.2 d; R.C.T. Parker, 1983: 186 8.

[63] Kopff, 1977 and Nussbaum, 1980: 78f. take a particularly gloomy view of the end of the play, and are opposed by Harvey, 1981.

The discovery of the contrasting comic aspect may begin from the parabasis. In the epirrhema, the Chorus refer to a divine blessing conferred on Athens:[64] 'they say that bad planning is endemic to this city, but that the gods turn to the better any mistake you make' (587–9). Strictly interpreted, this means that it is impossible for the Athenians to go wrong: unlike the divine boons granted to Ixion or Athamas, this one can hardly be abused. Such a strict interpretation is not mere pedantry, but is borne out by the play. It is precisely Strepsiades' 'bad planning' in trying to escape his debts which leads to the destruction of the Phrontisterion, the expulsion of Socrates and his minions, and the restoration of belief in Zeus and the Olympians. The cost to Strepsiades may indeed be relatively high, not least in the philosophically justified maltreatment he will suffer at the hands of his son,[65] but it is greatly to the advantage of the *city*, which is of greater importance than the individual. The play thus turns upon a paradox: the Sophists and their ways are presented as something that no true Athenian should have anything to do with, but at the same time, the way to destroy them appears to be to involve oneself with them.

At the same time, one should not underestimate Strepsiades' blame for what befalls him nor forget the mitigating factors in the case of Socrates. He may be worthy of a smoky end because of his dethroning of Zeus (though the changing of the vowel-stem of *kardopos*, and worrying about the obliteration of the distinction between the genders in words like *alektruon* or in the vocative of names like 'Amynias', might seem to be less of a threat to Athenian integrity), but it is notable that he is less keen to teach Strepsiades 'the argument that does not repay' (244f.), despite 'a thousand requests' (738f.; cf. 655f.), than Strepsiades is to force him to do it. After all, the Phrontisterion is the home not just of the Weaker or Unjust Argument, but of the Stronger or Just, and it is Strepsiades who insists: 'See that he learns both of those arguments, the stronger, whatever that is, and also the weaker, which overturns the stronger by its corrupt arguments – and if that isn't possible, at least teach him the unjust one, come what may' (882–6).

There is another point, too. If, *prima facie*, the destruction of the Phrontisterion is a 'good thing' for the city, on reflection one might argue that to bring violence (*bia*) against those who use argument and persuasion (*logos, peitho*) is not unproblematic, in that it goes against the value the Athenians placed on discussion as the basis of the settling of disputes, and recalls the many cases in tragedy and elsewhere where persuasion is presented as a more civilized device than violence.[66] Aristophanes can be said to have replied to the Sophists with words, but they are words in which an act of violence is inscribed. Indeed, violence is notably prevalent at the end of the play, in Strepsiades' attacks on creditors and Phrontisterion, and in Pheidippides' attacks on him (all of which are, ironically, the response to involvement with philosophical discourse): if we are shocked by Pheidippides' maltreatment of his father, should we not also be shocked by Strepsiades' treatment of Socrates? Should violence be the response to the challenges of philosophy?

Here it is instructive to consider Aristophanes' position. In the 'parabasis proper', he complains tactfully but clearly, that the audience whom he had supposed to be *sophos* ('wise') and *dexios* ('clever'), did not appreciate the excellence of the original version of the *Clouds*, composed by one who was himself possessed of the same qualities: 'I don't seek to deceive you by bringing on the same thing two or three times, but I play the *sophos* and put on ideas that are always new and clever and not like each other at all' (546–8). In the light of these claims it is striking that in the body of the play these qualities of wisdom,

---

[64] Also *Eccl.* 473–5 (with scholia); Dem. 19.255f. (quoting Solon, fr. 4).

[65] On the seriousness of this, cf. X. *Mem.* 2.2; [Arist.] *Ath. Pol.* 56.6; Lacey, 1968: 290 n. 113; Rhodes, 1981: 629. The relationship between Pheidippides and Strepsiades could also be analysed in terms of myths of conflict between father and son, on which see for instance Sourvinou-Inwood, 1979.

[66] Buxton, 1982.

cleverness and novelty are characteristics of the villains. *Kainos* ('new') is used once of Socrates, three times of Pheidippides after his conversion and four times of the Worse Argument.[67] *Sophos* ('wise') and its cognates are used seven times of Socrates and the Phrontisterion, six times and twice of Strepsiades and Pheidippides when they have become involved with the Phrontisterion and three times of the Worse Argument.[68] *Dexios* ('clever') shows a similar distribution.[69] The qualities that bring about the downfalls of Socrates and Strepsiades are thus exactly the ones arrogated to himself (and applied, with greater irony, to the audience) by the poet.

It is clear too that Aristophanes himself has become acquainted with a wide range of philosophical and scientific doctrines on religion, meteorology, grammar, rhetoric etc. in order to write *Clouds*,[70] so that he, like his Cloud-Chorus, turns into a figure of sophistic *goeteia* in order to make fun of contemporary philosophy. Had he not done so, *Clouds* could never have been written, nor the Phrontisterion burnt: it is, after all, he who has 'made the weaker argument the stronger' and sent a young man down the primrose path of philosophy. 'Aristophanes' is therefore an ambiguous figure in the text, who both displays and ridicules philosophical activity, and we have already seen that that ambivalence is enshrined in his self-presentation in the parabasis as the possessor of precisely those qualities which are said to make the Sophist so dangerous.

Any apparently uncomplicated 'message' that Socrates and his ilk represent a threat to Athens and its religion, which threat is condignly punished by divine agents, is thus deconstructed not just in the way in which characters who bear the names of real Athenians differ from the 'reality', so that 'Socrates' is a major distortion of the original, but more particularly in the way the moral status of all the characters is ambivalent and the author himself is characterized as closer to the Sophists than to 'ordinary' men in the audience.

Furthermore, these men have shown, by their failure to appreciate the first *Clouds*, that they are perhaps not best placed to make judgements about the place of philosophic argument in a state. Indeed, one could say they were little better than Strepsiades, their representative: their attitude to *Clouds* (first version) and Strepsiades' to Socratic teaching were of a piece, and Aristophanes' defeat by 'buffoons' (523–5) looks not unlike Socrates' at the hands of the *agroikos*.

---

[67] Socrates: 479f.; Pheidippides: 1397, 1399, 1423; Worse Argument: 896, 936, 943, 1031.

[68] Socrates: 94, 205, 331, 412, 489, 491, 517, 841, 1370; Strepsiades: 517, 765, 773, 1202, 1207, 1309; Pheidippides: 1111, 1370; Worse Argument: 895, 899, 1057. At 1378 it is applied to Euripides; 955 is neutral and only at 1024 is it used of a 'good' character.

[69] Of the Sophists and their learning: 148, 418, 428, 757, 834, 852; of Pheidippides: 1111, 1399.

[70] This range can be seen from Dover, 1968a: xxxi–lvii: the breadth of his knowledge combined with the mockery to which he subjects it may account for the competing claims that Aristophanes was for and against intellectual endeavour.

Acknowledgements

Grateful acknowledgement is made to the following for permission to reproduce material in The Offprints:

Momigliano, A.D. (1966) 'The place of Herodotus in the history of historiography', *Studies in Historiography*, Weidenfeld and Nicolson.

Dodds, E.R. (1966) 'On misunderstanding the *Oedipus Rex*', *Greece and Rome*, 13, Oxford University Press, reprinted by permission of Oxford University Press.

de Ste Croix, G.E.M. (1954–5) 'The character of the Athenian empire', *Historia* III, 1954–5.

Lissarrague, F. (1994) '*Epiktetos egraphsen*: the writing on the cup', in Goldhill, S. and Osborne, R. (eds) *Art and Text in Ancient Greece Culture*, Cambridge University Press; *Figures 3a, 3b, 3c:* British Museum.

Walcot, P. (1973) 'The Funeral Speech: a study of values', *Greece and Rome*, 20, Oxford University Press, reprinted by permission of Oxford University Press.

Hardwick, L. (1993) 'Philomel and Pericles: silence in the Funeral Speech', *Greece and Rome*, 51(2), Oxford University Press, reprinted by permission of Oxford University Press.

Gould, J.P. (1980) 'Law, custom and myth: aspects of the social position of women in classical Athens', *Journal of Hellenic Studies*, vol. C.

Finley, M.I. (1974) *Studies in Ancient Society*, Routledge (first published by the Past and Present Society).

Muir, J.V. (1985) 'Religion and the new education: the challenge of the Sophists', in Easterling, P. and Muir, J.V. (eds) *Greek Religion and Society*, Cambridge University Press.

Bowie, A.M. (1993) '*Clouds*', *Aristophanes: Myth, Ritual and Comedy*, Cambridge University Press.

Every effort has been made to trace all copyright owners but, if any has been inadvertently overlooked, the publishers will be pleased to make the necessary arrangements at the first opportunity.